SEARCHING FOR AN ADEQUATE GOD

SEARCHING FOR AN ADEQUATE GOD

A Dialogue between Process and Free Will Theists

DAVID RAY GRIFFIN
NANCY R. HOWELL
DAVID L. WHEELER
RICHARD RICE
WILLIAM HASKER

Edited by
John B. Cobb Jr. and Clark H. Pinnock

William B. Eerdmans Publishing Company
Grand Rapids, Michigan / Cambridge, U.K.

255 Jefferson Ave. S.E., Grand Rapids, Michigan 49503 /
P.O. Box 163, Cambridge CB3 9PU U.K.

Printed in the United States of America

05 04 03 02 01 00 7 6 5 4 3 2 1

Library of Congress Cataloging-in-Publication Data

Searching for an adequate God : a dialogue between process and free will theists / David R. Griffin . . . [et al.] ; edited by John B. Cobb, Jr., and Clark H. Pinnock.

p. cm.

Includes bibliographical references.

ISBN 0-8028-4739-0 (pbk.)

1. Process theology. 2. Free will and determinism — Religious aspects — Christianity. I. Griffin, David Ray, 1939- II. Cobb, John B. III. Pinnock, Clark H., 1937-

BT83.6 .S43 2000
231′.044 — dc21

00-027978

Contents

Contributors

John B. Cobb Jr. professor emeritus of theology, Claremont School of Theology, and author of *Christ in a Pluralistic Age*.

David R. Griffin professor of philosophy and theology, Claremont School of Theology and Claremont Graduate School, and author of *Evil Revisited: Responses and Reconsiderations*.

William Hasker professor of philosophy, Huntington College, and author of *God, Time, and Knowledge*.

Nancy R. Howell Academic Dean, Saint Paul School of Theology, and author of *A Feminist Christology*.

Clark H. Pinnock professor of theology, McMaster Divinity College, and author of *Flame of Love: A Theology of the Holy Spirit*.

Richard Rice professor of religion, Loma Linda University, and author of *Reason and the Contours of Faith*.

David L. Wheeler senior pastor, First Baptist Church, Los Angeles, CA, and author of *A Relational View of the Atonement*.

Introduction

Clark H. Pinnock

Process theists have engaged in many dialogues with parties situated on the liberal wing of the church and beyond Christianity, while classical free will (or openness) theists have mainly engaged parties on the evangelical/fundamentalist flank. Until now (however) they have not been much in dialogue with each other. It is time to change that because there is a lot for us to talk about. Any honest person on either side will acknowledge that we share many convictions and find much to appreciate in the other. A dialogue needs to happen because each position has assets that the other can appropriate and each can be stimulated by the other's acumen.

The fact is that process and openness theists share important convictions. We both value natural theology and appreciate the contribution of process philosophy to modern versions of it. We agree that this way of thinking also has something to contribute to interpreting the biblical faith and the Christian message. As is rare among modern philosophers, process makes the love of God a high priority and a central theme. Consequently it holds to a dynamic understanding of the world and God's interactive relations with it. It recognizes bipolarity in God, human self-determination, and divine persuasion. We both accept the need to critique classical substantive metaphysics and we both reject the notion that God is an absolute being, unaffected by the world.

We both insist that God is love and therefore filled with compassion and sensitivity. We do not believe that God determines the course of events unilaterally. We believe that the future is open and that some kinds of change even belong to the divine perfection and are not alien to it. We believe that God not only affects creatures but that creatures affect God. We both think that God suffers when things go badly for creatures. We both hold to the reality of libertarian freedom and consequently we both recognize that genuine evils exist. Both models are impressive ways to get at important things we both care a lot about.

It is also true that each side has real hesitations about the other that need to be faced up front. Starting with openness theists, one can say that their hesitations are for the most part biblical and theological in nature. For example, they repudiate the view that God does not exist apart from a world and (therefore) does not freely create any world in an ultimate sense. They have great difficulty accepting a source of creaturely power other than God with the implication that God cannot override it, even if God chooses. For God not to be able to do so for openness theists creates problems in the realm of miracles such as incarnation and resurrection and raises difficulties for the understanding of petitionary prayer. They think that, if God were tied in a metaphysical way to influencing the world and being influenced by the world in the uniform ways process dictates, this would diminish the freedom of God. It seems to openness theists that according to the process model God is locked into a way of relating to the world that leaves little room for divine initiatives in the history of salvation. Openness theists have the sense that the process God is more passive than the God of the biblical witness. Even though they want to replace a static view with a more dynamic view of God, not just any dynamic view will suffice.

In terms of philosophy, to engage in understatement, openness theists are less engaged generally speaking in metaphysics than process theists and they worry about the health of religion if it becomes too reliant on a particular philosophy. Christianity, when interpreted in a Whiteheadian conceptual environment, comes out looking a little different, they find. When the faith is translated into those categories, too many redefinitions of terms have to occur. For openness theists the ultimate metaphysical fact is God, not God and the world. Insistence on the world's necessity for God seems to conflict with God's free and sovereign love. These considerations, more than any arising from a close engagement with the niceties of the process vision, are what stick in the evangelical throat. Although they grant that the use of metaphysical categories is inescapable in theology, they think that theologians have to be more careful not to identify religious beliefs with a metaphysical system that is autonomous. We can adapt a metaphysics but we should not adopt one. We can utilize process insights to help us communicate the Christian faith without accepting the total system.

Process theists on the other hand are also hesitant and skeptical about the coherence of free will theism. They are convinced that they (the process theists) are the real free will theists and that the openness model is still too closely tied to classical theism to be effective. For the model to be intelligible, it would have to align itself more closely with process thought. As things stand, it is an unstable middle position, being neither fish nor fowl. There is still just too much coercive power, too much of the power to intervene, remaining in the openness position, even though it tries to distance itself from classical theism. From the process standpoint, the God of the openness model is still capable of coercion, and such a God who is only self-limited could at any time be un-limited. In the openness model, God still reserves the power to control everything, whereas in process thought God cannot override the freedom of creatures. This is a fundamental and crucial difference.

While openness theists affirm that God voluntarily gives freedom to the creature, process theists see freedom as an essential characteristic of the creature. God never overrides and always acts in love. The openness model gives the impression that God might love or might not love, depending on his will and freedom at the time. Though it sounds good to say that God can triumph over evil in the end, they make it sound as if God achieves this by putting love aside and by resorting to bullying tactics. Process theists have great trouble accepting that God's love for the world is voluntary. They are convinced that God, if not essentially related to the world, is only allowing Godself to be affected by the world and is not necessarily affected by it. They object to the idea that God only chooses to love and is not required by nature to love. A stronger doctrine of divine love would require us to think of God as essentially related and (therefore) essentially open to the world.

Furthermore, if God can really intervene in nonpersuasive ways, why doesn't God do so in relation to more genuine evils? It sounds as if

God does not stop them, though he could do so, because God likes the free will universe. But process theists want to know why God does not do more, if God really has the power to determine events unilaterally. And what kind of risk taker is a God who has the capacity for coercion? What risks are there that God could not avoid? In the end does God not permit gratuitous evils to occur because they suit him? There are a whole set of problems associated with the interventionist, supernaturalist model of the openness of God that naturalistic theism avoids.

There are important differences, then, to work through. But a dialogue that is respectful, uncontrived, and serious might just prove to be mutually beneficial. It could provide a stimulus to better work on both sides. As the proverb goes, iron sharpens iron. What good is idle praise? What we all need are hard questions. We need to have our feet held to the fire. That is how we grow in understanding.

Let's be honest – there is risk for us both in this dialogue. The conservatives will undoubtedly say: "There, we told you so – the openness theists are talking with the process theists! Did we not warn that they are covert processians who aim to smuggle these process ideas into evangelical thinking?" And certain liberals and modernists will say: "Why do you process theists bother with fundamentalists? Why do you lower yourselves to appear in print together with them? Where is your self-respect? Are you so desperate to find acceptance in the mainline?" Together we say to the critics – we will not allow ourselves to be led by such fears.

Conversations like this between different positions can be valuable, if each maintains respectful openness to the other. When competing positions speak truthfully about themselves and address valid criticisms, further reflection can be provoked. After all is said and done, differences are not something to be done away with but something to be embraced because, when we embrace them, a larger sense of the truth can emerge. So we do not have to try to assimilate the other or try and fit the other opinion into our framework. We do not have to exclude the other and make enemies. We can practice a hermeneutic of charity. We can repudiate our fears.

John B. Cobb

Perhaps we can summarize our differences as follows. On the one hand, openness theists are closer to the Bible and affirm its tendencies to anthropomorphism in its representation of God. To them this is more important than rational coherence of doctrine or avoiding various intellectual problems. They have adopted openness theism because this is more expressive of their understanding of the biblical God than classical theism rather than because it fits better with modern or postmodern thought.

Process theists, on the other hand, are keenly aware that supposing that God must be thought of anthropomorphically has led many moderns (and postmoderns) to reject all belief in God. They find in process thought a way to affirm what seems Christianly most important in anthropomorphic theism without being anthropomorphic. But the resultant doctrine does not include some of the ideas that openness theists associate with God's freedom. In terms of the late medieval debate between Thomists and nominalists, process theists believe that God's acts flow from the divine nature, whereas openness theists see God's will as free over the divine nature, in a manner analogous to human beings.

The difference is, in part, one of the understanding of history. On the whole, openness theists are less impressed than process theists are by the human importance of the changes in culture and worldview that have occurred since biblical times. Therefore, they are more comfortable with formulations that are less consciously modified to reflect these changes. By contrast, process theists suppose that theology can be convincing today only if it makes contact with contemporary scientific and historical knowledge.

In interaction, the differences can be reduced. Openness theists do not lack interest in rational coherence, and process theists do affirm the variability of divine action in the world. Openness theists are open, among other things, to philosophical reflection. That is why they are interested in discussion with process theists. Process theists are deeply concerned to think in a way that is continuous with the Bible. It is the greater continuity of process metaphysics with biblical categories that has attracted them. This means that the criticisms each directs to the other are meaningful to the recipients. Openness theists are uncomfortable in acknowledging incoherences in their position. Process theists are uncomfortable in being unbiblical.

Furthermore, openness theists know that we do not live in the same thought world as that in which the Bible was written. Process theists believe that there was much truth in that ancient thought world that has been lost as it has been largely replaced by another one. Thus openness theists are prepared to adapt to a new cosmology. Process theists seek a cosmology that makes it possible to recover Christian truths that, for so many thoughtful people, have been covered over by changing cosmologies. In all these ways there are inclinations in each community that move toward the other.

The social and ecclesiastical locations of the two groups also differ. Openness theists come from conservative evangelical traditions and undertake to free them from some of the rigidities that limit their creative development. Process theists are more often members of old-line denominations and seek to give content and assurance to the waning beliefs of their members. Both groups have significant influence but neither represents the mainstream of the churches in which they chiefly operate. Should they gain greater influence in their respective churches, we could look forward to reduced mutual suspicion and closer ecumenical relations.

The order of the chapters that follow creates a kind of spectrum running from David Ray Griffin's strong endorsement of process theism to William Hasker's equally confident exposition of free will (openness) theism, in which there is opportunity for these two eminent philosophers to reply. In the middle section of the book are three chapters by theologians who explain how they relate to this discussion, not only intellectually but experientially. Nancy R. Howell and David L. Wheeler are able to integrate process insights quite freely in their evangelical experience, while Richard Rice, though appreciative of process thought, is much more wary. Again the opportunity is given for each of them to reply to each, which adds much by way of nuance and depth.

1 *Process Theology and the Christian Good News: A Response to Classical Free Will Theism*

DAVID RAY GRIFFIN

To get right to the point, the issue of this book is whether process theology or classical free will theism provides a better framework for interpreting and defending Christianity's gospel, its good news. Advocates of classical free will theism have been forthright in stating their attitude toward process theology. Although they are extremely critical of the all-determining theism of Augustine, Thomas, and Calvin, they regard process theology as even worse (O 107, 141; NPT 316).[1] Having been asked to develop the case for process theology in response to classical free will theism, I will be equally frank in my statement of what I regard as serious problems in this position. My case is developed in the following way. In the first section, I make some preliminary points about the three terms in the title of this essay. In the second section, I lift up the main points on which process theism and classical free will theism differ. In the third section, I give some reasons for not finding

1. In citing the writings of classical free will theists, I have referred to two volumes of essays. "O" refers to Clark Pinnock, Richard Rice, John Sanders, William Hasker, and David Basinger, *The Openness of God: A Biblical Challenge to the Traditional Understanding of God* (Downers Grove, Ill.: InterVarsity Press, 1994); "NPT" refers to *Process Theology,* ed. Ronald Nash (Grand Rapids: Baker, 1987).

classical free will theism satisfactory. In the final section, I suggest that process theology provides a better framework for interpreting the Christian good news than its conservative critics, and even most of its advocates, have thought.

Preliminary Matters

Before beginning the argument, I need to make some preliminary points about the three major concepts involved: process theology, classical free will theism, and the Christian good news.

Process Theology's Core Doctrines

Process theology can be formally defined as the type of theology that derives its conceptuality for speaking of God, human existence, and the world primarily from the philosophy of Alfred North Whitehead and Charles Hartshorne. Acceptance of this formal definition, however, still leaves open the substantive character of process theology.

Much confusion and irrelevant polemic has been involved in discussions of the merits of process theology because of a failure to distinguish between process theology itself and various ideas that have been advocated by various process theologians. To be sure, much of the criticism of process theology originating in conservative circles involves outright distortion, based perhaps on careless reading, a desire to portray it in the worst possible light, or some combination of the two – outrage can be blinding. (We all probably need to make more effort not to violate the Ninth Commandment.) But much of the criticism takes the following form:

A. So and so, who is a process theologian, says X.
B. X is bad.
C. Therefore, process theology is bad.

This argument is obviously fallacious. It could be made valid only by inserting the idea that X belongs to, or follows from, process theology itself, or what could be called the "core doctrines" of process theology.

For example, process theology is sometimes said to be inadequate for interpreting Christian faith because it rejects life after death, limiting our hope to "objective immortality" in the divine experience. That indeed is the position taken by many well-known process theologians, such as Charles Hartshorne and Schubert Ogden. But it is not entailed by process metaphysics. In fact, Whitehead himself said that his metaphysical position on the soul-body relation allows for the soul's survival of bodily death, so that the question should be settled by empirical evidence.[2] Indeed, some process theologians, including John Cobb and myself, have affirmed the reality of life after death. The denial of life after death does not, accordingly, belong to the core doctrines of process theology. What does belong to the core doctrines of process theology, as even Hartshorne admits, is that life after death is possible.

That critics have often failed to make this distinction is not entirely their fault, because process theologians themselves have usually not clearly indicated which of their various views belong to the core doctrines of process theology and which ones are merely allowed by, without being entailed by, these doctrines. Indeed, prior to my own recent essay, "Process Theology: What It Is and Is Not,"[3] I know of no attempt to point to these core doctrines. One reason for this failure may be a resistance to "essentialist" thinking. But unless we are willing to give some indication of what we take to be the essence of process theology, we cannot use the term intelligibly. In particular, unless we process theologians, who know the position from inside, are willing to distinguish its core doctrines from adiaphora, we can hardly expect outside critics to make this distinction.

Without claiming that it is exhaustive, I proffer the following list of core doctrines:

1. The acceptance of the inevitable presuppositions of practice, which I have called "hard-core commonsense notions," as the primary test of adequacy for any philosophical or theological position. For ex-

2. Alfred North Whitehead, *Religion in the Making* (New York: Macmillan, 1926), 111. (This edition has been reprinted, with an introduction by Judith A. Jones; New York: Fordham University Press, 1996.) See also Whitehead's *Adventures of Ideas* (1933; repr. New York: Free Press, 1967), 208.

3. Originally delivered at Brigham Young University in December of 1996, this essay will be published in David Paulsen and Donald Musser, eds., *Twentieth-Century Christian Theology and Mormon Thought: Encounter and Dialogue* (forthcoming from Scholar's Press).

ample, we all inevitably presuppose in practice the reality of human freedom. Accordingly, any doctrine that implies that we are not free, because our actions are fully determined by God above or molecules below, is ipso facto inadequate.

2. Panexperientialism with organizational duality. Whiteheadian panexperientialism is the doctrine that all fully actual entities have at least some iota of spontaneity (self-determination) and experience. The term *organizational duality* refers to the distinction between two types of societies of these individual actual entities: (1) those, called "compound individuals" by Hartshorne, that have a higher-level, dominant member, giving the society as a whole a unity of self-determining experience, with living cells, squirrels, and human beings as examples; and (2) those merely aggregational societies, such as sticks and stones, that have no such unity. Given this distinction, the "pan-" in "panexperientialism" does not refer to "all entities" whatsoever but only to all genuine individuals. Although this distinction is central to Whiteheadian-Hartshornean process theology, some criticisms of this position have been based on ignoring this distinction, thereby implying that process theology holds that all entities, including rocks, have freedom. In any case, this doctrine provides the basis for a position that avoids Cartesian dualism while still affirming a distinction between the soul and the brain, a distinction that affirms the reality of human freedom and the possibility of life after death.

3. The nonsensationist doctrine of perception, according to which sensory perception, far from being our only mode of perception, is a secondary mode, being derivative from a more fundamental, nonsensory "prehension." Thanks to this doctrine, process theology holds that religious experience can involve a genuine perceptual experience of God.

4. The doctrine that all enduring individuals are personally ordered societies of occasions of experience. This doctrine, according to which the things that *endure* are analyzable into things that *occur,* is fundamental to process theology's reconciliation of final and efficient causation (or freedom and determinism): Each actual entity exists in two modes, first as a subject, then as an object. Its existence as a subject begins with its reception of efficient causation from prior actual entities (its physical pole) and ends with its exercise of self-determination (its mental pole). Then, with the perishing of its

subjectivity, it exists as an object for subsequent subjects, which means that it exerts efficient causation on them. Thanks to this doctrine of the perpetual oscillation between subjectivity and objectivity, we can hold to our three hard-core commonsense doctrines about causation: that present events are influenced by prior events, that we and analogous subjects are not wholly determined by such causation but exert a degree of self-determination, and that present events exert causal influence on subsequent events. Process theology's way of explaining how God is providentially active in all individuals is also based on the doctrine that all enduring individuals are societies of momentary events. This doctrine is violated, incidentally, by Whitehead's own doctrine of God, according to which God is a single, everlasting actual entity – which illustrates the point that "process theology" is not to be equated with everything that various process theologians, including Whitehead and Hartshorne themselves, happen to say. That Whitehead's doctrine of God is inconsistent with the rest of his system has been pointed out by various process thinkers, such as Hartshorne and Cobb. That Whitehead's own doctrine was incoherent does not entail, accordingly, that process metaphysics itself is incoherent. Something negative about process metaphysics or process theology itself would be entailed only if it were impossible to develop an adequate doctrine of God that is consistent with the core doctrines, but other process theologians, such as Hartshorne and Cobb, have arguably shown that this is not so.

5. The doctrine of internal (as well as external) relatedness. According to this doctrine, it belongs to the very nature of an actual entity that prior actual occasions, in their objective mode of existence, are included within it, so that its relations to these past occasions are constitutive of it. (There is external relatedness as well, however, in the sense that future occasions, not yet being actual, cannot be constitutive of present occasions. This insistence on external as well as internal relatedness is crucial to the openness of the future.) This doctrine of internal relatedness is the basis for understanding causation as incarnation, for regarding the presence of God in all things and the presence of all things in God as fully natural, and for developing a fully ecological view of reality.

6. Naturalistic theism. This doctrine involves the point that di-

vine influence in the world is a fully natural part of the normal causal processes of the world, never a supernatural interruption thereof. This point is based on the more fundamental idea that the God-world relation is not arbitrary, not based on a contingent decision, but is natural, being rooted in the very nature of God. This idea does not entail that our particular universe, which evidently has existed for only ten to twenty billion years, exists naturally, but only that some world or other – some plurality of finite actualities – always exists. This idea also does not imply that God is "dependent" on the world in the sense of being dependent on something contingent, because although our particular world (our "cosmic epoch") is contingent, being indeed dependent on a contingent divine willing, the existence of some plurality of actualities is guaranteed by the very nature of God, and in that sense exists as necessarily as does the divine nature itself. What this idea does imply is that not all the principles involved in our world are contingent, but that some of them are truly metaphysical, being inherent in the very nature of things – being inherent in the nature of God and thereby the God-world relation. Included in these metaphysical principles are the basic causal principles involved in the causal relations between actual entities, including God and other actual entities – which is why divine causality in the world is always an exemplification of, never an interruption of, these principles.

7. Dipolar theism. The discussion of this doctrine has been confusing because process theology involves a twofold dipolarity, one of which has been stressed more by Whitehead, the other more by Hartshorne. One dipolarity, that between God as influencing the world and God as influenced by the world, is emphasized by Whitehead's language of God's "primordial" and "consequent" natures, respectively. The other dipolarity, that between God as unchanging and God as changing, is emphasized by Hartshorne's distinction between the "abstract essence" and the "concrete states" of God. Although each philosopher makes both distinctions, neither provides a satisfactory account of both. Hartshorne is weak on God's influence in the world; and Whitehead, due to thinking of God as a single actual entity, tries to make the distinction between the primordial and consequent natures account for both dipolarities. One result was the incoherence referred to in point 4. Another result was that God's action in the world seemed to be based entirely on a static vision, not on decisions made in re-

sponse to the world. Both dipolarities were finally articulated in a self-consistent way, however, in Cobb's chapter in *A Christian Natural Theology* on "A Whiteheadian Doctrine of God."[4]

The viability of Whiteheadian-Hartshornean process theology, I am arguing, must be judged in terms of these core doctrines, which determine what else can and cannot be said in an intelligible, self-consistent way, not in terms of the personal opinions of Whitehead, Hartshorne, or other process thinkers on various other topics. For example, most of Whitehead's statements about God that critics of process theology have found offensive – such as the statements that God's existence is the "ultimate irrationality" and that God is "in the grip" of creativity, being its "primordial . . . accident"[5] – had already been criticized by Hartshorne as suggesting meanings that are not entailed by, and are even inconsistent with, Whitehead's basic metaphysical position.[6] If one is to make a serious criticism of process theology, one must orient it around the core doctrines and their implications.

Classical Free Will Theism

Another preliminary matter to explain is my choice of "classical free will theism" as the term for the contrasting position in this book. Advocates have called it simply "free will theism," but the term does not point to a contrast with process theology because the latter is also a form of free will theism. Indeed, I have previously referred to this other position as "hybrid free will theism" because it, unlike the full-fledged free will theism of process theology, does not consider freedom to be in-

4. John B. Cobb Jr., *A Christian Natural Theology* (Philadelphia: Westminster, 1965), chap. 5.

5. See, respectively, Whitehead, *Science and the Modern World* (1925; repr. New York: Free Press, 1967), 178; idem, *Process and Reality* (1929), corrected ed. (New York: Free Press, 1978), 349, 7.

6. Hartshorne has said that "Whitehead's exposition of his natural theology was sufficiently defective (a fact of which he was aware) to make it impossible to find a trouble-free interpretation of all that he said on this subject. One is forced to suppose him mistaken, or at least ill-advised in his choice of words, in some passages" ("Whitehead and Contemporary Philosophy," in *The Relevance of Whitehead,* ed. Ivor Leclerc [London: Allen & Unwin; New York: Macmillan, 1961], 21-43, at 25-26).

herent in the world and (at least generally) does not posit freedom all the way down to the most elementary creatures of the world. The other term used by our conversation partners for their position is the "openness view" or the "open view of God," thereby indicating that the future is open for God and that God is open to being influenced by the world's freedom. In this twofold sense of openness, however, process theology's view of God is even more open. The problem is that both terms – "free will theism" and "openness" – were chosen to contrast this position with the more traditional form of classical theism, as enunciated by Augustine, Thomas, and Calvin, according to which God has foreordained (or timelessly determined) all events. Both are forms of classical theism, in that both hold that all power essentially belongs to God, so that God could, if God so chose, create a world in which all events are determined by God. The term "classical free will theism," accordingly, serves to differentiate this position from process theology, which rejects the classical idea of divine power, as well as from the all-determining form of classical theism.

Good News: Primary, Secondary, and Tertiary Doctrines

In speaking about our third major concept, the Christian gospel or good news, it is important to keep in mind the distinction between *primary* doctrines, which directly express this good news, and *secondary* doctrines, which have been fashioned in order to support these primary doctrines. There are even *tertiary* doctrines, fashioned to support this or that secondary doctrine.

Among the primary doctrines of the Christian faith are the following: (1) God, the creator of the universe, is loving; (2) the world is therefore essentially good, although it is now filled with evil; (3) it is God's purpose to overcome this evil; (4) this overcoming will include a salvation for us in a life beyond bodily death; and (5) God has revealed these truths and acted decisively to realize the divine purposes in the life, death, and resurrection of Jesus of Nazareth. Among the secondary and tertiary doctrines that have been enunciated to support these primary doctrines, under particular interpretations, were the virgin birth of Jesus and the immaculate conception of Mary (both of which became important to the sinlessness of Jesus after a particular doctrine of "original sin" had been accepted), the doctrine of the Trinity worked out at Nicea and Constantinople and the doctrine of Jesus' relation to God worked out at Chalcedon (both of which supported particular conceptions of Jesus' saving work), the doctrine of transubstantiation (which supported the idea that the Eucharist is literally the "medicine of immortality"), the doctrine of divine impassibility (which was used to support the divine steadfastness), the doctrine of divine omnipotence (which was used to support the hope that God would in the end triumph over the forces of evil), and the doctrine of predestination (which seemed to be entailed by the doctrines of divine impassibility and omnipotence and was used to support the idea that salvation is based on God's grace, not human works).

The distinction between primary doctrines, on the one hand, and secondary and tertiary doctrines, on the other, is crucial for any attempt to reformulate the Christian good news in the contemporary situation. The reason this distinction is so important is that secondary and tertiary doctrines, which at first have a purely instrumental function, can through what can be called "reverence by association" come to seem important in themselves, to seem to be integral to the good news itself. They can come in effect to seem more important than the primary doctrines, in the sense that theologians become willing to affirm them at the risk of rendering questionable the truth of the primary doctrines. Examples are provided by the doctrines of divine impassibility and double predestination, both of which undermined the doctrine that God is "pure unbounded love." We need to remember that secondary and tertiary doctrines, no matter how revered they have become through association with a particular interpretation of the good news, are not themselves part of the good news, so that they should be rejected whenever they can be seen to undermine, rather than support, the good news and to be otherwise unwarranted.

This is a point on which process and classical free will theologians agree. For example, Clark Pinnock says: "We cannot allow undue loyalty to traditional paradigms and esteemed theologians to prevent needed revision of the doctrine of God for today" (O 107). Providing an example, William Hasker speaks of the doctrine of divine timelessness as "a mere remnant of tradition – a tradition that . . . might better [be] reexamined critically" (O 195). From the point of view of process theology, however, free will theists are holding onto other doctrines that, being mere remnants of tradition, should be critically examined and rejected, because they, besides not being rationally or even biblically supported, undermine the good news of God's pure unbounded love. I will explain this point after, in the next section, lifting up the main points on which the two views differ.

Process Theism and Classical Free Will Theism: The Central Differences

Although I focus on differences, the two positions agree on many points. One of those involves the criteria for judging a theological position. Although the classical free will theists may more readily invoke the normative status of the Bible, they are aware that no simple biblicism is possible. For one thing, they are aware that the Bible contains "vast and varied material" so that on most topics, such as the nature of God, it contains "diverse statements if not diverse perspectives" (O 15, 16). Rather than basing doctrines on proof texts, accordingly, one should look at the "broad sweep of biblical testimony" to try to discern the "spirit of the biblical message" (O 15). What one discerns this spirit to be, furthermore, will depend on one's "angle of vision" (O 57). Also, although the insights of revelation must be normative, theologians "should try to integrate all of the truth that they know from any quarter" (O 106), which would include all scientifically established truths. Christian doctrines must also be consistent with each other. With regard to the doctrine of God, "Each attribute needs to be explained coherently and the attributes together shown to be compatible with one another and with the vision of God as a whole" (O 101). Theologians should, furthermore, be concerned about the ways in which "God's name is dishonored because of poor theologies of God" (O 104). A succinct summary of the central criteria is provided in Pinnock's exhortation not to portray God "in biblically flawed, rationally suspect and existentially repugnant ways" (O 104). Process theologians agree with Pinnock that those criteria are violated by classical all-determining theism, but I also believe that they are violated, if less egregiously, by classical free will theism.

The issue between the two positions can be couched in terms of divine perfection. We both affirm the Anselmian formal definition, according to which God is that greater than which nothing can be conceived. And we agree that, in Hasker's words, "difficulties have arisen because people have been too ready to assume that they can determine, easily and with little effort, what perfection *is* in the case of God" (O 132). More particularly, we agree that the idea of divine perfection accepted by Anselm himself, according to which God is all-determining and impassible, is unacceptable from a Christian viewpoint, because it violates both the active and the responsive dimensions of the divine love. But our intuitions about divine perfection have some remaining disagreements. These can be explored in terms of what can be called the "generic idea of God,"[7] which has been held in societies in which biblically based religions have been dominant. According to this generic idea, God is:

1. alone worthy of ultimate devotion and commitment,
2. the supreme power in reality,
3. the creator of our universe,
4. providentially active in nature and human history,
5. a personal, purposive being,
6. perfectly good and loving,
7. the ultimate source of norms,
8. the ultimate guarantee of the meaning of life,
9. the trustworthy ground of hope for the ultimate victory of good over evil.

In contrast with the doctrines of God developed by most modern liberal theologians, the doctrine of God affirmed by process theists, like that of classical free will theists, involves – or at least can involve – all nine of these affirmations. The two positions, however, proffer different interpretations of some points. The issue, accordingly, is not whether the two positions are equally forms of theism, but only which interpretation of the disputed points is preferable. The contrasts between the two views can be brought out by looking at the disputed points, which are 2, 3, 4, 5, 6, and 9.

On point 2, both views accept not only the idea that God is the su-

7. I have discussed this generic idea of God in *God and Religion in the Postmodern World* (Albany: SUNY Press, 1987).

preme power in reality but also the idea that God is perfect in power, having all the power it is possible for any being to have. They differ, however, on what is possible. Holding that God always exists in relation to a multiplicity of finite centers of power, process theology says that God cannot be all-powerful in the sense of literally having all the power. By contrast, classical free will theism is classical precisely in holding that this is possible – that God can exist all alone and, indeed, did so prior to creating the universe. It differs from all-determining theism by holding that God has chosen to give at least some of the creatures the power of self-determination. It can thereby, in agreement with process theology, accept the biblical view not only that "God has rivals and has to struggle with them" but also that "evil is mounting a challenge to God's rule with considerable effect" (O 115). It also agrees that, insofar as the world has power with which it can either resist or cooperate with God, God is "dependent on the world in certain respects" and that "this dependence does not detract from God's greatness" (O 16). It holds, however, that this dependence on creaturely cooperation does not detract from divine perfection only because it is entirely voluntary, whereas process theology's vision of divine perfection does not require that God essentially have a monopoly on power. Classical free will theists do require this view, saying that God has "the power to control all things" (O 113). Indeed, they hold that Calvinism is right about God's power, because "God is completely capable of creating a universe every detail of whose history is solely determined by his sovereign decree" (O 151).

With regard to point 3, both views believe in a God who created our universe. In line with our belief that God always exists in relation to some multiplicity of finite actualities, however, process theists reject the idea that our universe was created literally out of nothing, in the sense of a total absence of finite actualities, whereas classical free will theists affirm this doctrine, regarding it to be essential to a Christian view of divine perfection. Although they would not consider it one of the primary doctrines of the Christian message, they do believe that it, besides being biblically based, provides essential support for the Christian good news.

With regard to point 4, both views hold, against most forms of modern liberal theology, that God is providentially active in both nature and human history. Process theologians may indeed have a stronger doctrine in one sense, insofar as we hold that God exerts variable divine influence in every individual event (every "occasion of experience") whatsoever, whereas at least some classical free will theists seem to hold that God is not directly involved (aside from God's general sustaining power) in most events, in that divine influence is not constitutive of the *whatness* (as distinct from the mere *thatness*) of the events. In another sense, however, they regard themselves as having a stronger doctrine of divine providential activity, insofar as they say that God can and occasionally does "intervene in the world, interrupting (if need be) the normal causal sequences" (O 109). By contrast, process theology says that God "intervenes" in every event, so that divine influence is a natural part of the world's normal causal sequences, and denies that God ever interrupts these normal sequences. In other words, divine influence never cancels out a creature's power of self-determination or its power to exert causal influence on other creatures. No event in the world, accordingly, is ever brought about unilaterally by God; divine-creaturely cooperation is always involved. This fact reflects the very nature of the divine-world relation, not simply a voluntary self-limitation.

With regard to point 5, both views not only hold that God is a personal, purposive being but add that this involves the twofold idea that temporality is real for God and that God interacts with the world, responding to the world as well as acting in it. Some classical free will theists even point out that they were influenced on this point by process theism, adopting its dipolar view that, although God's character and basic purpose are unchanging, God's experience and particular purposes must change in response to changes in the world (O 47-48, 118). The two views differ, however, with regard to the question as to whether God is *essentially* personal in this sense of being responsive to a world of finite actualities. Process theology, in line with its view that God is always interacting with some world or other, says yes, whereas classical free will theism, in line with its doctrine of creation ex nihilo, says no, that "God's openness to the world is freely chosen" (O 112). It can combine this voluntaristic denial that God is essentially responsive to a world with the affirmation that God is essentially personal by virtue of its acceptance of a social trinity, according to which God is a "community of persons" everlastingly interacting with each other (O 108).

With regard to point 6, both views agree that God is morally perfect and that love is of the divine essence. Indeed, given the long history in which classical theists subordinated the divine love to the divine power, process theologians are thrilled to find this new breed of classical theists saying that "love rather than almighty power is the primary perfection of God" (O 114), that "God is not a center of infinite power who happens to be loving" but that "love is the essence of the divine reality, the basic source from which *all* of God's attributes arise," so that "the assertion *God is love* incorporates all there is to say about God" (O 21). Again, however, there is a difference: Process theists hold that these statements refer to God's love for the world, that it belongs to the divine essence to love the world. For classical free will theists, by contrast, God is essentially loving in the sense that the members of the Trinity love each other. God loves the world only because of a voluntary decision (O 108-9).

Point 9, involving hope for God's ultimate victory over evil, is the one on which the two positions have generally been thought to differ most radically, insofar as most process theologians have not affirmed salvation in a life beyond death. As mentioned earlier, however, some forms of process theology, including my own, do affirm this hope, so there is no necessary difference between the two positions on this issue. There is a difference, nevertheless, insofar as process theology insists that any final victory of good over evil will be brought about wholly by the power of divine persuasion, whereas classical free will theists, believing that God has generally been holding all-controlling power in reserve, predict that the end of history will involve the "full display of God's sovereignty" (O 117).

Problems in Classical Free Will Theology

Having clarified the main differences between process and classical free will theologies, I argue in the present section that, for several reasons, the latter position provides a less satisfactory framework for the Christian good news than does process theology.

"The most striking difference between process and classical theism," advocates of the latter say rightly, "concerns the power of God and God's way of acting in the world" (O 138). Whereas process theism insists that "God's power is always persuasive, and never coercive" (O 138-39), classical free will theists say that, although it is good to emphasize God's persuasive power (O 140), we must not "reduce God's power to persuasion" (O 116). Rather, we must attribute to God two modes of action: sometimes God depends on the cooperation of the creatures, but at other times God brings about effects unilaterally (O 37-38). The analogy is with parents: Although they adopt the policy of normally using only persuasive power, "coercive power is there in reserve, should the child start to run out into a busy roadway" (O 142).

Their interest in supporting this doctrine of the dual mode of divine action in the world, which is a secondary doctrine (designed to support their Christology, eschatology, and acceptance of miracles, such as the parting of the Red Sea [O 140]), is evidently their main reason for upholding the tertiary doctrines of creation ex nihilo and the social trinity. In contrast with process theology, classical free will theism's affirmation of creation ex nihilo implies that God is "an agent unlimited by metaphysical necessities beyond his control" (NPT 321), so that "God remains gloriously free to act upon the world and be an agent in history" (NPT 320). At least equally tertiary is the doctrine of the social trinity, insofar as it supports this doctrine of creation ex nihilo by explaining how God could have been essentially loving before having had a world with which to relate.

This way of supporting their interpretation of the Christian good news, however, creates many problems. The most obvious is the problem of evil, which throws into question the (primary) doctrine of God's perfect goodness and love. The classical free will theists believe that they can deal with this "vexed problem" (O 117) better than can Calvinism, insofar as "Calvinism asserts that . . . God has deliberately chosen to cause all of the horrible evils that afflict our world," whereas their affirmation of genuine free will means that they can "attribute much evil instead to the rebellious wills of creatures" (O 152). They acknowledge, however, that they still have a problem: "Admittedly, some difficulty still remains so long as we [unlike process theologians] hold that God had the power to intervene to prevent these evils but did not do so" (O 198 n. 50).

In spite of its candidness, this statement, in saying merely that "some difficulty still remains," seems to minimize the seriousness of the problem faced by classical free will theists. Clark Williamson, a process theologian who has written a post-Holocaust Christian theology, has endorsed the dictum that we should make no theological assertions that could not be made in the presence of burning children.[8] Could we, in the presence of burning children, proclaim that God "remains gloriously free" to intervene in history? Do we want to say that, just as a parent can snatch its child from the path of a speeding vehicle, God could have snatched the Jews from the trains to Auschwitz – but failed to do so? Classical free will theists maintain that "God retains the power and moral prerogative to inhibit occasionally our ability to make voluntary choices to keep things on track" (O 159). This implies that God could have inhibited Hitler's choice to eliminate European Jewry but decided that this was not necessary to "keep things on track." Could we say this in the presence of burning children while maintaining with a straight face that love is "the primary perfection of God" (O 114)? All-determining theists have sought to reconcile the perfect goodness and love of God with the facts of the world by arguing that all the prima facie evils of the world are only apparently evil, being in reality necessary in some mysterious way for the greatest possible good. Classical free will theists, however, rightly reject this dodge (which contradicts the hard-core commonsense conviction, which we inevitably presuppose in practice, that some things are genuinely evil, making the universe worse than it might have been). This means, however, that they say that God, while having the power to have prevented them, permits particular evils that are "not the means of bringing about any greater good" (O 152). Their justification for this divine policy of nonintervention is that "God so values freedom . . . that he does not normally override such freedom, even if he sees that it is producing undesirable results" (O 156). That may sound acceptable in the abstract, but could one really maintain it in the presence of the parents of burning children? Has this theology really fulfilled its own dictum that we not portray God in "existentially repugnant ways"?

Besides the fact that classical free will theism is unable convincingly to portray God as perfectly good and loving in the face of humanly caused evil, it is even less able to explain natural evil, in the sense of evil produced by nonhuman nature (which, by hypothesis, has no power of self-determination vis-à-vis God). For example, after having criticized Calvinism for saying that "God has deliberately chosen to

8. Clark M. Williamson, *A Guest in the House of Israel: Post-Holocaust Church Theology* (Louisville: Westminster/John Knox, 1993), 13.

cause all of the horrible evils that afflict our world," Hasker says that his view attributes "much evil" to the creatures' rebellious wills, thereby implying that some of these horrible evils, those not due to free agents, are directly attributed to God's decision. For example, although the question of who gets cancer and AIDS would seem to depend, at least partly, on human decisions, that such diseases exist would be directly attributable to God, and one would have to accept the traditional characterization of hurricanes, tornadoes, and earthquakes as "acts of God." The classical free will theists assert, in any case, that God can and does occasionally intervene to override the natural order (O 168), which means that, even if they deny that God directly causes such events, they agree that God could have prevented any particular tragedy. Furthermore, their attempt to explain evil on the basis of freedom granted to human beings provides no help with the problem of animal suffering, at least insofar as this suffering has not been due to human agency. They have not, therefore, given any explanation for the vast majority of the suffering that has occurred during the history of our planet. This problem, which so bothered Darwin, further undermines the (primary) Christian affirmation that the world is the product of a perfectly good creator.

In addition to the fact that classical free will theism cannot, with process theism, characterize the divine causality in the world unambiguously as "creative love," it also undermines the conviction, which process theology regards as absolutely fundamental to the Christian good news, that responsive love to the world characterizes the very heart of God. In spite of all the distortions of this conviction introduced by all-determining, impassible theism, should we not now say unequivocally that the New Testament's declarations that "God is love" and that "God so loved the world" mean that responsive, compassionate love for the world's creatures is so fundamental to the very nature of God that God could not *not* love the world? Classical free will theism, however, explicitly denies this, insisting instead that God's love for the world is purely voluntary on God's part, being due to a free choice, a "decision to love" (O 119). But if divine compassion for creatures is purely voluntary, not inherent in the very nature of who God is, we cannot say that God simply *is* love.

We cannot say this, that is, with regard to God's relation to the world, but only with regard to God's inner trinitarian nature. Just after his warning about "undue loyalty to traditional paradigms" and his appeal to the normative status of biblical revelation, Pinnock begins his discussion of the attributes or perfections of God with the doctrine of the social trinity, which he calls "the centerpiece of Christian theism" (O 107). Careful students of the Scriptures since at least the time of Newton, however, have pointed out that this doctrine, articulated only in the fourth century of the Christian era, is not in the Bible. This doctrine, which Jews have always rejected as heretical, was surely not in the mind of Jesus of Nazareth, whose allegiance to the Shema cannot be doubted.

This doctrine, furthermore, is heralded by the classical free will theists because it allows them to say that God is "self-sufficient in fullness," so that to be loving God "does not need the world" (O 108). Is this view of divine self-sufficiency not simply a modification of Aristotle's deity, with the only change being that God, instead of simply being "self-thinking thought," is now "self-loving love," as if it were beneath the dignity of God essentially to be world-loving love? Classical free will theists know, of course, that this doctrine of divine self-sufficiency is not itself the Christian good news – as if we were to proclaim: "God does not need the world! Hallelujah!" But they do regard it as an essential support for the good news. We process theists regard it, however, as a threat to this good news, according to which it belongs to the very nature of God to love us – to love all of us, to love us without qualification, to love us even if we are not (yet) lovable. The idea that God's love for the world is voluntary, a matter of divine decision, keeps open the possibility that God might have decided to love only some of us, that God – as all-determining theism implied and sometimes said explicitly – is indifferent or even hostile to some of us. This suspicion that the attitude of the God of classical free will theists toward some of us may be less than fully loving seems confirmed insofar as they hold, as at least some of them seem to, that salvation will not be experienced by those who have not consciously appropriated God's saving work in Jesus. If God has instituted an economy of salvation from which some people will be excluded through no fault of their own, but only because some believers did not have sufficient missionary zeal or skill to convey the message to them in a convincing way, we have yet another reason to doubt the good news that the creator of the universe is pure unbounded love. Insofar as this idea is undermined by the doctrines of the social trinity and creation ex nihilo, do we not have here a clear example of subordinating a primary doctrine to a secondary or tertiary doctrine from a previous era?

This insistence on the essential independence or self-sufficiency of God, as we have seen, is for the sake of retaining the classical concept of divine power, according to which God could fully control the world and can and does, in our present world, intervene at will. This retention, however, is in strong tension with the insistence that love, not power, is God's primary attribute. Indeed, the question as to which of these is primary seems to reflect the central conflict within the thinking of classical free will theists. For example, although Pinnock says that "love rather than almighty power is the primary perfection of God" (O 114), his actual discussion of the perfections of God begins with the social trinity and the doctrine of creation ex nihilo (O 107-9), both of which he uses to support the essential omnipotence of God. And, although Pinnock says that "we must not define omnipotence as the power to determine everything," he had done just this on the previous page, saying that "His is the power to exist and the power to control all things" (O 113).

This tension is reflected in discussions of the divine modus operandi. For example, in a passage that could have been written by a process theologian, Pinnock says:

> God does not overcome his enemies (for example) by forcing but by loving them. God works, not in order to subject our wills but to transform our hearts. Love and not sheer power overcomes evil — God does not go in for power politics.
>
> We could also say that love is the mode in which God's power is exercised. . . . The question is not whether but in what manner God exercises power. The model cannot be domination but is one of nurturing and empowering. (O 114)

This equation of persuasion with love's modus operandi is made even more explicit in a later passage. Saying that persuasion is a noble form of power, which has been neglected by traditional theologians because of their equation of power with coercion, Pinnock writes: "The power of God's love (for example) does not command but woos and transforms us. This power can deliver us from evil and transform the wicked heart" (O 116). It would seem that Pinnock had thereby said that, because God is love, persuasion must be the way in which God acts, and that this mode of acting can accomplish all that needs to be accomplished. But he draws back, saying that process theology's "reduction" of God's power to persuasion is an "overreaction against almightiness" (O 116). The classical free will position is superior, he believes, because it says that God can act coercively as well as persuasively. He makes this point, interestingly, just after saying that "total control is not a higher view of God's power but a diminution of it" (O 114).

This tension between love and power, or between persuasive and coercive power, is involved in the question of the normative status of the revelation in Jesus. Following Whitehead's statement that "the essence of Christianity is the appeal to the life of Christ as a revelation of the nature of God and of his agency in the world,"[9] Christian process theologians have taken Jesus as revelatory not only of the divine character and purpose but also of the divine modus operandi. Classical free will theists also move in this direction. For example, Richard Rice makes a strong statement of the revelatory significance of Jesus.

> The familiar word *incarnation* expresses the idea that Jesus is the definitive revelation of God. . . . The fundamental claim here is not simply that God revealed himself in Jesus, but that God revealed himself in Jesus *as nowhere else*. In this specific human life, as never before or since, nor anywhere else in the sphere of creaturely existence, God expresses his innermost reality. (O 39)

He then suggests that this revelatory significance of Jesus should include the divine modus operandi, that the biblical account of Jesus' temptations, which suggests that Jesus had the power to accept or to resist the divine will, "supports the conclusion that the fulfillment of God's plans for humanity generally requires the cooperation of human agents. It is not something that God's will unilaterally brings about" (O 44).

The word *generally* in this statement, however, leaves the door open for saying that this is not the only way God acts. Indeed, Rice points out that the Bible portrays God as acting in two ways: "At times,

9. *Adventures of Ideas,* 167.

God acts to bring things about unilaterally, as it were. Some things God wants done, so he does them. . . . At other times, however, God interacts with creaturely agents in pursuing his goals. He works in and through situations where people are variously receptive and resistant to his influence" (O 37). The Bible does indeed express this twofold view. But does this mean that *we* should? On the issue of predestination versus an open future, the Bible also expresses two views, but the classical free will theists do not thereby feel constrained to say that both views must somehow be true. Rather, taking into account the "overall biblical portrait of God," they reject the predestinarian picture in favor of the openness of the future (O 15). Why not likewise take as normative that strand of the Bible that portrays God's action as persuasive rather than coercive? This would seem doubly appropriate, given the fact that the persuasion model fits with the openness of the future, while the coercion model fits with the rejected predestinarian picture, and the fact that the persuasion model is also suggested by taking Jesus as revelatory of the divine modus operandi. To affirm that God acts coercively as well as persuasively is in effect to deny that "God revealed himself in Jesus *as nowhere else.*" It is to imply that something else is to be taken as a superior, or at least equal, revelation.

This "something else" seems to be the traditional interpretation of Genesis 1. For example, Hasker seems to take it for granted that God is portrayed as creating the "heavens and the earth out of nothing" in "traditional theology and indeed in the Bible itself" (O 140). Pinnock says that Genesis 1 implies that God "created out of nothing" (O 112; NPT 318). Most Hebrew scholars, however, say that the best translation of the first two verses of Genesis is: "When God began creating the heavens and the earth, the world was void and without form." It teaches, in other words, creation out of chaos, not out of absolute nothingness. This, scholars agree, is the teaching of at least the overwhelming majority of the rest of the relevant passages in the First Testament.[10] A school of thought committed to taking "the broad sweep of biblical testimony" as normative, therefore, would seemingly have to reject creation out of nothing. In opposing the idea that divine knowledge includes the future, Pinnock says: "The popular belief in God's to-

10. See Jon D. Levenson, *Creation and the Persistence of Evil* (San Francisco: Harper & Row, 1988).

tal omniscience is not so much a biblical idea as an old tradition" (O 122). The idea of creation ex nihilo, however, has even less biblical support than the idea of divine foreknowledge.

Having noted the dictum of the classical free will theists that we should avoid a doctrine of God that is existentially repugnant, biblically flawed, and rationally suspect, I have argued that the doctrine that God has coercive as well as persuasive power, as supported by the doctrines of the social trinity and creation ex nihilo, fails the first two of these negative criteria. This doctrine is also rationally suspect, for various reasons. First, it is in tension with the contemporary view of the Bible, which is accepted by the classical free will theists, according to which the Bible contains diverse perspectives on various issues. If salvation is the most important issue, if a correct understanding of God is important for salvation, and if God could have provided an infallibly inspired and thereby crystal clear statement of these matters, then we should expect, given God's perfect goodness, that God would have done so. God is said to intervene occasionally to "keep things on track." Nothing would have been more helpful for keeping the human race on track than a completely consistent, unambiguous revelation of God's will for the human race.

The doctrine that God can act coercively in relation to the creatures is also in tension with the evolutionary account of the world. I refer here not to the specifically neo-Darwinian account, which should in no way be considered scientific fact, but simply to the idea, now confirmed beyond any reasonable doubt, that our universe in general and our planet in particular have been many billions of years in the making. If, as classical free will theists evidently believe, the universe exists exclusively or at least primarily for the sake of the divine-human drama of salvation, why would God have spent some 10 to 20 billion years merely setting the stage for the main act? This incongruity is bad enough when we consider that human beings, in the sense of Homo sapiens, have evidently existed for only 100,000 years or so, and thereby less than one-thousandth of one percent of the history of the universe. The incongruity surely becomes even worse when we are considering *Christian* Homo sapiens, who have existed for only 2,000 years. If God really created the universe primarily with Jesus and us in mind, and if God need not work persuasively but can, when really wanting something done, simply bring it about unilaterally, is it plausible that God would have employed such a long, slow, suffering-filled evolutionary process to get the world ready for the events planned for "the fullness of time"? As the classical free will theists insist, none of us can prove that our own view is correct. "Rather, one simply finds that a particular way of understanding the things of God makes the most sense, and provides the greatest illumination, in the overall context of one's thinking and living" (O 154). Although the idea that God has coercive as well as persuasive power may, by various far-fetched hypotheses, be made (barely) compatible with the evil and the evolutionary nature of the world, it certainly does not illuminate these facts.

The conflict with science is not limited to this conflict with the age of our universe. A more general conflict is with the fundamental assumption accepted by the scientific community for the past century and a half, namely, the assumption that there are no interruptions of the world's basic causal processes. One can point out, of course, that this assumption cannot be proved. But there are good reasons to accept it, and there are no facts that demand its rejection. Modern biblical criticism has removed, for example, any reason for thinking that the writing of the Bible involved any interruption of the normal thinking processes of the authors. Parapsychology, besides showing that those types of events traditionally considered miracles are not different in kind from events reported in most religious traditions, also provides reason to believe that they are explainable in terms of natural, albeit extraordinary, powers possessed by certain human beings, so that no supernatural act of God need be invoked.[11] The idea that there are no such supernatural interruptions of the world's causal nexus is, in any case, an assumption that the scientific community is most unlikely to relinquish. If we are to have any hope of overcoming the long-standing belief that the scientific worldview conflicts with Christian faith, which has been one of the two major causes of the decline of faith in the past centuries, especially among intellectuals, we need a form of Christian faith that does not presuppose supernatural interventions. The importance of this point becomes even more evident when one recalls that the same idea of divine power lies behind the problem of evil, which has been the other major cause of the loss of faith.

11. This is one of the main points of my *Parapsychology, Philosophy, and Spirituality* (Albany: SUNY Press, 1997).

Having argued that classical free will theism's view of divine power is rationally problematic, I now add a final complaint about its existential or pragmatic effects, which is that it encourages complacency about the future of our planet. Although the recent warnings about the dangers to the continued viability of the planet should have created great concern in the churches, given the Christian belief that the world is God's beloved creation, this concern has been undermined by other traditional doctrines, especially the doctrine that this world is primarily a proving ground for heaven and that, in any case, the end of this world will be brought about by an unprecedented (at least since the creation) display of divine power. Classical free will theism continues to underwrite those views. As an example of the idea that God acts in two ways, Pinnock says that, although God's present exercise of power is "subtle," the end of history will involve the "full display of God's sovereignty" (O 114, 117). Hasker says that the God of his theology "is able to do more [than the God of process theology] to ensure the completion of his plans" (O 199 n. 53). Basinger, building on these ideas, draws the complacent conclusion:

> Since the God of the open model can unilaterally intervene on occasion, we who affirm this model do not believe that humanity bears quite as much responsibility for what occurs as process theists believe. Specifically, unlike process theists, we believe that God has a very general plan for humanity that he will not allow human decision-making to alter. For example, we believe that whether our race survives is ultimately dependent on God and not on us. (O 173)

Translation: We can quit giving money to peace and environmental organizations, we can quit worrying about human overpopulation, depleting and polluting technology, and the clash between a finite earth and an economic system predicated on endless growth, and we can certainly dismiss the claim that global democracy is necessary if human civilization is to survive much longer. This is exactly the message that we do not need.

Process Theology and Christian Faith

Although classical free will theists will not agree that all of my criticisms point to true weaknesses in their position, they do agree that process theology is stronger in some respects, especially with regard to the problem of evil. For example, Hasker says that, given the view that God's power is exclusively persuasive, "the problem of evil, as an objection to belief in the existence of God, virtually disappears" (O 139). Furthermore, this way of understanding divine activity is seen to be "more congruent with God's actual ways of dealing with us" (O 139), which is no small point. Why would these Christian thinkers sacrifice these and the other strengths of process theology by retaining the idea that God is essentially omnipotent and can thereby act coercively, given all the problems this idea creates? The reason is that process theology's idea of divine power, they are convinced, cannot do justice to the central truths of Christian faith, especially the doctrines of creation, redemption, and eschatology. I agree, as I intimated at the outset, that much process theology has been deficient in these areas. I now suggest, however, that process theology can develop much more robust forms of these doctrines than has hitherto been customary. For good measure, I discuss two other doctrines on which process theology has often been criticized: trinitarianism and sin. Given limitations of space, my discussion of these complex and controversial issues is necessarily sketchy.

God as Trinity

I have developed a trinity of trinities,[12] each of which, I believe, expresses an important dimension of Christian faith. Two of these trinities are economic, but they are supported by a doctrine of a threefoldness in the inner nature of God. Whereas the social trinity was developed in part to suggest that God's activity in Jesus was different in kind from God's activity in all other events, this process trinitarianism makes the opposite point, that God's activity in all events is formally

12. "A Naturalistic Trinity," in *Trinity in Process: A Relational Theology of God,* ed. Joseph A. Bracken, S.J., and Marjorie Hewitt Suchocki (New York: Continuum, 1997), 23-40.

the same (although it can differ drastically in content and effectiveness).

Some economic trinitarian language is *epistemic,* referring to three ways of knowing God: (1) through the creation, (2) through the history of Israel in general and the life, death, and resurrection of Jesus in particular, and (3) through immediate human experience. The language of "Father, Son, and Holy Spirit" is best understood in this way. Applying the idea that all three "persona" are *homoousios,* the point would be that the God known in the creation, in the incarnation in Jesus, and in our immediate experience is acting in one and the same way. Our most immediate access to God is, of course, to God as Holy Spirit acting in our present experience. God thus experienced is a God who works persuasively, by presenting us with values and novel possibilities. To apply the principle that all three persona are *homoousios,* accordingly, would be to say that God acted in Jesus and even in the creation of our world in the same way that God acts in our present experience.

Some economic trinitarian language, such as Creator, Revealer-Redeemer, and Consummator-Sanctifier, is *temporal,* referring to God as acting at the beginning, the middle, and the end of this world. Applying the idea that all three persona of the Trinity are *homoousios,* the point would be that the Divine Reality acts in the same way in creating the world, in revealing itself redemptively in human history, and in bringing about a sanctifying consummation to human history. This trinity, accordingly, makes much the same point as the epistemic trinity, except that it adds the point about eschatology.

Underlying these economic trinities is an immanent threefoldness: Divine Creativity, Divine Creative Love, and Divine Responsive Love. Whereas God is the ultimate actuality of the universe, creativity is the ultimate reality, being the twofold power of self-determination and other-influence (efficient causation) embodied in all actualities, divine and creaturely. As such, creativity is the ultimate transcendental, corresponding to being itself. God is not identical with creativity (or being) itself, however, nor could God be the only embodiment of creativity, because it is the very nature of creativity to receive influence from others and then to exert influence on others. God is, however, the primordial and ultimate embodiment of creativity, being the only individual who everlastingly embodies creativity and the only all-inclusive, omnipresent individual. In one sense, Divine Creativity,

creativity as embodied in God, is like creaturely creativity, creativity as embodied in finite actualities. In another sense, however, it is qualitatively different, which brings us to the other two dimensions of the immanent threefoldness of God.

Whereas in finite actualities, creativity can be characterized by indifference or even hostility to other embodiments of creativity, Divine Creativity is eternally and necessarily characterized by Creative and Responsive Love. That it is characterized by Responsive Love means that God by nature always sympathizes perfectly with the weal and woe of all others, rejoicing with their joys and suffering with their pains. That Divine Creativity is eternally characterized by Creative Love means that God by nature always wills and influences the creatures toward the best possibilities open to them, toward their maximal fulfillment.

To express the connection between this immanent trinity and the economic trinities, I quote a passage from an essay in which I have developed these ideas more fully:

> It is because the immanent trinitarian nature of God requires that creativity be embodied in the creatures, so that they are not *mere* creatures but partially self-creating creatures, that the various distinctions we make in regard to God's activity in the world (creation, redemption, revelation, and so on) cannot involve different modes of divine operation. Divine activity cannot alternate between coercion and persuasion. Nor can it always be coercion, as traditional theism in its rigorous form said. The creativity of the creatures is nonoverridable, noninterruptable, in either its self-determining phase or its phase of causal efficacy. . . . God's activity at all stages of the world must be exclusively persuasive.[13]

Creation through Persuasion

Given a nonevolutionary view according to which our world is only a few thousand years old, we could assume that it had been created virtually all at once through overwhelming coercive power, a form of divine power different in kind from the persuasive power of God that we di-

13. Ibid., 38.

rectly experience. By contrast, divine persuasive power, which must wait upon the response of the creatures, could not bring a world such as ours into existence in six thousand years, let alone six days. Given a universe that has been billions of years in the making, however, the idea that it was formed solely through persuasive power becomes plausible. Indeed, as I have suggested, it becomes more plausible than the view that coercive power was employed.

Besides the fact that the idea of creation through divine persuasion now seems possible in principle, the character of the evolutionary process seems to require it. That is, the neo-Darwinian account requires that every step in the process be extremely tiny — tiny enough to have plausibly come about through the environmental selection of purely random (undirected) variations. The idea of significant jumps, or saltations, is ruled out, especially in sexually reproducing species: If it is virtually impossible to believe that a purely accidental saltation could result in a viable organism, because such a saltation would necessarily require dozens of accidental but compatible changes to occur simultaneously, the idea that such accidents could simultaneously produce two such organisms who could mate is wholly beyond belief. In conjunction with various conceptual factors, however, the empirical evidence suggests that evolution has proceeded by saltations — a fact that has been publicized by the notion of "punctuated equilibria." The basic idea is that macroevolution, rather than proceeding by means of steady, very gradual changes, seems to involve long periods of virtual stasis or equilibrium punctuated by occasional rapid changes. The theory popularized by Niles Eldredge and Stephen Jay Gould under the name "punctuated equilibria" is an unsuccessful attempt to reconcile the evident facts with neo-Darwinian nominalism (according to which there are no efficacious forms in the nature of things) and atheism (which supports nominalism).

In response, several classical (supernaturalistic) theists have argued that the facts point to the truth of "progressive creationism," according to which the development of life on our planet did indeed take several billion years, as conventional scientific theory holds, but that each species was created by God ex nihilo, so that no species evolved out of earlier ones.[14] Besides being in tension with all the evidence that

14. See my "Christian Faith and Scientific Naturalism: An Appreciative Critique of Phillip Johnson's Proposal," *Christian Scholar's Review* 28/2 (1998): 308-28, or the sec-

the various species *are* historically connected, however, this view also confronts the problem discussed above: If God can create any species, including the human species, ex nihilo, why create the world so slowly and with so much evil? The supernaturalist account of the creation of our world seems as inadequate to the facts as the atheistic account.

A far better account, I have argued at length elsewhere,[15] can be based on process theology's naturalistic theism. By virtue of its naturalism, this view is consistent with the long, slow, evil-filled nature of the evolutionary process. By virtue of its theism, it can explain the saltations that are inexplicable to neo-Darwinism, given its atheistic nominalism. Given the idea that God proffers initial aims to creatures, which consist of more or less novel possible forms for them to actualize, we can think of the saltations as neither divinely determined nor wholly accidental but as self-determined responses to felt possibilities. Furthermore, some of Whitehead's technical ideas, especially his concept of "hybrid physical prehensions," can explain how the gradualistic nature of divine activity required by a naturalistic theism can produce punctuated results. The upshot of this discussion is that process theology, while insisting that God works entirely by persuasive power, offers a robust doctrine of God as the creator of life and all of its species, in that the first emergence of life and every emergence of a new species thereafter required a specific form of divine creative-providential activity. Random variations and natural selection are relegated to a subordinate role, being important primarily in microevolution. In macroevolution, God is the primary agent.

A natural response at this point would be that, although it is possible that divine persuasion can account for the evolution and even the origin of life, it cannot account for the origin of the universe itself. At this point, many will claim, we need to appeal to divine coercion, especially given the growing evidence that the universe has been able to exist so long and to produce life only because it was "fine-tuned" at the outset. If any one of numerous variables, such as Planck's constant or the gravitational constant, were just slightly different, the universe

---

tion on Johnson and Alvin Plantinga in chap. 3 of my *Religion and Scientific Naturalism: Overcoming the Conflicts* (Albany: SUNY Press, 2000).

15. "Creation and Evolution," which is the final chapter of my *Religion and Scientific Naturalism.*

would not have developed in such a way that life could have evolved. A God with only persuasive power, it is widely assumed, could not account for such fine-tuning: the various constants must have been coercively imposed on the universe.

This conclusion, however, does not necessarily follow. The reason why divine persuasion cannot normally bring about effects unilaterally, or even virtually so, is that the divine influence always faces so much competition from the past world, with its well-entrenched habits. But prior to the beginning of our particular universe, or "cosmic epoch," the realm of finite actualities was (by hypothesis) in a state of chaos, which means that there were no enduring individuals. There were no molecules, atoms, electrons, protons, or photons, not even any quarks. There was a multiplicity of finite actualities, but they were extremely trivial events, happening at random, embodying no principles other than the purely metaphysical principles, which are instantiated in every world, even an otherwise purely chaotic world. An enduring individual, such as a quark or an electron, involves a serially ordered society of actual occasions, in which each occasion primarily repeats the more-or-less complex contingent form embodied in its predecessors in that society. In other words, each such enduring individual embodies a habitual way of being, which through its long-standing repetition of a contingent form gives this form considerable power to implant itself in future events. But in a state of chaos, prior to the emergence of any such habits, the divine influence, in seeking to implant a set of contingent principles in the universe, would have no competition from any other contingent principles.

In the first instant of the creation of a particular universe, accordingly, the divine persuasion would produce quasi-coercive effects. We can say, therefore, that the Genesis account is essentially correct: The divine spirit, brooding over the chaos, only had to think "Let there be X!" with X standing for the complex, interconnected set of contingent principles embodied in our world from the outset. From then on, however, the divine persuasive activity would always face competition from the power embodied in the habits reflecting these contingent principles, so that divine persuasion would never again, as long as this world exists, be able to guarantee quasi-coercive results.

Even if process theism, with its doctrine of exclusively persuasive power, can provide a plausible account of the origin and evolution of our universe, some will be inclined to think that it is nevertheless an inadequate framework for Christian faith, because its distinction between God and creativity involves a dualism unacceptable to Christian faith. This conclusion, however, would involve a failure to make necessary distinctions. Christian faith is indeed opposed to various forms of dualism, but not every doctrine that can be called "dualistic" is ipso facto antithetical to Christian faith. We need to see what it was about certain kinds of dualism that made them antithetical to Christian faith.

One form of dualism that has been emphatically rejected is Mazdaism, or dualistic Zoroastrianism, according to which the good creator is eternally opposed by an evil, destructive spirit of equal power and scope. This kind of dualism is problematic because it implies that the power of good will never overcome the power of evil. Another rejected form of dualism is Manicheanism, according to which our world was created not by the good, saving deity but by an evil spirit. This doctrine is unacceptable because it rejects the biblical conviction that our world is essentially good because the creation of a good creator, who is also our savior. When the (tertiary) doctrine of creation ex nihilo was finally affirmed by a council, the Fourth Lateran Council (1215), the doctrine was directed against Catharism, which held Manichean views.

In process theology's distinction between God and creativity, by contrast, there is no dualism between two cosmic actualities: God is an actuality, but creativity is not. By the ontological principle that only actualities can act, creativity as such cannot do anything. To distinguish between God and creativity, accordingly, is not to imply that God faces another agent, another "god." Creativity, furthermore, is not inherently evil. Taken abstractly, it is neutral, beyond good and evil. In actuality, furthermore, it always has a bias toward goodness, even as embodied in creatures, in that it is always qualified at the outset by an initial aim reflecting the Creative-Responsive Love of God. The dualism – or, better, semi-dualism – between God and creativity is not in tension with any primary Christian doctrines.

Another version of the charge that process theology involves an unacceptable dualism is that, in saying that our world was created not out of nothing but out of preexisting materials, process theology violates the biblical conviction that nothing exists prior to the creative activity of God. This criticism, however, involves a confusion between two meanings of "preexisting." By hypothesis, a chaotic realm of actual occasions preexisted the creation of our universe, but they did not exist apart from the creative activity of God. Every finite actual entity receives an initial aim from God, being thus evoked into existence by prevenient grace. God never confronts any finite actualities that were not themselves called into existence by a prior exercise of the evocative power of God.[16]

In sum, the charge that process theology involves an unacceptable dualism turns out, on examination, to be a red herring. The only real issue is whether the doctrine that divine power is exclusively persuasive can do justice to primary Christian convictions. I continue, accordingly, with this subject.

The Existence of Demonic Evil

It belongs both to Christian faith and to our hard-core common sense that there is genuine evil. From the perspective of common sense, some event is genuinely evil if it makes the universe worse, all things considered, than it might have been. From the perspective of Christian faith, something is genuinely evil insofar as it is contrary to the will of God. Because the will of a creator characterized by Creative-Responsive Love would naturally be for the greatest possible good of the universe, these two definitions coincide.

It has also historically been central to Christian faith to affirm the existence of demonic evil, meaning a power that (1) is diametrically opposed to the will of God and also (2) has sufficient power to threaten divine purposes. In the New Testament this demonic power was understood to be in control, if only temporarily, of our world. The Gospel of Luke (4:5-6) has the devil say that the kingdoms of the world are under his control. The Gospel of John (14:30; 16:11) speaks of the devil as "the ruler of this world." The First Letter of John (5:19) says that "the whole world is in the power of the evil one." And Paul (2 Corinthians 4:4) speaks of Satan as "the god of this age."

This New Testament picture is, we can say, mythical but realistic. It is mythical insofar as the demonic power is portrayed as an actual in-

16. Clark Williamson has stressed this point in *Guest in the House of Israel,* 220-23.

dividual who, in rivaling God in cosmic scope, knowledge, and power, is assigned attributes that no creaturely individual could have. But this picture is realistic insofar as it, by assigning real autonomy to Satan, portrays a real battle between divine and demonic power. The realism of this picture is especially evident today, as we realize that the continuation of the present trajectory of civilization in the twenty-first century will mean unprecedented suffering and destruction, perhaps even leading to the vastly premature extinction of the human race and most other higher forms of life.

Classical all-determining theism has been unable to do justice to this picture of a real battle between divine and demonic power. For example, Augustine retained the mythical aspect of the New Testament picture, portraying demonic power as an individual center of consciousness and will. Augustine gave up the realism of the New Testament picture, however, because of his view of divine power, according to which "nothing . . . happens unless the Omnipotent wills it to happen."[17] He therefore had to portray Satan as simply carrying out the will of God. The ostensible battle between God and the demonic, accordingly, was a sham. At the root of this conclusion was Augustine's monistic version of monotheism, according to which there is not only one power worthy of worship (monotheism), but only one power, period (monism).

Classical free will theists, insisting that God has given real power to the creatures, can affirm that the battle between divine and demonic power is a real battle. But they must hold that God freely caused or at least allowed this diabolical power to emerge even though there was no metaphysical reason for doing so. Whether they affirm a literal Satan or a demythologized version of demonic evil, they must hold that God, as essentially the only being with power, could have created a world essentially the same as ours but without this demonic power. Furthermore, although by affirming a divine self-limitation they can portray the battle as real, it need not, as we saw earlier, be taken with ultimate seriousness: We can count on God, at some time, to throw off this self-limitation and take unilateral charge of the outcome of the world.

17. Augustine, *Enchiridion* 24.95. This translation can be found in *Basic Writings of St. Augustine,* ed. Whitney J. Oates, trans. J. F. Shaw, 2 vols. (New York: Random House, 1948).

By contrast, process theism can portray the battle between divine and demonic power as a real battle for the soul of civilization and thereby the life of the planet. It can also show that the possibility of this battle could not have been avoided if there was to be a human race at all, because the possible emergence of demonic power was an inevitable by-product of the creation of human beings. This explanation lies in process theology's nonmonistic version of monotheism, with its distinction between God and creativity.

This distinction is at the root of process theism's theodicy. The idea that any individual created by God necessarily has its own creative power — which includes the power of self-determination and then the power to influence other creatures — lies behind process theology's dictum that God's power in the world is always persuasive, never coercive (in the sense of unilateral control). This point explains why, although God is perfectly good as well as perfect in power, there can be genuine evil in the world. A second point, which explains why there can be *so much* genuine evil, is that every increase in the possibilities for good necessarily means a correlative increase in the possibilities for evil. That is, God's purpose, by hypothesis, is to bring forth creatures with ever-greater capacities for realizing and influencing others in terms of the higher forms of positive value. However, this purpose necessarily means evoking into existence beings with ever-greater capacities for using their power in ways that are contrary to the will of God. The world has so much evil because the conditions for the greater goods are necessarily also the conditions for the greater evils.

This same twofold point provides the basis for explaining the rise of demonic power. With the emergence of human beings, creaturely creativity crossed a threshold. Thanks to the opposable thumb, through which we can literally grasp and manipulate things, combined with symbolic language, through which we can conceptually grasp and manipulate abstract concepts, creaturely power as embodied in human beings could become qualitatively greater than the power embodied in all other creatures. With the rise of human beings, it became possible for creaturely power to become demonic. Because of our unique capacity for transcending our immediate experience both temporally and spatially, we can formulate vast projects that influence life all over the planet and far into the future. Because of our unique capacity for self-determination, we can formulate these projects on the basis of decisions that diametrically oppose the will of God. Because of our capacity to be shaped and to shape others in terms of symbol systems, we can create ideologies in which such projects can be perceived as fulfillments of the will of God. Through these symbol systems and also through a level of usually unconscious influence that occurs between souls directly, a civilization can develop a kind of quasi-soul that subtly but continuously influences all its members. Accordingly, although there is no literal demonic soul, there can be a demonic quasi-soul, with effects equally destructive.

The above account, which explains how the rise of a demonic power is ontologically possible in a monotheistic universe, can be combined, furthermore, with a historical explanation of when and why this demonic power actually arose. In other words, process theology can talk about a literal historical "fall," in which the subjugation of the human race to demonic power began. My own account explains this fall in terms of the rise of civilization, with its cities and agriculture, which brought with it the war system. Given anarchy, in the sense of the absence of an overarching government, each community had to build up its power to match or exceed the power of all the surrounding communities. From this perspective, which Andrew Bard Schmookler calls "the parable of the tribes,"[18] the basic story of civilization since the rise of agriculture and city-states some twelve thousand years ago has been an ever-ascending spiral of power. In this process, every development that increased the power of one tribe would be retained and soon spread to the other tribes. The most obvious of these power-increasing developments are technological, such as advances in weapons, transportation, and communications. Also of obvious importance are economic and political developments that allow a state to raise and supply increasingly larger military organizations. But of equal if less obvious importance are ideological developments, such as those that increase a people's bellicosity and its willingness to sacrifice its young men and women in battle.

By filling in this sketchy account of the possibility and the rise of

18. Andrew Bard Schmookler, *The Parable of the Tribes: The Problem of Power in Social Evolution* (Boston: Houghton Mifflin, 1986). I have developed the ideas in this paragraph more fully in "Postmodern Theology and the Church," a three-part lecture series printed in *Lexington Theological Quarterly* 28/3 (1993): 201-60, esp. the second lecture, "Why Demonic Power Exists: Understanding the Church's Enemy," 223-39.

demonic power, process theism can provide a theological basis for understanding the New Testament picture, which is even truer now, of our world as subjugated to demonic power, even though this world is a creation of a good, loving God. The demonic is a creature: without God's constant creative activity in the evolutionary process, demonic power would not have arisen, because human beings, with their qualitatively unique embodiment of creaturely creativity, would not have emerged. But the demonic is not simply a creature, in Augustine's sense of a being wholly subordinate to divine power. Rather, now that demonic power has arisen, it cannot be simply controlled by God. The battle between divine and demonic power is a real battle, with the stakes becoming increasingly higher.

Salvation from Demonic Evil

Salvation has meant many things in Christian history. In the message of Jesus and the New Testament more generally, however, the primary focus was on salvation from demonic power. This salvation had two dimensions: salvation of the individual in a life beyond death, and salvation as the replacement of the reign of demonic power on earth with the reign of God. In process theology, hope for salvation can affirm both of these dimensions. Critics of process theology have often said that its greatest inadequacy is its restriction of salvation to a purely objective immortality in the consequent nature of God. As I indicated earlier, however, that criticism involves the fallacy of identifying the genus with one of its species. Process theology as such can speak both of hope for a salvation in a life beyond bodily death and of hope for a world ruled by divine rather than demonic values.

Although hope for salvation in a life beyond bodily death has traditionally been regarded as the Christian doctrine that most required the attribution of controlling omnipotence to God, process theology can affirm this hope while maintaining its dictum that God acts exclusively in terms of persuasive, evocative power. The two traditional images of life after death have been "immortality of the soul" and "resurrection of the body." Either of these, it has been thought, would require a supernatural act. Process theology, however, can speak of the "resurrection of the soul" (which was arguably the earliest Christian view).[19] Like the doctrine of the resurrection of the body, this doctrine says that fresh divine influence is involved in the soul's transition to a new mode of existence. Like the doctrine of the immortality of the soul, however, this doctrine indicates that this fresh divine activity need not be a supernatural exception to the kind of prevenient grace involved in all events, because the soul's ability to live apart from its bodily environment reflects a capacity induced by God long ago. That prior inducement, furthermore, also did not require any exception to God's normal way of acting. It simply involved one of the latest of many threshold crossings in the evolutionary process brought about by the Creative Love of God.

Given process theology's naturalistic theism, of course, we cannot understand this resurrection of the soul by itself as salvation from the demonic, because divine power cannot transfigure a soul unilaterally. We can, however, understand it as a necessary condition – as the opening into a continuing journey with and toward God.[20] Just as the great extension of time backward opened up by the evolutionary perspective has enabled us to understand how divine power that is exclusively persuasive could have created our world, an analogous extension of the time God has to work with us can allow us to understand how this same divine power may yet "transfigure you and me."

Turning now to the hope, repeated every time we utter the Lord's Prayer, for a time in which God's will is done on earth, we must recognize that this hope has traditionally been closely connected to the idea that the reign of demonic values will be overcome by an overwhelming display of destructive omnipotence. Such a display would surely have been necessary if this replacement was to occur, as at least some early Christians thought, within a few years. That expectation, however, proved to be false. The question before us now is whether there is any realistic way, given the present trajectory of civilization and excluding the idea of supernatural intervention, to conceive of the emergence of a

19. See Gregory Riley, *Resurrection Reconsidered: Thomas and John in Controversy* (Minneapolis: Fortress, 1995). See also John B. Cobb Jr., "The Resurrection of the Soul," *Harvard Theological Review* 80/2 (1987): 213-27. I employ this notion in a chapter called "Parapsychology, Miracles, and the Resurrection of the Soul" in a work in progress to be entitled "The Divine Cry of Our Time."

20. I have provided my reasons for believing in life after death as a continuing journey in *Parapsychology, Philosophy, and Spirituality.*

mode of civilization in which divine values would gain ascendancy over demonic ones. As a process theologian, my own view, as implied in the foregoing discussion of the actual rise of demonic power in history, is that this emergence would require, as its necessary condition, the overcoming of global anarchy through the development of a global democratic government. This idea is, of course, extremely controversial, even in Christian circles, but all the objections – to its necessity, its desirability, and its possibility – can arguably be answered.[21] The most serious criticism involves the question of possibility. Indeed, the transition from global anarchy to global government would involve the most drastic change in human political life since the very beginning of civilization. This transition would involve not a gradual evolution but a quantum leap to a radically new mode of existence. As suggested earlier, however, a review of the evolutionary history of our world through process theistic eyes suggests that God, by presenting radically new possibilities as attractors, has evoked analogous leaps many times before.

In conclusion: In the previous section I gave several reasons for thinking that classical free will theism is an unsatisfactory framework for articulating Christianity's good news. In the present section I have sought to show that process theology, besides avoiding the inadequacies of that position, does not have the even worse inadequacies often attributed to it by evangelical theologians. Of course, a complete response to this criticism would require a discussion of some issues not discussed here, such as Christology and biblical inspiration. But I hope that, by dealing with some of the complaints most often voiced, my discussion will lead evangelicals to look more seriously at process theology as a framework for articulating Christianity's good news.

21. I argue this in a work in progress on the need for global democracy, which is closely connected with "The Divine Cry of Our Time."

In Response to David Ray Griffin

WILLIAM HASKER

David Griffin has given us a strong affirmation and defense of process theism vis-à-vis the open view of God, which he terms "classical free will theism."[1] His discussion touches on a large number of important issues, and I can comment on only a few of them. Griffin's delineation of the core doctrines of process theology is welcome, and should assist critics in directing their attention to the central elements of the process position. His assessment of the differences between process theology and the open view is careful, insightful, and on the whole scrupulously accurate. I have to say, however, that he has not been so careful in some of his other assertions about free will theism. At several points he criticizes this position on the basis of views that are not entailed by it, and that adherents of the position might well repudiate. (This clearly violates Griffin's own principle, that a position should be criticized on the basis of its core doctrines and not on the basis of views that "are merely allowed by, without being entailed by, those doctrines.")

One such view (and one that I personally reject) is the idea that "the universe exists exclusively or at least primarily for the sake of the divine-human drama of salvation." Given the unimaginable size and

1. I agree with Griffin that this label is helpful in distinguishing our view from process theism, which could itself be termed "free will theism" or the "open view" of God. Nevertheless, I shall in this comment continue to use the latter two designations; there will not, I think, be any danger of confusion.

immense age of the universe, it strikes some of us as highly unlikely that there is nothing going on in any other part of it that is of great interest to the Lord! Even more objectionable is the attribution to us of the view that "God has instituted an economy of salvation from which some people will be excluded through no fault of their own, but only because some believers did not have sufficient missionary zeal." None of the coauthors of *The Openness of God* accepts this view, and two of them (Pinnock and Sanders) have authored volumes championing the "inclusivist" view according to which many will be saved through Christ even though, through no fault of their own, they have had no opportunity to make a specific response to the Christian message.[2] Most egregious of all, however, is the attribution to David Basinger of the view that "We can quit giving money to peace and environmental organizations, we can quit worrying about human overpopulation, depleting and polluting technology, and the clash between a finite earth and an economic system predicated on endless growth." To speak frankly, this is a cheap shot that is not worthy of the scholarly and constructive tone maintained by Griffin in other parts of his essay.

Aside from these lapses, however, Griffin has on the whole directed his criticisms at central elements of the open view. I shall in turn focus my rejoinder on key themes of process theology as expounded by Griffin. I begin by looking at his major criticisms of free will theism, and then turn to some considerations with regard to theological method, concluding with reflections on the doctrine of the Trinity.

Power

I now address three interrelated topics featured in Griffin's critique of free will theism: the relation between persuasive power and coercive power, the problem of evil, and the love of God. Griffin finds our view that God exercises both persuasive power and coercive power – or, as I prefer to say, determinative power – to be highly problematic. But the

2. See Clark Pinnock et al., *The Openness of God: A Biblical Challenge to the Traditional Understanding of God* (Downers Grove, Ill.: InterVarsity Press, 1994); Pinnock, *A Wideness in God's Mercy: The Finality of Jesus Christ in a World of Religions* (Grand Rapids: Zondervan, 1991); and John Sanders, *No Other Name: An Investigation into the Destiny of the Unevangelized* (Grand Rapids: Eerdmans, 1992).

basic situation is not at all difficult to understand. Persuasive power is inherently preferable, and is God's most usual way of dealing with human beings, because only persuasion leaves the freedom and integrity of the human subject intact, and only persuasion is able to elicit a genuinely free and personal response from the human subjects. (Examples such as I have used previously, involving the restraint of children, may make the use of force seem less problematic than it actually is. Forcible interference with the actions of a competent adult is a serious matter, and is generally recognized as such.) But persuasion is not always sufficient, because some persons become obdurate and persist in doing evil in the face of even the most intensive application of loving persuasion. That is certainly our experience in dealing with our fellow human beings, and a theological perspective that asks us to ignore that experience when we think about God's power bears a heavy burden of implausibility.

Griffin thinks to have found a contradiction in Clark Pinnock's treatment of divine omnipotence. Pinnock says of God, "His is the power to exist and the power to control all things," yet he goes on to say, "we must not define omnipotence as the power to determine everything."[3] But there is no contradiction, as Griffin should have seen had he taken note of the second part of the latter statement. In full, the statement reads, "we must not define omnipotence as the power to determine everything, but rather as the power that enables God to deal with any situation that arises."[4] God's power is not the power to determine everything, because he has chosen to people his world with free creatures, and it is contradictory to suppose that God himself determines those things he has entrusted to the creatures to determine. But he remains in control, in that it is God who has given this power to creatures, and furthermore God retains the power to intervene and to overrule creaturely actions when he sees that it is wise and good to do so. As I argue in my paper (chapter 5 below), our intuitions strongly support the view that a God able to use both persuasion and determinative power is greater than one who is limited to persuasion only. The question is whether such a great God actually exists, and whether the assertion that he exists can run the gauntlet of the objections raised against it.

3. *Openness of God,* 113, 114.
4. Ibid.

Evil

Chief among these objections, of course, is the problem of evil. In this connection Griffin endorses Clark Williamson's dictum that "we should make no theological assertions that could not be made in the presence of burning children." Let us suppose, then, that we find ourselves, along with Williamson, Griffin, and others, in a room where young children are being deliberately burned to death. There is, furthermore, a barrier between us and the children that makes physical interference impossible, while leaving us fully able to see them and hear their screams of agony. What, I wonder, would Griffin do in this situation? Would he cry out in protest? Burst into tears? Would he pray? Or would he stand mute, stunned by the enormity of what he is witnessing? Of one thing we may be confident: he would not launch into a learned discourse on theodicy. None of us would do that, and if we take Williamson's dictate at face value there is an end of any sort of formal theological reflection. But Griffin would not accept this, any more than I would. So Williamson's maxim does not mean what it seems to say, and one is left to wonder what meaning is really intended. One might tend to suspect that the saying is being used as a means of intimidation – a sort of emotional blackmail – in order to foreclose certain possibilities from being expressed. Perhaps, though, this judgment is overly harsh. It may be that what is meant is merely that whatever view we espouse must be able to give some credible account, in a way that is not existentially repugnant, of such horrible evils as the burning of children to death. If that is the intention the challenge is a fair one, and one the open view is willing to accept.

Supposing, then, that we are allowed to speak to the issue, what can we say about the problem of evil? What strikes me at this juncture (I had not seen this clearly before now) is the *similarity* of the problem of evil as viewed from the perspectives of process theism and free will theism.[5] Both views employ versions of the free will defense, attributing human-caused evil to the undetermined free choices of human beings. Process theists, to be sure, claim that freedom is a necessary part of cre-

5. What follows involves a correction of my earlier assertion that, for process theism, "the problem of evil, as an objection to belief in the existence of God, virtually disappears" (*Openness of God,* 139).

ation, and not the result of a decision on God's part. But while freedom in some form or other may be necessary according to process theism, the complex and sophisticated variety of freedom involved in human agency is not; God could have refrained from "luring" the world in the direction that led to the development of such freedom. Or, freedom in this form having entered the world and having proved too costly, God could simply allow the world to revert to its earlier, less highly evolved state. Free will theists will agree with process theists that "God's purpose . . . is to bring forth creatures with ever-greater capacities for realizing and influencing others in terms of the higher forms of positive value," and that "this purpose necessarily means evoking into existence beings with ever-greater capacities for using their power in ways that are contrary to the will of God." In other words, both in free will theism and in process theism it is God who is responsible for the existence of creatures who have the freedom and power to bring about great evils. Both versions of theism, then, must hold that this choice of God's is worth the risk it entails. Further, both views will agree, one may hope, that a policy of frequent interference on God's part, whenever the creatures choose a destructive course, would undermine the possibilities for good brought about through the existence of free created persons.[6]

While Griffin concedes some degree of efficacy to the free will defense, he considers the problem of natural evil, in the form of animal suffering, to be intractable for free will theism. My own view is that the world of nature, human depredations aside, is indeed the good creation of God, and that animal suffering, an inescapable part of a world so constituted, does not negate the world's goodness overall. Griffin evidently disagrees with this, but what is the precise nature of his complaint? One possible view is that the world of nature as we know it is a bad thing, so bad that its existence is worse than its nonexistence, and a good person would never have brought it into being. This, however, is profoundly inconsistent with the ecological consciousness, involving a celebration of the world of nature, that Griffin, along with John B. Cobb Jr. and many other process thinkers, thinks we should cultivate. It

6. I am not forgetting that, on the process view, God lacks the determinative power that would be needed for such interference. But process theists are not unwilling to make hypothetical judgments about what God should do were he to possess this sort of power – indeed, such judgments form a major part of their critique of classical theism.

is also inconsistent with the process idea that God has "elicited" the existence of this very world by his guidance of the evolutionary process.

Griffin's view, then, must be a different one. The most plausible alternative is that the world of nature, though not bad overall, is nevertheless distinctly inferior to alternative worlds we can envisage that a God endowed with classical omnipotence would have brought into existence in preference to the present one. Such a perspective is often thought to be plausible, but I believe it faces at least two serious objections, one derived specifically from process theism and the other quite general in its application. From the standpoint of Griffin's process theism, it is hard to see why the world of nature should not have come out very much as God wanted it to be. In the chaos preceding the present cosmic epoch, "the divine influence, in seeking to implant a set of contingent principles in the universe, would have no competition from any other contingent principles," and would thus be able to "produce quasi-coercive effects." What this means is that the fundamental laws of nature, established in the first moments of this cosmic epoch, will be exactly as God desires them to be.[7] Subsequent to this evolution takes over, but an evolution that is not explainable along exclusively Darwinian lines. (About *that,* at least, Griffin and I are very much in agreement.) The "saltations," or major advances in the evolutionary process, are brought about by "a specific form of divine creative-providential activity." Since it is these evolutionary "jumps" that determine the new types of creatures that appear, and these jumps are the direct result of special divine activity, it seems likely that the new forms are very much as God wanted them to be. And it is, of course, these new forms that determine the future lines of evolutionary development and thus, ultimately, the overall shape of the natural world God is luring into existence. It is conceivable, to be sure, that the creaturely response to the divine initiative was not what God desired, and things went awry as a result. Perhaps God was trying to produce a super-antelope, and a saber-toothed tiger emerged instead. But how plausible is this? I conclude that, on process assumptions, it is quite unlikely that the world of nature differs radically from what God intended it to be.

7. It will be recalled that Griffin needs to hold this in order to account for the "fine-tuning" that, according to the best current physics, was required for the production of a cosmos that would be friendly to carbon-based life.

The other objection to the theory in question (that the world of nature, though not bad overall, is less good than other worlds we can see to be possible) is that we just do not know nearly enough about possible alternative systems of nature to have any reliable views about what is and is not possible or desirable. Science-fictional fantasies and idyllic paintings of the "peaceable kingdom" just are not enough to go on here. Indeed, our best present knowledge suggests strongly that even minor modifications in the fundamental laws of nature would result in a universe in which human life, and any form of carbon-based life, simply could not exist.

With respect to all these considerations, process theism and free will theism seem to be very much on all fours with each other. (Both of them, let it be said, enjoy distinct advantages compared with other views such as Calvinism and Molinism.) There remains the fact that according to free will theism, but not according to process theism, God has the power to intervene in particular cases, so as to prevent disasters from occurring. Since God has the power to do this, one may ask why, in a particular case, he has not done it. It seems, then, that there is still a question the free will theist must face, whereas for the process theist no such question exists. In this respect, one may think, process theism still enjoys an important advantage.

I believe, however, that this advantage mostly disappears, once we realize that frequent and routine interference by God, whether with human actions or with natural processes, would be counterproductive and would frustrate the purposes for which God created in the first place. Process thinkers such as Griffin routinely overlook this; they seem to assume that if God has the power to intervene in any one of a number of situations he could equally well intervene in all of them. This may be true so far as raw power is concerned, but God's actions are constrained by factors other than a limitation of power. In my paper (chapter 5 below) I sketch out an argument showing that it cannot be the case that God is ethically required to intervene routinely in order to prevent harmful events from occurring.[8] I will not repeat that argument here, but will merely restate the main point: If we were able to count on God for such interference, this would undermine the sense of

8. For the full argument, see my "The Necessity of Gratuitous Evil," *Faith and Philosophy* 9/1 (1992): 23-44.

need and responsibility that impels us to correct the evils of existence or to stop them from occurring in the first place. This general point applies to both natural and moral evils, but in each case there is an additional consideration. Frequent interference with human action would undermine the economy of moral life according to which we are responsible to and for each other. And routine intervention in the natural order would negate the integrity of God's creation, suggesting that God was a bumbling artisan who just could not get it right.

But if this is correct – if it is not possible, consistent with the divine purpose for the world, that God should intervene routinely so as to prevent pain and suffering on the part of the creatures – then surely it is no strong argument against the divine goodness and governance of the world that God has not acted to prevent some particular evil that we find especially vexing. God has taken the enormous risk of so arranging things that, to a great extent, the prevention and alleviation of evils in this world are left as tasks for us his children. In this age of the world, God's hands are our hands; may we use them well in his service!

Love

Process theists and free will theists are agreed that love is God's preeminent moral attribute, but Griffin contends that free will theism is unable to give an account of this love that is adequate and convincing. One sort of objection is seen when he juxtaposes Pinnock's assertion that "love rather than almighty power is the primary perfection of God"[9] with the observation that Pinnock's "actual discussion of the perfections of God begins with the social trinity and the doctrine of creation ex nihilo, both of which are used to support the essential omnipotence of God." This assertion is, however, highly questionable, since the page and a half on the Trinity has much more to say about love than about omnipotence: "This doctrine does not portray God as a solitary, domineering individual but as the essence of loving community. . . . When seen as social trinity, God is the ultimate in community, mutuality and sharing."[10] In any case, something more substantive

9. *Openness of God,* 107.
10. Ibid., 108.

than this is required, if Griffin is to make good his claim that the open view lacks an adequate conception of divine love.

Griffin finds additional backing for his claim in an assertion that is indeed central for free will theism, namely that God, as the Trinity, is a loving God even apart from creation. This means that a created world is not necessary for God to be able to exercise his love; the creation of a world, then, is a free and gracious decision on God's part. Griffin comments: "The idea that God's love for the world is voluntary, a matter of divine decision, keeps open the possibility that God might have decided to love only some of us, that God – as all-determining theism implied and sometimes said explicitly – is indifferent or even hostile to some of us." Thus the doctrine of the Trinity, taken together with the contention that God has no need for a creation in order to exercise his love, casts a shadow over the claim that God loves every one of his creatures. But this argument is easily answered, and I give the answer in my paper (chapter 5 below): It is true that, on the open view, "the love and relationality of God *toward the creation* are merely contingent"; nevertheless, "given that there is a creation, it is necessarily the case that God is related to it and loves it." It is contingent that we human beings exist to be the objects of God's love – but it is not contingent that he loves all those who exist to be loved.

Almost certainly, Griffin's conviction that free will theism has an inadequate conception of divine love rests most heavily on the final point touched on in the discussion of the problem of evil: If God could have prevented some tragic evil that befalls us but did not do so, then he is less loving than he could be, and perhaps hardly loving at all. This contention sets up a direct trade-off between the love and the power of God: the more power God possesses, the less loving he is, and vice versa. We have already seen that this version of the problem of evil has little force, far less than Griffin and other process theists attribute to it. But it is worth pointing out that in the Bible itself there is a persistent tension that is highly relevant to the issue. At times, we see the biblical writers rejoicing in the manifest goodness of God. But at other times – not infrequently in the Psalms, for example – we find the writer wrestling with a seeming insurmountable situation, and wondering out loud why God has done nothing about it:

> Will the Lord spurn forever,
> and never again be favorable?

Has his steadfast love ceased forever?
  Are his promises at an end for all time?
Has God forgotten to be gracious?
  Has he in anger shut up his compassion?
(Psalm 77:7-9, NRSV)

Always, however, there is the conviction that God can alleviate the situation, and the hope that he will do so. Sometimes, too, another theme emerges that has become familiar in these pages: God is withholding the decisive exhibition of his power, in order to exercise his persuasion in the hope that men and women will repent and willingly turn to the Lord: "Or do you show contempt for the riches of his kindness, tolerance, and patience, not realizing that God's kindness leads you toward repentance?" (Romans 2:4, NIV). Thus we have the abiding tension for the pilgrim people of God: living in the present beset by various evils, troubled sometimes that God's deliverance has not yet come, but confident both in God's power and in his ultimate victory over all that harms and oppresses us. Process theology, sadly, finds itself unable to sustain this tension: rather than waiting patiently for the final deliverance, it must deny God's power to deliver us in order to keep from thinking God unloving because he has not already done so.

Method

Several topics discussed by Griffin can be placed under the general rubric of theological method. Of interest in this connection is his classification of doctrines as primary, secondary, and tertiary. Some classification of this general type is likely to be at work in any theological system, even if it is not explicitly pointed out as such. But these classifications are of limited use in polemical situations, because different theological positions will have different lists of primary doctrines and different interpretations of the ones they do agree on. To take only a single example, Griffin's classification of the doctrine of the Trinity as "tertiary" for the open view is quite mistaken, as we shall soon see in detail.

Here is a question about theological method for Griffin: What is the source of the "Christian good news" of which he speaks? The source is not to be found in process philosophy, which rather serves as the "framework for interpreting" the good news. The source can hardly be the tradition of Christian theological reflection, which is usually mentioned only to be rejected and dismissed. Perhaps the Bible is a better candidate, but Griffin's treatment of the Scriptures as a source is perplexing. At times the Bible is appealed to with apparent confidence, but on other occasions biblical teachings are rejected with little indication of regret or concern. But how does Griffin decide what to accept and what to reject?

An answer to this question occurs to me, but I am not sure if it is the right answer. I surmise that the source of the good news is indeed the Bible, especially the New Testament – on those occasions when what the Bible says harmonizes well with the dictates of process thought. If this is correct, then the congruence between the good news (as understood by Griffin) and process theism is unsurprising – and by the same token, this congruence does not amount to much as support for the truth of the process perspective.

It is not correct to say, as Griffin does, that free will theists and process theists agree on "the criteria for judging a theological position." Though we do embrace the dicta that Griffin quotes with approval from *The Openness of God,*[11] our commitment to Scripture as the Word of God, and to the most central affirmations of the creedal tradition, is of a different order than the "pick and choose" attitude toward these sources adopted by process theology. For a representative statement on theological method from the perspective of the open view, one can hardly do better than Pinnock's development of the "Wesleyan quadrilateral" of Scripture, tradition, experience, and reason, which is beautifully summarized in Nancy Howell's essay (chapter 2 below).[12]

11. I need to point out, however, that Griffin has misused my reference to divine timelessness as "a mere remnant of tradition." I did indeed say, with regard to the Reformed theologian Louis Berkhof, that "the doctrine of timelessness is not a living part of Berkhof's theology but rather a mere remnant of tradition" (*Openness of God,* 195). No doubt there are others about whom this could be said, but I would never say it about all contemporary adherents of divine timelessness. (Eleonore Stump, Brian Leftow, and William Alston are all noteworthy examples of thinkers for whom timelessness is much more than a tradition.)

12. Howell's summary is particularly welcome to me, because it provides something that is lacking in my own essay (chapter 5 below), which refers to the quadrilateral but does not develop it in any detail.

Trinity

These varied aspects of theological method all find a focus in the doctrine of the Trinity, which is given prominent attention by Griffin in the closing pages of his essay. This is actually somewhat surprising, in view of his earlier remarks that the doctrine was "articulated only in the fourth century," "is not to be found in the Bible," "has always been rejected as heretical by Jews" (this should be taken as an objection by *Christian* theologians?), and "was surely not in the mind of Jesus of Nazareth." Nevertheless, Griffin develops three distinct trinitarian patterns in relation to God, referencing a recent article in which he set forth these same ideas more fully. One cannot but admire the imagination and ingenuity with which this material is developed. Nevertheless, there is here a striking lack of continuity with the biblical and patristic sources from which the doctrine of the Trinity originally developed. The term *homoousios* is retained, presumably out of some sort of loyalty to the tradition, but the content associated with it is only distantly related to its original meaning as employed by the Nicene fathers. Griffin puts his finger on the crucial issue: "Whereas the social trinity was developed in part to suggest that God's activity in Jesus was different in kind from God's activity in all other events, this process trinitarianism makes the opposite point, that God's activity in all events is formally the same (although it can differ drastically in content and effectiveness)." One need only add that, not just the "social trinity" (which Griffin seems to regard as a modern invention), but the doctrine of the Trinity itself was developed precisely in order to affirm and celebrate the uniqueness of the divine presence in Jesus, "the only Son of God, eternally begotten of the Father." If one denies that uniqueness, then any "doctrine of the Trinity" that remains can only be an empty shell.

Griffin claims that social trinitarianism is a "tertiary doctrine" on the ground that, by explaining how God can be loving apart from the creation, it "protects" the doctrine of creation ex nihilo, which he classifies as a "secondary" doctrine. Now, the doctrine of the Trinity does have this use among others, and it is so employed in my own essay (chapter 5 below). But this is far from being the primary rationale for the doctrine. A full account of the doctrine of the Trinity would take us far beyond the reasonable bounds of this discussion. But one crucial bit of biblical evidence, interpreted as all the church fathers interpreted it, propels us far along the road toward the Nicene doctrine. Stated baldly, the point is as follows: The relationship between Jesus and the Father, as portrayed in the Gospels, was understood as a relationship between Father and Son within the Trinity.[13] As an illustration of this point, one quotation from Augustine must suffice: "For to this His words come, 'That they may be one, even as we are one'; namely, that as the Father and Son are one, not only in equality of substance, but also in will, so those also may be one, between whom and God the Son is mediator, not only in that they are of the same nature, but also through the same union of love."[14] Here it is crystal clear that Augustine is applying the words of Jesus to the Father as a description of the intratrinitarian relationship of Father and Son. This point, once accepted, establishes at a single stroke the fundamental conception of "social" trinitarianism, namely that the persons are distinct subjects who enter into personal relationships with each other. If this point is combined with a few other extremely plausible theological assumptions,[15] the inference to the Nicene doctrine of the Trinity becomes quite compelling. That doctrine may be "secondary" in an epistemological sense, in that it represents an inference (albeit a compelling inference) from several other theological propositions. But this by no means entails that it is "secondary," let alone "tertiary," in Griffin's sense, namely that its importance is only to provide "protection" for other, supposedly more significant, beliefs. For orthodox Christians, there *are* no more significant beliefs.

13. For more about this, see my article, "Tri-Unity," *Journal of Religion* 50/1 (1970): 1-32.

14. Augustine, *On the Trinity,* trans. A. W. Hadden (Edinburgh: T. & T. Clark, 1973), 4.9, p. 122. The notion that Augustine's doctrine was "an approximation to Unitarianism," as alleged by William Temple, is a drastic misconception. See my "Tri-Unity."

15. Among these would be the following: There is one God, and only one, so the Father and the Son cannot be separate divine beings; thus, the doctrines of the unity of the divine *ousia* and of the "generation" of the Son and the "procession" of the Holy Spirit. Furthermore, the dichotomy God/creatures is exhaustive; there are no "semi-divine" beings such as were posited by Neoplatonism and, in a different way, by Arianism. Finally, there was the recognition that the Spirit is a third divine *hypostasis,* distinct from and equal to the Father and the Son.

Coda

Whitehead once described Christianity as "a religion seeking a metaphysic."[16] There is wisdom in this description. Christianity involves deeply metaphysical claims about the nature of God, human beings, and the natural world, and for its full articulation it does indeed have need of a metaphysical scheme in which these claims can be set out and assessed. For this reason there has historically been a succession of different versions of "Christian metaphysics"; none of these has been without its uses, and none has been free of drawbacks. Has the Christian faith now found its best, and final, metaphysical home within Whitehead's own system? We open view theists beg leave to doubt this. Whiteheadian metaphysics can be helpful and has in fact been helpful to many, especially in breaking the grip of the prevailing scientific naturalism.[17] But when given excessive authority, so that it becomes the yardstick by which the gospel itself is measured, the Whiteheadian scheme can become a prison for theology. Thus we are moved to echo Karl Barth's insistence that theology needs to be a *free science* — free, above all, from any presupposed philosophical schema that would limit, and hinder, the church's ability to hear the Word of God spoken to us in Jesus Christ, and to bear witness to that Word.[18] It is this Word that we seek to have as the measure and the substance of our own theological witness, and we invite process theists, and others, to join us in that quest.

16. From F. C. S. Northrup and Mason W. Gross, eds., *Alfred North Whitehead: An Anthology* (New York: Macmillan, 1953), 485.

17. For a generous acknowledgment of the merits of the Whiteheadian system by one who finds it ultimately unsatisfactory, see the essay by Richard Rice, chapter 4 below.

18. See Karl Barth, *Evangelical Theology: An Introduction,* trans. Grover Foley (repr. Grand Rapids: Eerdmans, 1980), 7-9.

2 *Openness and Process Theism: Respecting the Integrity of the Two Views*

NANCY R. HOWELL

Autobiographical Context

My readiness as a process theologian to engage in dialogue with evangelical theism is, in part, autobiographical. My formation as a young Christian and as a seminary student responding to God's call to ministry occurred in an evangelical context among Southern Baptists. Southern Baptist affirmations of faith remain important to me. The centrality of the Bible as the historical, sacred text of the Christian tradition, the priesthood of all believers who have made a profession of faith that Jesus Christ is the revelation of God, the competency of believers under the guidance of the Holy Spirit to read and interpret Scripture, and religious freedom of the individual from state or ecclesial authority (among other historical values) continue to form my theology in profound ways that bind me to the community of evangelicals. As I have taught and worked among Methodists and Lutherans, these marks of Southern Baptist tradition and faith – these commitments – tangibly remind me that my heart recalls important roots of my faith.

Given the recent decade of Southern Baptist denominational history, it is incredible to remember that I learned about process theology (and other contemporary forms of theology, which influence my constructive scholarship) from the theological education that I received at Southeastern Baptist Theological Seminary. As I became more committed and cognizant of the history of my denomination, process theology became an important theological tool in my spiritual growth and assisted my intellectual articulation of theological doctrines. For example, I found Whitehead's language about the persuasive lure of God and John Cobb's process theism that described God's call forward especially enriching for interpreting what I meant and experienced as God's call to ministry. The lure of God and the call forward spoke to me about a personal relationship with God as an ongoing divine influence in the intimate spaces of my life where I felt compelled to respond to adventures and unknown futures envisioned by God for my vocation. The metaphysics and language of process theology aided me in expressing a vital part of my Christian journey. That God's power was described as persuasive rather than coercive rang true to me since it was clear to me that everyone from Adam to Moses to me had been able to resist God's intentions. Against strong interpretations of God's control and omnipotence, the creative, responsive love of God described by Cobb and David Griffin resolved a tension between neoclassical theism and my understanding of the God of Exodus whose mind changed under Moses' counsel and whose revelation in Jesus Christ was compassionate rather than controlling. Process theology did not distract me from my faith commitments, but drew me into a more textured theism consistent with my Baptist tradition.

My experience was not that I was being drawn away from an evangelical faith by a liberal theology that was inconsistent with it, but that multiple languages of faith were enriching my understanding of God. Ironically, I did experience the Southern Baptist Convention moving away from its heritage toward a more fundamentalist and creedal stance. The inerrancy debate seemed less like faith that the Holy Spirit would guide the believer in interpretation of Scripture and more like an authoritarian imposition of a single reading of the text and encroachment upon religious freedom. Reviving an earlier denominational controversy over reading Genesis creation accounts, Southern Baptist spokespersons were moving away from what I experienced as the power of God's observable, continuous creation, which reasonably should be apparent to scientific observation if God is still creator. The silencing of women at the Southern Baptist Convention meetings and the withdrawal of funding for appointments of women in Home Mission sites directly contradicted the affirmation of the priesthood of all believers. Process theology did not lead me to reject evangelicalism, but it did offer a place to think with other open minds when Southern Baptists began to close conversations.

Evangelicals

My experience as a Southern Baptist makes quite clear to me that there are varieties of evangelical perspectives and that the term *evangelical* is not limited to use by conservative Christians. First, it is important neither to collapse evangelicalism into fundamentalism (which has been described as a strident and militant antimodernist Christian movement defending thoroughgoing biblical inerrancy and dispensationalism)[1] nor to let the term suggest identity between the Evangelical Lutheran Church in America, an old-line denomination, and more conservative Christians.

Henry H. Knight III has sorted out the many historical uses of the term "evangelical" in his excellent book, *A Future for Truth: Evangelical Theology in a Postmodern World.*[2] One use of "evangelical" arises from the Protestant Reformation and nearly equates the term with "protestant," which is the usage common in Lutheran contexts. This usage reflects Reformation theology and refers to common doctrinal tenets such as salvation by grace through faith, Christ as Savior and Lord, and Scripture as uniquely authoritative. A second use reflects the eighteenth- and nineteenth-century awakenings and focuses on personal conversion, holiness, evangelism, and (often) social reform. A third use of "evangelical" emerged in the United States in the 1940s as a postfundamentalist neo-evangelicalism. A rejection of militant, separatist fundamentalism, neo-evangelicalism aspired to "a renewed intellectual engagement with science and culture and a vigorous, biblically based social concern."[3]

1. William Vance Trollinger Jr., "Fundamentalism," in *A New Handbook of Christian Theology,* ed. Donald W. Musser and Joseph L. Price (Nashville: Abingdon, 1992), 195.

2. Henry H. Knight III, *A Future for Truth: Evangelical Theology in a Postmodern World* (Nashville: Abingdon, 1997), 20-22.

3. Ibid., 20.

Knight understands Gabriel Fackre's typology of evangelicals to be influenced consciously by the historical meaning of evangelicalism in the awakenings and implicitly by the postfundamentalist sense of evangelicalism. Fackre names five categories of evangelicals: (1) fundamentalist evangelicals, who are separatist, militant, and committed to strict biblical inerrancy; (2) old evangelicals, who are concerned with the pious life, conversion experience, evangelism, and disciplined Bible study; (3) new evangelicals, who are similar to old evangelicals with added emphasis on apologetics (as rational defense of the faith) and social issues (in relation to personal piety); (4) justice and peace evangelicals, who engage in radical social critique most often from Anabaptist, Calvinist, and (adds Knight) Wesleyan backgrounds; and (5) charismatic evangelicals, who emphasize personal experience in the forms of baptism of the Holy Spirit, the gift of tongues, and "a fervent life of prayer, praise, and personal testimony."[4]

Knight cites also Donald Bloesch's recent typology of evangelicals in *The New Handbook of Christian Theology* as an even more inclusive understanding of evangelical diversity, which implicitly reflects the three historical understandings of "evangelical" (protestant, awakening, and postfundamentalist). Bloesch names seven categories of evangelicalism: (1) fundamentalism; (2) confessional orthodoxy, emphasizing strict adherence to Reformation creeds and doctrines; (3) evangelical pietism, including the Holiness movement; (4) neo-evangelical theology, combining a high view of biblical authority with historical criticism; (5) charismatic evangelicalism, including Pentecostalism; (6) neoorthodoxy (which is not usually included in the diversity of evangelicals although it is committed to reappropriation of Reformation theology); and (7) Catholic evangelicalism.[5] Bloesch is careful to note the tensions created by the diversity within evangelicalism – tensions that range from biblical inerrancy and infallibility, the role of the sacraments in effecting salvation, and the doctrine of hell to the role of women in ministry and the impact of ideologies, such as socialism and feminism, on the church and social action.[6]

4. Ibid., 21. Knight cites Gabriel Fackre, "Evangelical, Evangelicalism," in *Westminster Dictionary of Christian Theology,* ed. Alan Richardson and John Bowden (Philadelphia: Westminster, 1983), 191.

5. Knight, *Future,* 21-22. Knight cites Donald G. Bloesch, "Evangelicalism," in *New Handbook of Christian Theology,* 170-71.

6. Bloesch, "Evangelicalism," 173.

Knight's analysis finds Fackre's and Bloesch's typologies helpful in describing the diversity of evangelicals, and Knight's historical analysis suggests that the reason for the diversity lies in historical tensions between scholasticism and pietism that were resolved either by denying one side of the tension, giving each a separate sphere of influence (dualism), or integrating theology and piety (reason and experience).[7]

Second, it is helpful to suggest what commonalities there are among self-identified evangelicals. Some characteristics of evangelical faith include the importance of a personal relationship with God through Jesus Christ and the authority, if not the inerrancy, of the Bible. Bloesch identifies a dozen key doctrines, which might be held in common by most evangelicals: (1) a high view of Scripture, including the divine authority of Scripture, primacy of Scripture over other sources, and veracity or truth of Scripture; (2) salvation by grace alone; (3) Christ as the preexistent Son of God, who is the incarnate and divine Savior; (4) the crucial importance of conversion; (5) the pursuit of holiness that advances the process of sanctification; (6) the ontological Trinity; (7) the sovereignty of God; (8) the church as the believing people of God; (9) the crucial role of preaching; (10) the priesthood of all believers; (11) the universal call to sanctity; and (12) the urgency of the Christian mission.[8]

David Wheeler has suggested that the National Association of Evangelicals' statement of faith exemplifies well the essence of evangelicalism (see chapter 3 below). This statement first affirms that the Bible is the inspired, infallible, and authoritative Word of God; second, that there is one God who exists in the Trinity of Father, Son, and Holy Spirt; third, that the virgin birth, sinless life, vicarious and atoning death, bodily resurrection, ascension, and second coming are central to belief in Jesus Christ as Lord; fourth, that regeneration by the Holy Spirit is essential for regeneration of sinful persons; fifth, that the Holy Spirit sustains a present ministry and indwells Christians to enable them to live a godly life; sixth, that there is a resurrection of the saved to life and a resurrection of the lost to damnation; and seventh, that there is spiritual unity among those who believe in Jesus Christ as Lord. This is one statement of what it means to be evangelical from the standpoint

7. Knight, *Future,* 24.

8. Bloesch, "Evangelicalism," 172.

of evangelicals who formed an organization that serves as an alternative to global ecumenism, which was affirmed by institutions such as the World Council of Churches. Certainly, as Wheeler points out, some of these affirmations may be held by Christians who are not evangelical, but it should be noted also that these affirmations are open to nuanced interpretations by diverse evangelicals and that the range of evangelical faith statements is not limited to the National Association of Evangelicals' statement.

One particular example of evangelicals who offer options within evangelical theology are those whose theism is consonant with that described by Clark Pinnock, Richard Rice, John Sanders, William Hasker, and David Basinger in *The Openness of God.* Bloesch categorizes Pinnock, at least, among neo-evangelicals who identify with a reformed or refurbished evangelicalism.[9] Since it is these theologians of the open view or free will theism that I engage in conversation here, I begin by expressing my understanding of what that theological standpoint is.

In the preface of *The Openness of God,* Pinnock describes the open view of God: "God, in grace, grants humans significant freedom to cooperate with or work against God's will for their lives, and he enters into dynamic, give-and-take relationships with us."[10] Such an evangelical view is grounded in biblical, theological, philosophical, and practical (which, I judge, entails experiential) evidence that God is responsive to human responses to divine work in the world.[11] The open view rejects classical theism on the grounds that it is not faithful to the biblical portrayal of God and, in rejecting classical theism, retrieves a view of a God who takes risks.[12] This biblically recovered picture of God differs from the classical omnipotent God who operates in the world through mastery and control, who endures unaffected by creaturely experience, and who wields changeless, immutable, supreme power.[13] Pinnock describes reciprocity in the dynamic relationships between God and humans:

9. Ibid., 171.

10. Pinnock, "Preface," in *The Openness of God* (Downers Grove, Ill.: InterVarsity Press, 1994), 1.

11. Ibid., 1, 9.

12. Ibid., 1; Richard Rice, "Biblical Support for a New Perspective," in *Openness of God,* 15.

13. Pinnock, "Preface," 1; Rice, "Biblical Support," 11-13.

> The Christian life involves a genuine interaction between God and human beings. We respond to God's gracious initiatives and God responds to our responses . . . and on it goes. God takes risks in this give-and-take relationship, yet he is endlessly resourceful and competent in working toward his ultimate goals. Sometimes God alone decides how to accomplish these goals. On other occasions, God works with human decisions, adapting his own plans to fit the changing situation.[14]

My reading of Pinnock's description of God's relationality and power is that God is receptive to humans, engages human freedom, and simultaneously remains the powerful and responsive deity to whom Scripture attests. Key to the open view of God is the prominence of divine love. In relation to God's power, love is the critical divine attribute that moves power to sensitivity and responsiveness.[15]

Process Theology

Process theology in large measure agrees with the defining points of the open view of God, yet process theology is more typically associated with liberal rather than evangelical theology. John P. Crossley Jr. defines liberalism in theology as the "deep respect for authority of reason and experience in religion, an openness to culture, a willingness to adapt theological expression to cultural forms, and continuing flexibility in interpreting the sacred texts and practices of its tradition."[16] As theology adapted itself to the Enlightenment trust in reason and experience, liberal theology expressed its flexibility in four areas: (1) scientific analysis of sacred texts and practices, (2) humanistic and social scientific formulations of human nature, (3) scientific understanding of the nature and origin of the universe, and (4) understanding of morality as independent of divine or scriptural command.[17] The liberal traditions in theology differ from conservative

14. Pinnock, "Preface," 1.
15. Rice, "Biblical Support," 15.
16. John P. Crossley Jr., "Liberalism," in *New Handbook of Christian Theology,* 285.
17. Ibid., 286.

views characterized by priorities that place biblical authority above reason, experience, and culture.[18]

Making reference to Kenneth Cauthen and Henry Churchill King, Henry H. Knight III has described theological liberalism and evangelicalism historically and comparatively. The liberal apologetic approaches theology with three themes in mind: continuity, dynamism, and autonomy. First, continuity minimizes or eliminates distinctions between the supernatural and the natural. The dichotomy of God and the world is bridged by focus on the significant immanence of God, which makes God accessible to anyone, not just the Christian, who seeks understanding of nature and humanity through reason and experience. Second, dynamism is the primary way that liberal theology understands reality. Contrary to a static view of God and the world, the immanent God of liberal theology permeates a changing world of history and culture (and, I would add, biological evolution). Third, the autonomy of reason and experience is emphasized, giving faith a subjective dimension. Reason and experience ground historical criticism of sacred texts and contextual readings of Scripture and tradition as expressions of historical experiences of God.[19] The contrasts with evangelical theology are clear. While liberal theology affirms the immanence of God in history, evangelicalism affirms a transcendent God who acts in history. While liberal theology values the truth that emerges from reason and experience, evangelical theology affirms the authoritative truth of Scripture and tradition that give testimony to divine activity in history.[20] As one might expect, the apologetics of liberalism do not absolutely distinguish its theology from evangelicalism, which developed its own apologetic appeal to reason (e.g., in the evidentialist apologetics of Princeton theologians and in the neo-evangelicalism of the 1940s).[21]

Closer to the conversation intended by this essay, Delwin Brown, a process theologian, and Clark Pinnock have engaged each other in dialogue to discern the commonalities and distinctions between liberal and evangelical perspectives. On the one hand, in a fair-minded and

18. Ibid., 285.
19. Knight, *Future,* 42.
20. Ibid., 43.
21. Ibid., 45.

generous passage, Pinnock characterizes liberal theologians as creative people less concerned about heresy and continuity with tradition and more concerned with making sense of Christianity for reasonable contemporaries. Thinking more inductively from human experience than deductively from Christian tradition, liberal theologians make modest truth claims in light of human inability to possess divine truth, which generates in liberalism greater relativism toward other religious and theological perspectives.[22] On the other hand, Brown defends liberal theology, which (he argues) may be deductive or inductive methodologically, as long as its forms (reason, sensory experience, intuition, or praxis) are defensible in contemporary discourse.[23] Pinnock contrasts liberal theology with evangelical theology, which guards (1) the truth of formative messages of the church and (2) doctrinal continuity with the historical church, Jesus, and the apostles. Pinnock describes evangelicalism as the theological option more convinced of the enduring articles of evangelical faith, which need no change, in contrast with creative liberalism, which is constantly open to theological revision – and, critically speaking, short-lived in its theological proposals.[24]

Perhaps the most crucial comment of all is Pinnock's point that "liberalism" and "evangelicalism" are diverse. Neither is fixed in history or finalized in theological position.[25] As a theologian influenced by process, feminist and womanist, and liberation theologies, I am reluctant to cast my lot fully with either liberalism or evangelicalism and yet find it impossible to deny the faith commitments that I share with each.

What then *is* the theism that forms and informs my faith commitments? I offer a brief definition of my relational theism, which is analogous with my brief sketch of the open view of God concluding the previous section.

My definition of process theology/theism might include that God is the visionary, purposive divine companion whose attributes include relational freedom, power, and experience, whose presence and power are unlimited, whose relation to the world (inclusive of, but not

22. Clark Pinnock, "Introduction," in *Theological Crossfire: An Evangelical/Liberal Dialogue* (Grand Rapids: Zondervan, 1990), 13.

23. Delwin Brown, "Theological Method: Section 1," in *Theological Crossfire,* 23-24.

24. Pinnock, "Introduction," in *Theological Crossfire,* 13.

25. Ibid., 12.

limited to, humans) is responsive and creative love. This sentence describing process theism is very dense as a compressed expression of what I mean to say about God, and I will elaborate briefly the significance of each point. First, process theism emphasizes the relational character of God. God stands in relation to the world as one who provides vision and purpose for the present and future. God's immersion in the experiences of the world and God's vision of beauty, truth, and goodness uniquely establish both divine companionship and purpose in the world. Second, the presupposition of relationship requires theological decisions about the nature of freedom, power, and experience. God's relationships do not eliminate God's freedom, but God is also not an individualist. Freedom has little meaning apart from relationships that create contexts for the experience of freedom. Divine freedom works in the world to actualize God's vision in highest regard for the freedom and experiences of creatures. Similarly, power means little apart from relationship. I understand divine power to be perfect power because it is relational rather than coercive. God's experience is likewise relational and perfect in that it is responsive to the world's experience and entails all experiences without reducing all divine experience to the world's experience. Third, God's power and experience are unlimited. By this conclusion from panentheism, I mean to affirm that God is both transcendent and immanent – embodying the world's experiences but not limited to the world. I reject unilateral transcendence, classical supernaturalism, pantheism, and anthropomorphism as incomplete renderings of the divine that compartmentalize God into limited spheres of power and experience. Finally, God's creative and responsive love brings God's visionary power into the world. God influences the world toward the divine vision and future, but does so clearly as one genuinely affected by the world's experience and relationships. The continuing creativity and responsiveness of God are not limited to human experience and relationships, but extend to nonhuman experiences and relationships so that God's vision is imparted to the entirety of history, culture, and nature.

The influence of Whitehead's metaphysics on my relational process theism is apparent; however, the standpoint of this paper will be process theology rather than process philosophy. While I am indebted to Whitehead's philosophy and while I understand philosophy, theology, and ethics as difficult to disentangle into separate disciplines, I find it more useful and appropriate in this conversation to concentrate on the theological constructions that are Whiteheadian rather than on Whitehead himself, who was not writing theology.

Theological Method

Obvious commonalities between the open view of God and process theism push comparison toward methodological considerations to discern some distinctions between the two highly relational and dynamic views of God. I begin by recalling what I understand from Pinnock and Rice to characterize theological method, and then I describe the method that informs my theology.

To begin, I must agree with the implications of a rhetorical question posed by Pinnock, "Does it not concern us that God's name is often dishonored because of poor theologies of God?"[26] The response that Pinnock's question evokes comes easily from me: It matters immensely how and what we say theologically because theology is not simply an intellectual task. Theology is a quest for God borne of faith. Theology, poorly undertaken and expressed, diminishes and dishonors God and the church. My search for distinctions between the open view and process theism begins with the affirmation that each perspective intends its theology to honor God and build up the church.

Theological method for the open view of God starts, characteristically for evangelicals, with revelation as the orienting center for theological sources. Pinnock affirms that theological method returns evangelicals to the fundamental fact of revelation, the divine disclosure of God in history. Pinnock's description of revelation suggests that it occupies two historical places. First, revelation is the self-disclosure of God in Jesus the Christ. Second, Pinnock expresses a more contemporary sense of revelation: "What revelation means for evangelicals is that we have seen God having been disclosed in history in the person of Jesus Christ for the purpose of reconciling and restoring the whole human race."[27] For Pinnock, revelation appears to be significant histori-

26. Pinnock, "Systematic Theology," in *Openness of God,* 104.

27. Pinnock, "Theological Method: Section 2," in *Theological Crossfire,* 39.

cally and experientially, disclosing God "in history and in every human heart."[28]

Pinnock understands that four sources for theology arise from the ultimacy of divine revelation. The four sources, which Wesleyans call the quadrilateral, are (1) Scripture, the written witness to revelation; (2) tradition, the community remembering the revelation; (3) experience, the existential appropriation of revelation; and (4) reason, a test for internal consistency and a means to think through revelation.[29]

Pinnock understands Scripture to be distinct from revelation and the unique source that gives later generations access to the original revelation. The power and authenticity in the witness to the original revelation resides in a written canon that preserves a primary witness, whereas an oral tradition would risk reinvention and distortion of the witness to revelation.[30]

To Pinnock's point that Scripture is a source for theology, both Pinnock and Rice add that Scripture is the norm for theology. Pinnock's theology intends to discern the distortions of hellenization in the doctrine of God and to allow the Bible to function more normatively in theology.[31] Rice claims that "agreement with Scripture is the most important test for any theological proposal. By definition, the task of Christian theology is to interpret the contents of the Bible."[32]

These important claims about the vital role of Scripture for theology do not imply that Pinnock and Rice are reductionist or literalist in their use of the Bible as a source for theology. Pinnock clearly holds that the Christian sacred text should be understood in light of its own claims about inspiration. The Bible is a human witness to divine revelation, but it is not merely a human source, as liberal theology tends to say. Further, it is inappropriate to exaggerate the divine character of the Bible, as some evangelical theology might. The modest claims of the Bible's doctrine of inspiration attest to "its complete profitability rather than any scholastic perfection."[33] The modesty of the Bible in its own claims about inspiration ought to be equaled by human humility in the

28. Ibid.
29. Ibid., 40, 43.
30. Ibid., 40-41.
31. "Systematic Theology," in *Openness of God,* 101.
32. Rice, "Biblical Support," 16.
33. Pinnock, "Theological Method: Section 2," 41.

face of formulating a doctrine of God. Pinnock reminds theologians of two important points. First is the relation of the reader and the text: "We insist on distinguishing between the Bible and our attempts to interpret it, and we believe that God always has more light to shed on his Word than we have received."[34] Second, it is wise to remember a priori notions that we bring to an interpretation of the text. Since it is inevitable that we bring presuppositions and interests to the task of interpretation, we need to recognize the approach to the Bible that we bring with us: "In the case of the doctrine of God, we all have a basic portrait of God's identity in our minds when we search the Scriptures, and this model influences our exposition."[35] Part of the theological task is testing our models of God in light of Scripture. The theologians who hold the open view of God find both classical theism and process theism insufficient when measured against the norm of Scripture and the biblical view of God.

The Bible does not function, however, as a literal yardstick against which to measure our models of God. Rice reminds us that the best scholarship suggests that nearly all biblical language about God is metaphorical, attributing comparatively the qualities of one thing to describe another. While most language used for God is metaphorical, it is unwise to distinguish too sharply between literal and figurative biblical language since biblical language is textured, and different metaphors function differently with respect to their various representations and their relative importance in relation to biblical themes. Rice argues that the open view of God is constructed by attention to those metaphors that play a more prominent role in the biblical account of God and that bear a stronger resemblance to divine reality. Such metaphors as divine suffering and divine repentance provide a strong hermeneutical key.[36]

The root metaphor for theology in the open view of God is persons in loving relationship.[37] Pinnock elaborates on the biblical view of God's sovereignty by opting against the view of God as aloof monarch and for the view of God as caring parent. The caring parent evokes the image of love, responsiveness, generosity, sensitivity, openness, and vul-

34. "Systematic Theology," 103.
35. Ibid.
36. Rice, "Biblical Support," 17.
37. John Sanders, "Historical Considerations," in *Openness of God*, 100.

nerability (to use Pinnock's list of attributes). Unlike the God described by Whitehead and some contemporary process philosophers and theologians, the open God is more than a metaphysical principle. The open view stresses the personhood of God, a divine image that John Cobb and some other process theologians also support.[38] The personhood of God is described relationally as one "who experiences the world, responds to what happens, relates to us and interacts dynamically with humans."[39]

Among theologians who hold the open view, the important argument for this type of theism is advanced using Scripture. The sustained argument by Rice looks to both testaments of the Bible to make the case. Rice observes that the Bible presents evidence of both divine responsiveness and creaturely freedom.[40] The Hebrew Bible attests to the social and dynamic character of God in descriptions of emotions, intentions, and actions that reflect how the world affects God.[41] The Greek Testament furthers the view of God as relational in the incarnation, life, and ministry of Jesus.[42] The biblical witness to the revelation of God in Jesus is an important reason to assert the relational character of God.

While the Bible has unique status among the sources, I should not neglect other theological sources that contribute to the open view. The second source is tradition, the historical community that remembers the revelation. Pinnock is critical of evangelical theologians whose concentration on the centrality of biblical authority obscures the memory of the tradition. Tradition, in Pinnock's view, is where the revealed Word of God is refreshed, rediscovered, reformulated, and restated: "In the history of interpretation and in tradition, like so many refractions of sunlight passing through the prism, the Word of God is continually pondered, treasured, and passed on to subsequent generations."[43] The historical refractions and reformulations in the tradition are not a threat to Christian integrity, but a commitment to preserving the value, meaning, and intelligibility of revelation. "Tradition is the pro-

38. Pinnock, "Systematic Theology," 103.

39. Ibid.

40. Rice, "Biblical Support," 18.

41. Ibid., 22.

42. Ibid., 39-40.

43. Pinnock, "Theological Method: Section 2," 41.

cess of the Word of God becoming historically effective."[44] Scripture is not forgotten or misplaced in using tradition as a source for theology because the sacred text remains the measure of faithfulness to the revelation. Scripture reforms and corrects tradition, holding its place of centrality and authority.

The third source for theology is experience, the existential appropriation of revelation. Present experience of believers is important, but it must always be correlated with tradition, the experiences of the community in history. Worship, preaching, liturgy, and teaching enable the integration of personal and historical, communal experience. Personal life and experience are transformed in encounter with the historical experience and social memory that have formed the church. The Holy Spirit works in both personal and communal experience to enliven the encounter of person, church, and experience with the Word of God. Important as personal experience of revelation is in Scripture, individual experience is not revelation and must be accountable to Christian norms arising from Scripture and mediated through tradition.[45]

The fourth source for theology is reason, which is important because of the intelligibility of God's Word and revelation. Pinnock names several important functions of reason in theological formulations: (1) avoidance of contradiction, (2) accountability to new information, and (3) attention to holistic (rather than fragmented) truth. The human gift and quest is intelligence, which seeks understanding in relation to faith. Pinnock asserts that "even revelation needs to be thought out and not left undigested."[46] While Pinnock contends that evangelicals should give higher regard to the role of reason in theology, he cautions that reason should not be given the highest place as final source and judge in theology. The role of reason is humble because it is subject to culture.[47]

Pinnock suggests that theology must hold the four sources (Scripture, tradition, experience, and reason) in tension and let them function together as the foundation for a solid theology. Theology gains its authenticity and stability not from the shifting tide of culture

44. Ibid., 42.
45. Ibid., 42-43.
46. Ibid., 43.
47. Ibid., 44.

but from the historical vision that grounds the church. The revelation of God deposited in Scripture is the Christian defense against passing cultural influences.[48]

Because there is significant agreement between the method that supports an open view of God and the method that informs my theology, I will discuss the process that shapes my work in dialogue with Pinnock and others who advocate an open view of God.

Recalling the biblical command to worship God with heart, soul, mind, and strength, Gordon Kaufman has described theology as "the mind's worship." Kaufman's name for theology has stuck with me because it suggests an attitude toward writing theology. The image of the mind's worship suggests to me that one writes from the standpoint of faith. Theology presupposes God, regardless of whether one is writing apologetically, and an experience of being in relationship with God. Because it is also worship, theological writing itself is a reverential experience with God, in openness and responsiveness to God and in communion with biblical and historical communities of faith. Because theology is the *mind's* worship, theological writing resembles contemplative and meditative disciplines and calls on committed and disciplined intellect.

Kaufman suggests further useful language to me when he describes theological writing as a constructive task that engages the received faith with the contemporary situation. Theology makes the received faith fresh again in light of new historical contexts. The received faith, to which we have access through revelation, Scripture, and tradition, is the context that suggests whether theology is *Christian* theology. The resources of the received faith are not simply normative or reductive parameters for assessing theology. Scripture, tradition, and revelation are better understood as interrelated components of a wisdom tradition that brings critical insight, meaning, evaluation, challenge, and vision to the contemporary situation. The contemporary situation contributes existential, cultural, and intellectual puzzles for consideration in light of the received faith. In dialogue that honors the received faith, the contemporary situation stimulates theology to reformation of unjust conclusions, uncommunicative language, and inaccurate presuppositions. Constructive theology that engages both the re-

48. Ibid.

ceived faith and the contemporary situation assumes God's creative and redemptive activity in the past and divine engagement with the world in the present and future.

My version of constructive Christian theology refers to six sources and stimuli for the theological task: revelation, Scripture, and tradition (often associated with the received faith), and experience, culture, and reason (often associated with the contemporary situation). These sources appear in different forms and relationships in other types of theology, and I do not intend for them to prescribe a correct theological method. They are clearly not interpreted identically with the ways that Macquarrie or Cone or Gutiérrez or Delores Williams or Ada María Isasi-Díaz or Kwok Pui-lan might use them. In truth, they are for me tools, stimuli, hints, and reminders rather than formulaic and rote sources. In other words, revelation, Scripture, tradition, experience, culture, and reason are living, breathing, dynamic, interconnected – and often serendipitous – voices in the task of theology.

Like Pinnock, I presume that revelation must inform theology. In particular, Christian theology is indebted to the centrality of the self-disclosure of God in Jesus the Christ. The special revelation of God incarnate is particularly paradigmatic and suggestive for a relational theology. My constructive theology would add remembrance of other divine self-disclosures. The Christian canon suggests what those self-disclosures might be – the creation, the *imago dei,* the chosen people of Israel, the prophetic voices, and the church, the body of Christ. All divine self-disclosure reflects the creative and redemptive activity of God in relation to the world. While I often associate revelation with the received faith, this larger sense of revelation patterned after divine self-disclosure in Scripture suggests to me that theology should be attentive to the creative, redemptive, self-disclosing God by remembering, watching, and anticipating the divine presence. The living Christ calls theology to expect revelation, not only to recall it. This emphasis on anticipation of revelation may differ from the open view.

Like Pinnock, I take Scripture to be a central and authentic witness to the revelation of God, especially the historical revelation of God in Christ. I am resistant to debates about inerrancy and infallibility of Scripture, in part, because they fall into a modernist, rationalist habit of ascribing proof where faith is sufficient. By contrast, I find literary-critical thinking about the Bible to be a valuable legacy from the Enlightenment that has enabled me to drink more deeply from the wisdom of the sacred texts. The more I can learn about literary genre, historical context, and cultural setting the more fully I appreciate Scripture and the models that it provides for theological integrative thinking about the received faith and contemporary situation. For example, Douglas Oakman (my colleague from Pacific Lutheran University) has given me insight about the Gospels through his research on the socioeconomic milieu of Jesus' culture, which has relevance to theology concerned about liberation and economic justice.

The greatest danger in theology is not the neglect of Scripture but the misappropriation and uninformed use of Scripture. A colleague once told me that one can tell when a theologian went to graduate school by how dated his or her knowledge of biblical scholarship is. To depend on biblical scholarship and yet be uncommitted to deep study of the Bible, its languages, and current scholarship is a limitation for theology. As Rice points out, we do bring a view of God to reading Scripture. Presuming models of God as we read texts runs a risk of habituated biblical study even when we take care to place theology firmly in the Christian community and hermeneutics under the leadership of the Holy Spirit. Another hazard to theology is unwillingness to challenge scriptural texts when we have good grounds. For example, I am unwilling to support as universal propositions passages that are unjust, such as the New Testament advice that slaves obey their masters or Hebrew texts that accept violence toward women. I accept that the canon holds plural and diverse perspectives about which we must be discerning. Above all, then, theology requires humility rather than arrogance in the interpretation of Scripture for the contemporary situation.

The third stimulus for my theology is tradition, which I find to be miraculous. It is remarkable to me that Christian traditions carry with them a power transcending the limitations of the persons, institutions, and cultures that create them. The traditions of Christianity hold for me an identity at once to embrace and to evaluate. The diversity within Christianity sets the range of options available for theology that wishes to be Christian, yet the tradition should be subject to scrutiny. For example, I am unwilling to give blanket endorsement to the traditions in Christianity that used Scripture and theology to justify slavery in the United States. Tradition is a dynamic source and stimulus for theology, but it is a dynamic source to which we add and from which we reform.

Experience seems to be an important source in the openness view, and it is a valuable stimulus for my constructive theology as well. I concur with Pinnock that personal experience is one dimension of this source, but I want to emphasize that communal experience is likewise useful as a theological source. In addition to religious experience, I would like to add that nonreligious experience also provides impetus for my theology. For example, liberation theologians have taught me to be attentive to the experience of the oppressed, as individuals and communities and in both religious and nonreligious experiences. Experiences of death and injustice suggest large questions for theology ranging from theodicy to salvation and Christology because death and injustice point toward a human condition in the contemporary situation. I am also attentive, however, to the religious experience of the oppressed that gives rise to base Christian communities, liberation hermeneutics and theology, and revolution. The religious experience of the oppressed moves North American constructive theology to address ecclesiology, missiology, and ethics. Experience goads my theology to give particular attention to places where experiences are neglected or marginalized, but where they have power to impact the world. The marginalized experience suggests questions for theology to address and holds theology accountable to justice.

Perhaps the greatest point of departure between my theological sources and the sources that inform the open view is my inclusion of culture as a source and stimulus. Culture is multifaceted. Its facets are literature and the arts (inclusive of pop culture and its media), news and events, social sciences (psychology, sociology, economics, politics), natural sciences (physics, biology, ecology), and world religions. Each of these sources suggests how we might understand the world and ourselves in relation, and they give theology dilemmas, information, issues, illustrations, and analyses to consider. A particularly important facet of culture for theology is language. Since religious language is metaphorical, theology must pay attention to where language shifts and develops in order to be responsible and clear about what it wishes to communicate about God. Even the same word used over different generations in the same city can be heard very differently between mother and child.

Theology is not just speech about God – it is hearing about God; thus theology must be accountable for how its words are received.

In agreement with Pinnock, I judge reason to be an important source for theology that wishes to be intelligible, coherent, consistent, and comprehensive. Logic and philosophy that speak to the community addressed by theology assist in making revelation available and language accessible. Theology must make sense. While I would agree with John Cobb that all theology is shaped by its culture's vision of reality (worldview), I choose to learn explicitly from philosophy. From a Christian standpoint, I interact with philosophies that are useful in generating questions, constructions, and worldviews. Like the theology that supports the open view, my theology interacts with relational metaphysics that provide alternatives to classical theism. Among relational philosophies and metaphysics, Whiteheadian and some feminist postmodern thought opens fruitful possibilities for my theology. Philosophy is not theology or even the starting point for theology, but philosophy can contribute depth and clarity to theology.

I see theology not just as interpretation of the Bible, but as the language that seeks the continuous relevance of God to the world in light of contemporary issues, struggles, and creativity. Calling on the Bible and other bearers of the communal witness, theology assists the church (Christianity) and churches (particular communities of faith – especially communities of "the least of these") in coming to voice and keeping the meaning of God and Christ fresh. This is a function of theology internal to Christianity for building up the church. Theology further equips the church and churches to speak to the world. This second function of theology is external, and it takes Christianity into the world as a creative and critical voice.

Theism

What difference do the commonalities and distinctions between the open view and process theology really make? An obvious example for analysis is theism, and I will focus on God as creator as I detail some points of agreement with the open view and reflect on the scope of our differences.

The focus on relationality in both the open view and process theism undergirds a good deal of agreement in principle about the creativity of God, theologically speaking. First, God is the free creator of significantly free human beings. Our theologies are committed to genuine, rather than illusory, human freedom without compromising the freedom of God. Second, God's power is conceived in relation to the freedom and decisions of others who have freedom and power. God's power and creativity do not negate human freedom, but relate to human freedom. Freedom is exercised by God and humans in relationships. Third, an implication of freedom in relationship is that God is responsive to our responses. If humans are truly free, then God's creativity and responses are in some sense contingent on how humans exercise freedom. The open view of God and process theism understand responsiveness in light of the love of God. Fourth, God does not unilaterally control all that happens. Human freedom would be a sham if God controlled all events. Therefore, God's power is not best understood as coercive or unilateral. Fifth, God is endlessly resourceful and competent in working out the divine goals. Although God's power is relational and responsive, God's freedom to work toward the divine goals is not lost. While process theology might describe God's creative activity in terms of a divine lure that mediates pure potential to the world and the open view might choose more traditional language, each intends to affirm that divine purpose endures and works transformatively in the world. Sixth, God's action is social and dynamic. Rice and Pinnock note supporting examples from Scripture and tradition: (1) creation and deliverance in the Hebrew Bible, (2) incarnation in the Greek Testament, and (3) the doctrine of the Trinity in the historical tradition. These sources inform both the open view of God and process theism in describing God as relational and changing.[49] Seventh, God interacts with creatures. God influences creatures and creatures influence God such that history is not a product of divine action alone. History is created in the dynamics between God and humans. Eighth, God depends on the world in certain respects – in such a way that dependence enhances rather than diminishes God. My agreement with Rice on this point is rooted in the social, relational, and responsive character of God. There are limitations to agreement between the open view and process theism on this point. We address the questions of whether God

49. Rice, "Biblical Support," 35, 39; Pinnock, "Systematic Theology," 97.

could exist without the world and whether God created the world ex nihilo quite differently. The open view affirms that God could exist without the creaturely world. The open view also affirms creation of the cosmos from nothing, but argues that creation ex nihilo does not entail that God controls and determines everything.

Underneath the points of agreement between process theism and the open view, there are sticking points in the details. One of those sticking points is in the tension between the metaphysics of creation and the theological purposes of biblical creation accounts. The open view might well call process theism to be more explicit about how biblical accounts of creation inform process theology. Both views might agree, however, on some of the theological purposes behind the Genesis 1-2 creation accounts. The Genesis texts on creation express theological commitments (1) to the dependence of the world on God, (2) to the presence of God in all dimensions of the cosmos, (3) to the created goodness of the world and God's delight in it, (4) to the purpose of humans in their origins, (5) to expression of an ancient cosmology in relation to God, and (6) to God's worthiness of worship. If we can agree that these points and perhaps some others express the central theological content of the Genesis creation stories, then perhaps we can agree that theological statements beyond these are more speculative in importance. As we move beyond the explicit theology (or theologies) expressed in the accounts of creation, we might acknowledge that both the open view and process theism begin to elaborate a worldview beyond what is included in the canon.

I have no reservations about the usefulness of metaphysical statements or philosophy to assist us in making the Christian story of origins meaningful in our time. However, some criteria for assessing the usefulness of metaphysics in the formation of a theology of creation might be in order. For example, the criteria might include whether metaphysics reflects appropriately upon biblical texts or whether the metaphysics discussion is evocative, informative and formative, illuminating, and relevant in the context of Christian community. It might be useful to see what differing criteria emerge from the relational metaphysics of the open view and process theism. We might all be able to see better where we leave tradition and Scripture and opt for speculative metaphysics in the formation of our theological alternatives.

A second sticking point is related to *creatio ex nihilo* and *creatio continua.* Both views embrace continuing/continuous creativity in God's ongoing relation to free creatures. But a serious difference emerges from the standpoint of the open view and *creatio ex nihilo.* I understand the problem in these ways. First, there is concern about the interdependence of God and the world. There is consensus between the open view and process theism that the world and humans depend on God for existence, in some sense, and God is related to the world by divine love and continuing responsiveness. What does it mean, however, to say that God depends on the world? On the one hand, if theology begins with the assumption of *creatio ex nihilo,* certain assumptions are made about dependence of the world on God. These assumptions might include that dependence is always framed in terms of the contingent existence or nonexistence of the world. If these assumptions are primary, then the reverse assumptions seem incomprehensible because the definition of dependence derived is objectionable when applied to God. On the other hand, if theology begins from the assumption that God did not create ex nihilo or that dependence means something else, then the dependence of God on the world might be less objectionable.

Let's start with the consensus in the two views that free creatures interact with God's desires for the course of creation and in exercising their freedom either further or reject the divine goals. Consequently, God responds accordingly to free human action. If we understand this mutual process of formation (in-formation) and influence (in-fluence) as interdependence, then the conflict between the open view and process theism is not so apparent – and this is my understanding of what pertains in each view. My sense of this agreement is based on a comment by Rice in *The Openness of God:*

> As an aspect of his experience, God's knowledge of the world is also dynamic rather than static. Instead of perceiving the entire course of human existence in one timeless moment, God comes to know events as they take place. He learns something from what transpires. We call this position the "open view of God" because it regards God as receptive to new experiences and as flexible in the way he works toward his objectives in the world. Since it sees God as dependent on the world in certain respects, the open view of God differs much from conven-

> tional theology. Yet we believe that this dependence does not detract from God's greatness, it only enhances it.[50]

While somewhat different metaphysics or reasons may be behind this point of agreement, the theological consequence is similar. This is a personal metaphor of interrelationship. The main point of disagreement, then, seems to be between proponents of the open view. For example, Rice and William Hasker seem to differ when Hasker appears to side with classical theism on the point of unilateral dependence of the world on God because of his focus on ontological dependence rather than relational interdependence.

Because of my reading of biblical scholarship on Genesis 1:1-2 (which suggests that God created from chaos rather than nothing) and because of the priority that the incarnation has in my theology, I am reluctant to endorse a theology of creation ex nihilo. The incarnation is the revelation of God, whose primary identity is understood in relation to the world and not in isolation. The doctrine of the Trinity, which is more a construct of the tradition than a biblical theology, may be best expressed relationally as a social trinity, but a social trinity is not the same as the incarnation, which reveals God foremost in relation to the world, not to Godself. Panentheism, which understands the world in ontological relationship with God, is analogous to the incarnation in Jesus the Christ, who was truly human and truly divine.

A second dimension of the tensions around creation out of nothing and continuing creation may relate to how we think differently about mind and body and organic views of God and the God-world relationship. I think that I understand the reluctance of some who hold the open view to embrace the organic model of God and the God-world relationship — in part due to Sallie McFague's criticism of the classical organic model. I want to hear more about the discomfort with the organic worldview of process thought from those who hold the open view. For now, however, I will side with them in rejecting a classical organic model. My reasons may be different and may hold different theological consequences. McFague finds the classical organic model to be objectionable on two grounds: the mind/body who symbolizes organicism is (1) a male body and (2) a human body. The androcentrism and

50. Rice, "Biblical Support," 16.

anthropocentrism of the classical organic model, therefore, are problematic for a gender-inclusive and nature-inclusive theology.[51] I applaud her metaphorical suggestion to expand the notion of body to include all bodies in nature from humans to the barest puff of existence.[52] This new metaphor of the world as God's body contains the plurality and diversity of nature. It continues to embrace the personal while expanding the metaphor in important ways for an ecological model of God. She resists describing God in terms of mind and body, because the mind/body distinction has tended to leave women and nature on the short end of the stick by associating rationality with masculinity. To replace mind/body, McFague turns to Spirit and Body. By "Spirit," McFague means the breath of God, which inspires and, in fact, breathes life into the world's creatures. Spirit as the source of vitality and life contrasts with the Mind, which orders and controls the world.[53] Note, by the way, that she moves us closer to a biblical metaphor than the importation of Hellenistic mind/body language does. Let me note also that McFague's theology has implications for the metaphor of the body of Christ, the church. My conclusion overall is that perhaps we have been arguing about the trees when the forest is green and rich with potential for growth.

Boundaries

I do not describe myself as an evangelical. I also do not describe myself simply as a process theologian or a liberal theologian. My theology is Christian (although trying to some Christians), feminist, relational (influenced by Whitehead's metaphysics, but not uncritical about how), and ecological. It has strong sympathies with liberation theologies from a number of oppressed communities in the global context and with religions of the world and religiously plural contexts. It carries the zeal and central commitments of my evangelical roots.

It is generally my perception that evangelicals left me rather than

51. Sallie McFague, *The Body of God: An Ecological Theology* (Minneapolis: Fortress, 1993), 30, 36-37.

52. Ibid., 37.

53. Ibid., 143-45.

that I left evangelicals. Regardless, I know why we parted company. Someone drew boundaries that for me compromised a biblical and theological strand of thought that focuses on the Christic revelation of God as love. Theologically, the doctrine of God as creator was compromised for me by blind disregard of the world during the political, conservative entrenchment of the Southern Baptist Convention.

Several issues are at stake for me: liberation of politically and economically oppressed persons, coequality or the valuation of women in their differences from men and in their diversity as women, affirmation of Christians and non-Christians who are gay or lesbian (at least on the grounds of a strong doctrine of grace), dialogue and transformation in a religiously and culturally plural community and church, and embracing of science for the sake of knowing the world created by God and for the sake of lending a nonmaterialist voice to appreciative observation of and interaction with the world.

Complementarity

In the course of thinking about this dialogue between evangelical theism and process theism, I have grown weary of any pressure to decide the superiority of one view over the other. I hope that I have indicated where I delight in our agreement, where I wish we were expending less abstract energy, and where I require process theology to explore some projects where evangelical theology alone would not assist me much. I regret most that there is no return to paradise where I first learned process theology in an evangelical context and worried little about hate in a caring Christian community.

I am not a process theologian who thinks that process theism is the only coherent and viable alternative to classical theism.[54] What I seek is not competition among the views, but coalition. Together we have rich agreements that can inspire Christian congregations of all types since both process theology and evangelical theology are not specific to particular denominations. What I urge is that we continue to develop rich language affirming God's love and responsiveness to the world. From Pinnock's delightful prose to Whitehead's intriguing met-

54. William Hasker, "A Philosophical Perspective," in *Openness of God,* 140.

aphors, we have a range of language capable of speaking to diverse Christian audiences. Why should we diminish God or the church by abandoning one or the other?

In Response to Nancy Howell

DAVID L. WHEELER

As I read the essays by my theological colleagues in this project, Nancy Howell and Richard Rice, and compare them to my own contribution to this volume (chapter 3), I am struck by the strong autobiographical flavor of each of the three pieces. I take it that this is more than simply deference, intended or unintended, to the recent ascendency of "narrative" and "niche" theologies. More and more, theologians are becoming aware – along with other contemporary thinkers – of the social construction of the self and the perspectival nature of all our doctrinal constructions. Or, to put it in terms of the Wesleyan quadrilateral, we are constrained to privilege "experience" – our own, concrete, particular experience – as a theological source. We may position our theologies as responses to culture (classical Protestant liberalism) or responses to God's culture-transcending self-revelation (evangelicalism), but our own journeys seem to mold powerfully both the method and the content of our theologies.

Nancy Howell declares: "Southern Baptist affirmations of faith remain important to me" and "tangibly remind me that my heart recalls important roots of my faith" (p. 53). Why is this so? We can give all sorts of explanations of the method, sources, norms, and loyalties of our theologies, and yet we are always – for better or for worse – inescapably in conversation with the harmonies and dissonances of our roots. A process account of this phenomenon might speak of the efficient causation of our unique material, biological, and cultural antecedents, and the fitting of God's lure to just that type and degree of actualization the theologian in question represents. Speaking psychologically, I have become convinced by my experiences among members of the professional philosophers' guild that choices of rational, mystical, or empirical perspectives on one's environment are to a great degree functions of temperament – a finding that could launch us on an interminable discussion of "nature" and "nurture" in the formation of personality. Suffice it to say that as different as we might otherwise be, Nancy Howell and I are by both history and temperament the sort of persons who are patient with and eager for dialogue between traditions, who are aware of our own limitations and the limitations of our own most cherished formulae; who genuinely want to learn, not simply to debate and refute. Further, I deeply resonate with Howell's experience that the evangelical faith of her youth and the process theism she discovered as a graduate student were not mutually exclusive alternatives but examples of "multiple languages of faith [that] were enriching my understanding of God."

I say all this not to boast, on my own behalf or Howell's. An irenic temperament is not an unmixed blessing; it does not fit one well for drawing lines in the sand and issuing challenges. "In the course of thinking about this dialogue between evangelical theism and process theism, I have grown weary of any pressure to decide the superiority of one view over the other," Howell says. To the extent one employs this irenic tendency for fostering dialogue and creating understanding, its presence must be considered a gift of grace. Nevertheless, Howell does identify herself at the beginning of her essay as "a process theologian"; it is interesting to note that Richard Rice wonders whether there is such a thing, or if instead there are simply some Christian theologians – in our cases – using process categories to locate ontologically our faith assertions (Rice, chapter 4 below). Howell herself declares at the end of her essay: "I am not a process theologian who thinks that process theism is the only coherent and viable alternative to classical theism. What I seek is not competition among the views, but coalition."

With her conciliatory language toward evangelicalism and her reluctance to choose among mutually exclusive alternatives, Howell does not generate energy from the discovery of "distinct alternatives" and "permanent divides" in the material content of doctrinal assertions as does Rice. But it does seem to me that she generates significant energy in her comparison of her theological method with that of her evangelical dialogue partners. The remarks in my opening paragraph about the widespread privileging of experience in contemporary theology notwithstanding, Howell is correct in stating: "Theological method for the open view of God starts, characteristically for evangelicals, with revelation as the orienting center for theological sources." She then describes Clark Pinnock's use of the Wesleyan quadrilateral, and what she sees as Pinnock's (and Rice's) privileging of Scripture as the original and normative source among the multiple revelatory sources described in the quadrilateral. She further cites Rice's claim that "agreement with Scripture is the most important test for any theological proposal."

Notwithstanding the pluriform nature of American evangelicalism surveyed briefly by Howell, I would argue that Rice's claim, along with the privileging of personal relationship to God through Christ, are the two tenets that constitute the bedrock identity of that often slippery and polemical designation "evangelical." I would further claim that the subjectivism inherent in that latter characteristic of evangelicalism is in inherent tension with the referral to inscripturated revelation by evangelicals as the objective benchmark for authentic Christian faith. But be that as it may, Howell correctly describes the model of God promoted by the "openness" evangelicals as "biblically recovered" — that is, a responsive God extracted from a Christian tradition in bondage to alien conceptualities by a heuristic use of biblical texts. Again, Howell is appreciative and conciliatory. "Like Pinnock," she says, "I presume that revelation must inform theology." And, "Like Pinnock, I take Scripture to be a central and authentic witness to the revelation of God." But the vital energy that structures her theology seems to originate elsewhere.

She speaks warmly and enthusiastically of her discovery, as a graduate student, of Whiteheadian language about God's persuasive love, which gave expression to her own previously existing "faith commitments." She speaks of her experience of "the power of God's observable, continuous creation." Later in her exposition, she gives her own enumeration of six sources of constructive Christian theology, divided into the received sources (revelation, Scripture, tradition) and the situational sources (experience, culture, reason), a typology reminiscent of Tillich. Then as she analyzes the use of these sources in constructive theology, we find a fascinating chain of "I" statements moving her exposition forward and staking out her loyalties. "I am unwilling . . ." "I concur with Pinnock . . ." "I am attentive to. . . ." Then comes her explicit identification of "the greatest point of departure between my theological sources and the sources that inform the open view," namely her "inclusion of culture as a source and stimulus." Pinnock and Rice are characteristically evangelical in privileging Scripture among theological sources, indeed, making it the normative source, as I have noted. Combining hallmarks of classical Protestant liberalism and the pietistic side of evangelicalism in her synthesis, Howell privileges experience, not only as a theological source, as we all do to some extent today, but as a methodological norm. "Experience," in this instance, means both her profound personal experience of the divine (self-authenticating and sui generis, as in James's *Varieties*?) and the transcendence-laden contents of culture – our shared experience symbolically produced, preserved, and transmitted.

One might think of inscripturated revelation *over* culture, as in the formulae of Pinnock and Rice, while for Howell Scripture and other explicitly Christian elements of tradition are guideposts to the transcendent dimensions of culture itself. Any and all elements of culture (e.g., Whiteheadian metaphysics) might rise to prominence in various given situations as bearers and interpreters of transcendent insight. "I see theology not just as interpretation of the Bible but as the language that seeks the continuous relevance of God in the world in the light of contemporary issues, struggles, and creativity. Calling on the Bible and other bearers of the communal witness, theology assists the church."

Dare I generalize that this methodological divide is not just an issue between Howell, Pinnock, and Rice, but that it comprises an essential difference between evangelicals – including openness theists – and process theists in general? It is not simply that the former submit to revelation and the latter generate putative religious truth out of arbitrarily selected experience. Both Howell and Rice, it seems to me, would acknowledge the necessity and gracious character of God's self-revelation for any who would hope to encounter "the visionary, purposive divine companion" and to understand and communicate that encounter. But Howell, it seems, would find that revelation in a constellation of sources, within which authenticity is a function of the consistency, coherence, and fruitfulness of the constellation as a whole (to be sure, to be a Christian is to privilege Jesus as the Christ among these sources).[1] Among these sources is the Whiteheadian metaphysics, carrying its power to illuminate experience quite apart from any intrinsic connection to Christian tradition. ("I have no reservations about the usefulness of metaphysical statements or philosophy to assist us in making the Christian story of origins meaningful in our time.") In contrast, Rice would privilege Scripture within a graded hierarchy of sources.

As I have wrestled with issues of theological method with my students for fourteen years, it has been helpful for me to tell the contrasting yet yoked stories of Karl Barth and Paul Tillich. As young pastors both found their theological training and acculturation catastrophically inadequate to deal with the tragedy of the First World War. "The Fatherhood of God and the Brotherhood of Man" indeed, when the "Christian" nations of Europe and the United States were using the technology of the new century to annihilate one another! In his *Römerbrief,* Barth spoke of a "Wholly Other" God who comes to humanity on his own terms, in his concrete, specific self-revelation that is – paradoxically – part of human history at the same time that it is underivable from any conditions existing in that history, and incommensurate with any and all canons of human knowing. Jesus Christ, testified to within and unifying Holy Scripture, is the reality of that revelation. Not only does Jesus Christ answer humanity's questions, but God through Christ actually sets the questions – sinful humanity cannot even know what it needs to ask, know, and be.[2] In contrast, Tillich, though he affirmed the reality of a divine self-revelation in Christ, developed his famous method of "correlation," in which the theologian seeks in the Christian revelation answers to the questions that arise in human culture.[3] If Christian faith is not applicable to real questions asked by real human beings, then it may be so "wholly other" as to be irrelevant.

Without presuming to reduce Howell and Rice methodologically to two deceased forerunners, I must say that I can see two rivers of method flowing through the twentieth century; one is named "Barth" and the

1. Cf. John B. Cobb Jr., *Christ in a Pluralistic Age* (Philadelphia: Westminster, 1975).

2. Karl Barth, *The Epistle to the Romans,* trans. Edwyn C. Hoskyns (London: Oxford University Press, 1933), 28ff.

3. Paul Tillich, *Systematic Theology,* 3 vols. (Chicago: University of Chicago Press, 1951-63), 1:59-66.

other is named "Tillich." They often are interlaced in the theological floodplain, and many thinkers – myself included – wade now in one and now in the other. One river flows from the twin springs of revelation and experience, and has birthed in our generation the various concrete theologies of experience – feminist, womanist, liberationist, and so on. The other purports to come solely from revelation, and would carry and shape experience in its torrents. In this theological parable, process theology is clearly birthed in the River Tillich, which in turn has emerged as one freshet from the aquifer named Schleiermacher, while American evangelicalism, however much its more conservative practitioners might protest, is hydrologically Barthian. Thus, even when Howell as a process theologian and Rice as an openness evangelical make common cause on the topic of God's receptivity to influences from the world, even "as dependent on the world in certain respects," they arrive at this agreement through contrasting paths – a sort of theological "convergent evolution." Of course, the methodological contrast is never absolute, as Howell demonstrates when she connects her negative assessment of creation ex nihilo to "my reading of biblical scholarship."

Personally, I am intrigued with trying to tease out these methodological contrasts because: (a) disparate starting points and methods can lead to widely different loyalties with a common tradition (e.g., Christian fundamentalists and mainline Protestants who neither understand each other's loyalties nor give each other the benefit of a presumption of good faith); (b) methodological differences can impede communication and hinder common tasks even when theological content is similar (e.g., the paucity of interchange between the two camps represented in this book); and (c) I must confess I have lurched along the boundary of these two methodological models throughout my own career as a theologian and church leader, seemingly unable to commit entirely to either model, and thus reduced to making suggestions about questions they might put to each other, as I do in my own essay in this symposium (chapter 3 below). I envy Howell and Rice their clearer identities!

In Response to Nancy Howell

RICHARD RICE

> *"Philosophy is not theology or even the starting point for theology, but philosophy can contribute depth and clarity to theology. I see theology not just as interpretation of the Bible, but as the language that seeks the continuous relevance of God to the world in light of contemporary issues, struggles, and creativity."*

Nancy Howell has some fine things to say about the nature of theology. As she describes it, theology is more a personal journey than a discipline or a task, and her own experience richly illustrates this account. Her journey led from a conservative Baptist upbringing, through an introduction to process thought, and on to an appreciation for a number of viewpoints and concerns. Accordingly, she declines the labels "evangelical," "process," and "liberal," although she appreciates the values associated with each of them. She affirms the zeal and central commitments of her evangelical roots – though evangelicals left her, she states, rather than the other way around. And she embraces the insights of process thought, without regarding process theism as the only coherent alternative to classical theism. "My theology," she says, "is Christian (although trying to some Christians), feminist, relational (influenced by Whitehead's metaphysics, but not uncritical about how), and ecological." Moreover, she calls for coalition, not competition, among these different views.

I like the irenic tone of Howell's reflections, and I think her description of the way her own outlook has developed applies to the experience of many theologians. I know it rings true to mine. Most of us do not deliberately select a theological perspective, gradually master an appropriate method, and then proceed with our work. We do not choose to be conservative or liberal, evangelical or process theologians. Instead, life's experiences bring us to a certain point as our convictions accumulate and modify. We take our bearings, survey the resources at hand, and work things out theologically where we find ourselves. Over time careful thinking and openness to evidence may change our views. But this happens in a holistic rather than discursive way. It is more a matter of what Bernard Lonergan calls conversion than the conclusion of a rational investigation.

In recent years many theologians have reconceived the nature of their discipline in a way suggested by Howell's remarks. Their goal is not to find the best theory for adjudicating the claims of Christian faith, but to bear witness to the distinctive insights of the Christian community. For example, Rebecca S. Chopp recasts the central theological task as a "poetics of testimony" designed to "describe or name that which rational discourse will not or cannot reveal."[1] The theorist judges witnesses and testimonies in order to assess their truth.[2] But the task of poetics is "not so much to argue as to refigure, to imagine and refashion the world." It allows testimony, "the discourse that refers to a reality outside the ordinary order of things," to retain its peculiarity. It also brings theory into the picture, not to judge but to serve the testimony, to give voice to particularity and difference inherent in testimony. Chopp's revisionary proposal gives theology a practical, moral task. Its purpose is not to order discourse in relation to reason, but to order discourse in response to the moral summons in testimonies, "to imagine and create new ways of envisioning human life."[3]

I sense a similarity between the theological reordering that Chopp calls for and the theological vision Howell offers us here, with her weariness of theological debate and her interest in the transformative power of various religious visions. I also see it in her list of six "sources

1. "Theology and the Poetics of Testimony," *Criterion* 37/1 (1998): 2.
2. Ibid., 5.
3. Ibid., 9.

and stimuli" for theological reflection." She describes them as "tools, stimuli, hints, reminders rather than formulaic and rote sources," as "living, breathing dynamic, interconnected – and often serendipitous – voices in the task of theology." It is clear that Howell does not conceive of theology as a meticulous application of various procedures, or a quest for the perfect theory. This is probably why she is less interested in process philosophy than in process theology. Her desire is to find out what process terms and categories can contribute to our vision of the way things are and ought to be, not to work out the details of an elaborate cosmological scheme.

I share that preference. I appreciate the fresh breeze that has blown through theology lately, drawing us to a new appreciation for the originating myths, symbols, and stories of the Christian community and directing us to their life-transforming possibilities. Thus, while I am interested in the ways process thought can help us express the fundamental insights of Christian faith, I have never had much interest in becoming a process philosopher, or even a process theologian, for that matter.

Howell raises an important issue when she questions the relation between philosophy and theology. It is a perennial concern for theologians. Theology cannot ignore philosophy, for reasons that Paul Tillich, among others, makes abundantly clear.[4] Yet there are always risks in turning to philosophy. One is the possibility that a particular philosophy will come to dominate one's theological perspective. A theologian may turn to philosophy for conceptual assistance in interpreting Christian insights and wind up viewing Christianity as an illustration of the philosophical system. The more powerful the system, the greater the risk. Process theologians and open theists share the view that classical theists succumbed to this temptation. They "bought into" a powerful philosophical perspective that elevated being above becoming, and excluded temporality from ultimate reality.

Open theists have somewhat similar concerns about process philosophy. There is no question that process philosophy is a powerful intellectual system, and process insights can be helpful in explaining as-

4. Particularly *Biblical Religion and the Search for Ultimate Reality* (Chicago: University of Chicago Press, 1955).

pects of Christian faith. But process theologians sometimes seem to let the process system determine their reading of Christian faith.

For this reason, the differences Howell perceives between process theism and the open view of God, the "sticking points," as she calls them, come to something more than conceptual quibbles, or mere variations on a theme. These divergent visions of God's relation to the world go to the heart of the Christian faith. At least, this is the opinion of influential process thinkers such as David Griffin. Their similarities notwithstanding, he argues in this volume (chapter 1 above), process thought provides a better framework for interpreting the Christian good news than does open theism, or as he terms it, "classical free will theism."

We cannot resolve these differences here, of course, but we need to note them. The most basic is God's relation to the world, an issue often associated with the problematic notion of creation ex nihilo. I assert, as Howell notes, that God depends on the world and that such dependence enhances, rather than detracts from, God's greatness. But what, precisely, is the nature of this interdependence between God and the world? This is where process thought and open theism come to a crucial parting of the ways.

For process thought, God-and-world is the fundamental metaphysical fact, the ultimate reality. Neither God nor world is comprehensible apart from the other. In fact, the two expressions are different ways of designating the same thing. "To think about God," says Charles Hartshorne, "is the same as to think about the world, except in emphasis." "God is 'the world' understood, the world is 'God' understood."[5] "God is the all-inclusive reality."[6]

The world is an aspect of God's reality; God is an aspect of the world's reality. To put it another way, ultimate reality is both necessary and contingent. As Hartshorne develops the cosmological argument, "God" denotes the necessary aspect of reality; "world" denotes the contingent aspect. There are things in reality that come and go, that might or might not have existed. But there is also something that cannot fail

5. Charles Hartshorne, *Man's Vision of God and the Logic of Theism* (Chicago: Willett, Clark, 1941), 339.

6. Charles Hartshorne, *A Natural Theology for Our Time* (La Salle, Ill.: Open Court, 1967), 12.

to exist, and this is what God is. The idea that God is sheer existence is inadequate, however, because nothing simply exists. Everything that exists experiences other things. Thus God would not exist without experience, and God must experience *something.* Consequently, God needs nondivine objects of experience. God's reality depends on the creaturely world. God's choices have a great deal to do with the character of the world (although they do not determine it), but the world as such does not exist because God decided to create it. It is just as important, just as fundamental, to the scheme of things as God is.

What is interesting about this view of God and the world is the way it resembles the classical view – not classical theism, but classical paganism. Greek religion humanized the divine, it is often noted, and Greek philosophy naturalized the cosmos. There is still a place for the divine in classical philosophy, but it is thoroughly anchored in the natural order of things. The controversial notion of creation ex nihilo developed as thinkers in the early Common Era came to see the contrast between the God of classical thought and the God of Christian faith.

According to historian Robert Wilken, the great physician Galen was the first critic of Christianity to see the implications of its view of God's relation to the world.[7] Like other Greeks, Galen believed that God created the world out of what already existed. In Plato's *Timaeus,* a widely read work at the time, God fashions existing matter like a potter fashions clay. In contrast, "The Mosaic view implies that the world was created out of what did *not* already exist. . . . [It] implies that matter came into existence only at the time of creation and did not exist prior to creation."[8] This is the idea that the phrase *creatio ex nihilo* came to express. It means that the world's existence is due entirely to God's decision. God creates because God chooses to create. God's relations to the world are based on freedom, not on necessity.

Although the phrase implies that there was a time before which God created, for many thinkers this is not its central idea. For Keith Ward, for example, "It is irrelevant to a doctrine of creation *ex nihilo*

7. Robert L. Wilken, *The Christians as the Romans Saw Them* (New Haven: Yale University Press, 1984), 89. According to Wilken, the first Christian thinker to develop the rudiments of a doctrine of creation ex nihilo was the Gnostic theologian Basilides. But it is not clear what, if any, influence his treatment of the topic had on subsequent Christian thinkers.

8. Wilken, *Christians,* 85.

whether the universe began or not." The doctrine "simply maintains that there is nothing other than God from which the universe is made, and that the universe is other than God and wholly dependent upon God for its existence."[9]

If Wilken is right, it was originally pagan thinkers who perceived that Christianity involved a new concept of God's relation to the world. The concept of creation ex nihilo developed as early Christians articulated the gospel in response to their critics. They saw that God is not a facet of reality or a principle within reality. God is the one reality on which everything else depends, and it exists by virtue of God's free decision.

That there is a world only because God has chosen to create one does not mean that the world as it exists perfectly reflects God's will, or that God could bring into existence any possible state of affairs by sheer fiat. Whether that is the case depends to a significant degree on the kind of world God has chosen to create. For open theists, as for process thinkers, the creatures have significant freedom and God respects the choices they make. Accordingly, God typically relates to the creatures through persuasion, much as process thought insists. Thus we should neither underestimate nor exaggerate the differences between process theism and open theism. While the two positions involve divergent views of the world's necessity, they share some important convictions about the nature of God's interaction with the creatures.

The sheer giftedness of creation, or the nonnecessity of the world, bears on a couple of the other points Howell raises in her discussion. First, God's creative and responsive love is a central element in her definition of God, and it is the central divine attribute for both open theists and process theologians. But the two groups develop their shared emphasis on God's love in different ways. For process thinkers, divine love implies a necessary world, for unless we think of the world as necessarily existing, we cannot think of God as essentially loving. If the world exists only because God chose to create it, they argue, then God's

9. Keith Ward, "God as a Principle of Cosmological Explanation," in *Quantum Cosmology and the Laws of Nature: Scientific Perspectives on Divine Action,* ed. Robert John Russell, Nancey C. Murphy, and C. J. Isham (Notre Dame, Ind.: University of Notre Dame Press, 1994), 248-49. Quoted in John F. Haught, *Science and Religion: From Conflict to Conversation* (New York: Paulist, 1995), 111.

love for the world does not express God's innermost, fundamental reality. It is merely incidental to God's nature.

For open theists, the notion of a contingent world argues for, rather than against, divine love. Creation is a choice, not a necessity, for God, but this does not make the world's existence incidental to God. To the contrary, it shows how important the world is to God. It provides a vivid manifestation of God's love. A freely chosen commitment can express one's deepest character every bit as much as one's response to something unavoidable. For many people, having children is a choice, not a necessity. But this hardly makes their children incidental to their identity.

Howell describes the Trinity as "more a construct of the tradition than a biblical theology," and asserts that the incarnation "reveals God foremost in relation to the world, not to Godself." But this misses the essential insight of the Trinity, namely, the close relation between God's inner reality and God's relation to the world. God's action in the world, in particular, the divine self-giving Christians see in the incarnation, mirrors, expresses, and ultimately fulfills the dynamics of God's inner life. God's love for the world freely extends the love that pulsates within the inner life of God.

Another aspect of Howell's discussion that invites comment is the notion that the world is God's body: "I want to hear more about the discomfort with the organic worldview of process thought from those who hold the open view." On the one hand, the organic metaphor is helpful for expressing God's intimate awareness of the creatures, but it has some liabilities. In contrast to some other familiar metaphors, it does not depict the world as an alien force that God subdues or as an artifact that God manipulates – both of which place God over against the world in unfortunate ways. The organic metaphor brings the world into God's own life, underscoring the importance of the world to God, the profound intimacy of God's knowledge of the world, and the tenderness of God's care for it.

On the other hand, the body metaphor does not express effectively the distinctly personal nature of our relation to God that is traditionally of such importance to evangelicals. I am aware of the cells in my body, certainly; I interact with them in profound ways, but I do not think of them as friends or counterparts. I do not engage them in personal relationship. Thus the incarnation is significant here not just because it shows God entering into a close relationship with creaturely reality, but because it shows God expressing God's self in personal form, in the form of someone who interacts with human beings as friend to friend, to cite a word that appears frequently in the farewell discourses of the Fourth Gospel.

In the final analysis, I think the most basic difficulty open theists have with process theism is the way it seems to limit God to cosmic, or cosmological, functions. It attributes various cosmic operations to a supreme instance of creativity. But in moving from the world to God, it refuses to conceive God as distinct from the world. In other words, it conceives God only in relation to the world. From my perspective, process thought is correct in what it affirms of God but wrong in what it denies. God is indeed the principle that renders the world intelligible. A theistic explanation of reality is the only one that ultimately makes sense. God is the necessary being on which everything depends, the source of novelty, the supreme orderer, and the all-inclusive experience that gives every feature of creation its lasting value. God is, as Hartshorne says, the one being who can be individuated by concepts alone. All this is true, but there is more to God as well. God is a specific person, with specific plans, specific actions, and specific means of self-expression. It is a mistake to equate these specific features in the Christian portrait of God with God's generic cosmic role.

The problem is clear when we look at process treatments of the Trinity. For process thinkers "Father," "Son," and "Holy Spirit" are historically relative expressions whose meaning can be articulated more adequately today by the sort of conceptual scheme that process philosophy provides. For Marjorie H. Suchocki, for example, the appellations "Father," "Son," and "Spirit" are historically relative and no longer convey their original meaning. To do justice to their original insights, we should employ terms such as "presence," "wisdom," and "power."[10] According to David Griffin, the Trinity is a "tertiary doctrine," something not part of the good news, but an historical accretion that needs to be separated from the primary doctrines of the faith when it interferes with them. He exchanges the Trinity of Christian orthodoxy for a "trinity of trinities," which applies three groups of three categories to God,

10. *God, Christ, Church: A Practical Guide to Process Theology,* rev. ed. (New York: Crossroad, 1992), 229.

including the description of God as Divine Creativity, Divine Creative Love, and Divine Responsive Love.[11]

But for many who have thought about the Trinity in recent years, such an approach misses the point. The Trinity is not a concept but a name. It identifies God in a way that cannot be reduced to or replaced by conceptual schemes. The designations "Father," "Son," "Spirit" are not an antiquated attempt to express the divine reality in thought forms drawn from common human experience. They express the distinctive features of God's self-revelation in history. To use David Griffin's expression, they are primary, not secondary or tertiary, elements in Christian faith.

This is similar to the point Colin Gunton makes in his study of Charles Hartshorne and Karl Barth. Anselm's famous argument for God is central to the work of both figures, Gunton observes, but they take it in completely different directions. The difference between them is the difference "between the concept of a God who reveals his 'name' on particular, concrete, occasions, and the God who is believed to be inferable from man's universal (metaphysical and linguistic) experience."[12]

This, then, is open theism's basic reservation with process theology. From the perspective of open theists, process philosophers and theologians identify God with an aspect of the world, whereas Christian faith identifies God as the one who is revealed in the particular, specific events of salvation history. These events are unique and unrepeatable. They may illustrate what God is always doing in the world, but that is not their primary, let alone their exclusive, concern. This is why the name of God that comes from them can never be equated with general terms and concepts.

Such differences notwithstanding, process theologians and open theists have a good deal in common. I like Howell's eclectic approach to theology; it suggests a way for us to work together. Like her, I feel that process thought provides a significant resource for Christian thinkers today. And like her, I hope that dialogue will continue between process theologians and open theists as we work out the implications of our

11. See David Griffin's contribution to this volume, chapter 1 above.

12. Colin Gunton, *Becoming and Being: The Doctrine of God in Charles Hartshorne and Karl Barth* (Oxford: Oxford University Press, 1978), 105-6.

common conviction that God is deeply involved with the affairs of the world God loves, and that our actions make a profound difference to the world's future and to God's.

3 *Confessional Communities and Public Worldviews: A Case Study*

DAVID L. WHEELER

Two Streams of Experience: An Autobiographical Reflection

From earliest childhood, my connection with the Sacred was forged by two separate but contemporary streams of experience. One stream of experience was born in the place my brother and I called "back in the field." The other burst forth and was fed in the Southern Baptist church life of my childhood and adolescence. When I was a young boy in Louisville in the early 1950s, our modest postwar subdivision lay on the far south end of town. Right across our back fence lay the old Douglas Park horse track, a feeder track for the world-famous Churchill Downs. The wooden bleachers in the grandstand had been ripped apart for salvage, but the cement foundations were still in place, littered with discarded parimutuel tickets, and a rusty starting gate on wheels still sat on the dirt track. Though races were no longer held there, the place still bustled with life. Small-time owners and trainers with big dreams still stabled and exercised their horses there. The rows of stables were filled with occupants and perfumed by fresh hay and new manure; horses whinnied and kicked stable doors; exercise boys and grooms bantered, smoked, and played with their scruffy dogs. Behind the stables was a second magical realm, of scrub woods, blackberry thickets, and Douglas Pond – the weedy remains of what had once been the cosmetic centerpiece of the racetrack infield. In the spring my brother and I would wade along the edge of the pond to scoop up tadpoles, which we carried home to keep vigil over through their magical transformation into tiny frogs. In the summer we gathered the wild blackberries and hawked them to our neighbors; in winter we tried to guess the identity of the tracks in the snow, and reconstructed in our imaginations the adventures of the absent creatures. In those innocent days, my mother never thought twice about her two primary schoolers vaulting the fence and disappearing for hours at a time into this exotic world.

When I was not "back in the field," I was reading. My mother bought a series of inexpensive *Time-Life* nature books. One was about the history of life on our planet. The illustrations of brontosaurus, triceratops, and tyrannosaurus rex were reproductions of the famous murals by Charles Knight in the Field Museum in Chicago. I became accustomed to thinking of life and its history in terms of millions of years. Later my parents made a major investment for a young family with one wage earner and four children spaced from elementary school to diapers: a set of *Compton's Pictured Encyclopedia*. I supplemented my forays into nature life by immersing myself in the pages of the encyclopedia, particularly the articles and full-color illustrations about forests, animals ancient and contemporary, stars and galaxies.

During this same period of time, my parents had joined the Beechmont Baptist Church in south Louisville. My siblings and I were part of the church from "cradle roll" on up. The church was the center of our social lives and networks of friends as well as the place where the values of our home were clarified and confirmed and our language about the Sacred was created and rehearsed. When Miss Lillian Douthitt laid out the six days of creation on her flannel board for the primary Sunday school class, I was introduced unawares to the theology of creation. God, the protective heavenly Father of my childish prayers, was also responsible for the fascinating array of natural wonders I explored back in the field and read about in the encyclopedia.

When I was eleven, our pastor, Brother Morton, came to visit the junior Sunday school department. Picking up a folding chair, he asked us if we believed it would support his weight. Of course we all did. "And so do I," he added with a flourish. "But the *proof* comes when I actually trust my weight to the chair," he said, sitting down with a thud. Thus we were introduced to the difference between faith as intellectual assent and faith as volition, and we were put on notice that it was time for each of us — individually, voluntarily, without pressure or even input from peers and parents — to make our own unique, eternally valid decision for Jesus Christ. In due course, I took my own turn in the baptismal pool, up behind the pulpit and the choir loft, where Jimmy Hahn's father had painted a Jordan River scene that looked for all the world like Beargrass Creek.

That same year I began what has become a lifelong practice of daily devotional Bible reading. Southern Baptists then and now have quantified all aspects of congregational life, and I could be 100 percent on the report sheet for Baptist Training Union on Sunday evenings only if I had done my daily Bible readings. But I already had a strong internal drive to make sense of my faith. "Making sense" of my faith, in the Southern Baptist context, meant learning *the Story,* for the principles of Christian belief and behavior are understood to be embedded in the Story, from whence they can be extracted by any normally intelligent believer who approaches the text in good faith. Issues of one's gender, social location, historical distance from the scriptural events, and so on were never broached by the preachers and teachers of my youthful experience; it was assumed that the Bible Story (singular) contained a consistent set of univocal truths that all Spirit-led interpreters could in principle identify and agree on, and this set of truths constituted, in the words of a pastor I once heard at a youth retreat, "the Manufacturer's Instruction Manual for the human race."

When I was thirteen, I first felt the need to do a synoptic reading of my two formative traditions. This need did not arise from a sense of anxiety or doubt, but simply from a natural desire to order and coordinate these important and — as far as I was concerned — manifestly true spheres of knowledge. I was reading H. G. Wells's *Outline of History,* which placed the emergence of Homo sapiens some thousands of years in the past. My father's *Halley's Bible Handbook* allowed as how there might be gaps in the litany of the patriarchs' ages in Genesis 11, thus releasing one from strict compliance with Archbishop Ussher's 4004 B.C. date for creation. I seized on these two insights to conclude that biblical and secular accounts of human and natural history could be compatible. For myself, I applied this principle to the kind of attempted correlation of Genesis and generic evolutionary sequence and chronology often attempted by biblical believers who combine some tolerance for typological readings of Scripture with a measure of scientific literacy.[1] The possibility of a nonliteral, nonchronological reading of Genesis was still several years in my future.

What strikes me, in retrospect, is that in contrast to many of my contemporaries raised in similar environments, I experienced no wrenching conflict between my faith convictions and the "scientific worldview" I had partially absorbed and partially constructed from the material of my childhood experience. I had an intuitive grasp of the oneness of the cosmos and the connectedness and flow of its constituents, alongside a personal awareness of the living Christ as my companion and moral compass, and these elements of my experience had always coexisted. In addition, I had a naive expectation that "truth" in my biblically based value system and "truth" in the structures and processes of the natural world I loved so much would ultimately be compatible. We chastened postmoderns now affirm that all our "truths" are contextual and partial, "prehensions" in the Whiteheadian sense. But dare we still hope that there is a growing, evolving comprehensive Truth, retained and enjoyed in the immediacy of the Divine Experience?

It was this inchoate hope that led me to Whitehead. I had bought a copy of *Process and Reality* when I was an M.Div. student. But I first began to read it the year I was a day care teacher for a class of four-year-olds in the basement of a Brooklyn church. I was "tentmaking" in the city between my M.Div. studies and the beginning of my doctoral work at the Graduate Theological Union in Berkeley. During the children's naptime, I would sit in the doorway of the darkened room with the door propped ajar to admit light from the hallway. I started right in on Whitehead's abstract categoreal scheme – what else was one to do? I do not know how much I really understood, but my religious faith had already convinced me that the quest for universally applicable insights, for Truth, is not a fool's errand. In this conviction, evangelical Christians and process thinkers are united.

1. See, e.g., Robert C. Newman, *Genesis One and the Origin of the Earth* (Downers Grove, Ill.: InterVarsity Press, 1977).

Locating and Evaluating Religious Experience: Three Theses

My colleagues and I in this project represent two important contemporary intellectual and cultural movements: evangelical Christianity and process-relational theism. The usages of the term *evangelical Christianity* are manifold and often ambiguous. Here I mean to refer to those American Christian communities, millions strong, that emphasize a personal faith relationship with Jesus Christ, the centrality and preeminence of biblical authority for faith and practice, and a vigorous defense of what the Methodist theologian Thomas C. Oden calls "classic Christian orthodoxy."[2] Evangelicalism thus characterized has a clear experiential basis, yet makes epistemological and ontological claims that purport to transcend and precede that experience. It is those claims that project evangelicalism, willingly or unwillingly, into the marketplace of ideologies. It is readily apparent from my autobiographical reflections above that each of the key characteristics of evangelical Christianity in my definition is clearly present in my youthful religious formation, and this is my "home place" in the faith.

By "process-relational theism," I refer to the associated concepts about the nature, character, and action of God implicated in the philosophical cosmology of Alfred North Whitehead, and developed in response to classical theological and devotional questions by many of Whitehead's primarily American interpreters – perhaps most notably, Charles Hartshorne and John B. Cobb Jr.[3] Process-relational thought is "cosmology" in the grand style of Plato, Aristotle, and Hegel: the at-

2. Thomas C. Oden, *After Modernity . . . What? Agenda for Theology* (Grand Rapids: Zondervan, 1990), 34ff.

3. Whitehead's cosmology receives its definitive expression in *Process and Reality* (1929), corrected ed., ed. David Ray Griffin and Donald W. Sherburne (New York: Free Press, 1978). More accessible expressions of his thought appear in *Adventures of Ideas* (1933; repr. New York: Free Press, 1967) and *Religion in the Making* (1926; repr. New York: Meridian, 1974). For insight into Charles Hartshorne's application of Whiteheadian thought to theological issues, see *The Divine Relativity* (New Haven: Yale University Press, 1964). For John Cobb's Christian process theology, see *The Structure of Christian Existence* (Philadelphia: Westminster, 1969) or *Christ in a Pluralistic Age* (Philadelphia: Westminster, 1975). Perhaps the best introduction to process theology in a Christian mode is John B. Cobb Jr. and David Ray Griffin, *Process Theology: An Introductory Exposition* (Philadelphia: Westminster, 1973).

tempt to frame and utilize a coherent and comprehensive explanation of "the way things are." For Anglo-American philosophy in the twentieth century, positivistic in spirit as it has been, obsessed with questions of linguistic meaning, and skeptical of our ability to make assertions about the world per se, cosmology has been out of fashion. But evangelical Christians and process theists find themselves today together among the intellectual minority who still engage in the ancient and honorable task: making sense out of the whole of life.

Some thinkers and believers both in the evangelical camp and among process theists might believe that they have little in common beyond the hopelessly broad "quest for ultimate truth," and therefore would have little to learn from one another. The largely critical essays in Ronald H. Nash's collection, *Process Theology,* would be an example of this attitude on the evangelical side.[4] My intellectual understanding of the way faith develops and flourishes and my own personal experience predispose me to the opposite view. My faith community ties, so important in my own faith awakening, from my childhood and young adulthood as a Southern Baptist through my present lengthy association with an American Baptist educational institution – located in one of the most conservative of American Baptist regions – have been thoroughly evangelical. The language of personal relationship to Christ and the new birth, and the practice of seeking God's voice in an authoritative Scripture, are deeply ingrained in my being. It was in the local congregation of baptized believers that my faith was birthed and nurtured. At the same time, I have found that the concepts and basic worldview of process-relational thought resonate deeply with my experience of a complex, interconnected physical world resplendent with beauty and intrinsic value at every level. Process-relational thought connects the micro- and macrocosmos, as well as disciplines as diverse as physics, aesthetics, and theology, and is consistent with – indeed, illuminative of – the two great scientific theories of late modernity, biological evolution and quantum physics. Thus I am inclined by experience, and perhaps by temperament as well, to bring cultural and intellectual traditions into dialogue, and in particular, these two traditions.

Let me share the following specific theses that guide my version of this dialogue:

4. Ronald H. Nash, ed., *Process Theology* (Grand Rapids: Baker, 1987).

1. Religious experience, though perhaps unique and particular to the individual subject, is never simply one's own rendition of some generic "God-consciousness." Like all artifacts of human culture, it is socially constructed, and comes clothed with the history, images, and ritual habits of some concrete faith community. As far back as 1821, the great, empirically oriented theologian Friedrich Schleiermacher spoke of the "positive" religions of humankind: "Each particular form of communal piety has both an outward unity, as a fixed fact of human history with a definite commencement, and an inward unity, as a peculiar modification of that general character which is common to all developed faiths."[5] Thus my brief evocation above of my own religious experience introduces the first key principle that governs my work as a theologian: the faith that has the power to move us and to form us is invariably *"experienced through the relationships, the rituals, the moments of adoration and the actions of the* communitas *which characterises specific living faith traditions."*[6]

In contrast, generic religious symbolism entertained by isolated individuals tends to be sterile and self-regarding. Consider, for example, the fantastic array of "New Age" religious ideologies in the United States. They tend to accept uncritically the most problematic feature of post-Enlightenment modernity, the absolutizing of the autonomous individual as arbiter and beneficiary of realized value, while refusing to subject their religious intuitions to critical analysis, as a consistent Enlightenment position would demand. By contrast, my own religious formation in community, imperfect as it may have been and imperfect and incomplete as my own character might be, urged me and moved me beyond self-involvement in crucial ways. The concern for one's personal salvation notwithstanding, the fundamental value at the center of this faith community was and is the glory of God. "*Thy* Kingdom come, *thy* will be done . . . ," we prayed. A sovereign and holy God is the ultimate reality; we are his creatures and the objects of his judgment and mercy. Jesus his Son is our common Savior, Lord, and ethical compass. Our personal stories are connected to and evaluated in terms of *the Story,* the biblical metanarrative whose coherence and universal ap-

5. Friedrich Schleiermacher, *The Christian Faith* (Edinburgh: T. & T. Clark, 1928), §10, p. 44.

6. David L. Wheeler, "Universal Concern and Concrete Commitments: In Response to Anderson," *Process Studies* 23/3 (1994): 194.

plicability postmodern thinkers may doubt, but whose power to lend meaning to and connect the disparate lives of my childhood brothers and sisters in the faith has been demonstrated in our community over and over again. Finally, Jesus in his Sermon on the Mount and Paul and James and John in their epistles provided principles and concrete examples for character formation and holy living that we, naively perhaps, translated directly into our own life situations.

In sum, living faith has a *home,* and disconnected from that home, it is isolated, effete, and abstract. Evangelical faith takes God's self-authenticating revelation to be the unique and sufficient basis of faith, and rejects Protestant liberalism's strategy of positing human experience alongside revelation as a correlative pole of faith. Nevertheless, the concrete life of faith called forth, we believe, by that divine revelation is the place where encounter with the Sacred is encouraged, interpreted, and reinforced. I must start here in my dialogue with other understandings of the Real, on my quest to believe better in order to understand better (cf. Anselm, *Proslogion* 1).

2. Having said this, let me acknowledge that, for any believer, faith's home is to some extent a function of the contingencies of one's birth, upbringing, and historical-cultural location, and to some extent a function of one's own temperament and choices. Fundamentalisms of every ilk ignore this truism, and indeed my childhood faith community, though not notably intolerant in practice or intemperate in language, naively assumed that sitting on the shoulders of the authors of Holy Scripture, they had a universal perspective. "All scripture is inspired of God" (2 Timothy 3:16); the Holy Spirit, as the universal and infallible interpreter, will "guide you into all truth" (John 16:13); and the Jesus known to us through his concrete history and his dwelling in our hearts is, unequivocally, "the way, the truth, and the life," and no one comes to the Father but by him (John 14:6). In contrast, I will proceed on the basis that concrete faith communities, no matter how great their vitality and their efficacy in producing concord and well-being for their believers, do not exhaust the possibilities of encounter with the Real, nor do they exclude the possibility of other faith communities and traditions.

By saying this, I do not wish to adopt a position of theological or ontological relativism. I believe that the core images and concepts of my faith tradition are "true," in the sense that they are a faithful response to God's self-communication within the limits of human symbol-forming capacity. But the Sacred Presence, or the Real, or whatever we may wish to call it, is always at the same time vaster and more subtle than all our categories and concepts. As my own experience has broadened from the extroverted, cognitively robust religion of my youth, I have become more aware of the ineffable, indefinable dimensions of that experience. My youthful experiences of the richness of earth's biotic communities, both those present and those extending into an almost unimaginably lengthy past, could never be resolved without remainder into the anthropocentric "salvation history" of Baptist proclamation. It is primarily Nature that has introduced me to that experience of the Sacred called "apophatic" by scholars of religion – the way of negation or emptiness, beyond image or concept.[7] Thus relationship with the Sacred may elude characterization because it cannot be limited to our faculties of conceptualization.

Then again, relationship with the Sacred may elude characterization because of its uniqueness for the experiencing subject and its intensely personal character. Students of Whitehead are reminded of his famous description of religion in *Religion in the Making:* "Religion is what the individual does with his own solitariness."[8] Many in our generation have resonated deeply with Martin Buber's description of those moments of intimate bonding with the other that constitute an "I-Thou" relationship. In those moments we do not define or characterize the other, nor assign it any utilitarian value, but simply dwell in the other. Buber's "I-Thou" relationship is not religious experience per se – it is simply experience, plumbing the depths of the wonder and mystery of being. But then, this is precisely where the Sacred is found – in the midst. "Extended, the lines of relationship intersect in the eternal Thou."[9] This openness to the Sacred in all experience can be taken to the Scriptures and to the defining beliefs and principles of action of one's faith community for illumination and evaluation; conversely, one's experience of the Sacred might dramatically reframe one's read-

7. Ironically, major western mystics have located the apophatic experience beyond the sensory and even beyond self and other (cf. Teresa of Avila, *The Interior Castle*), whereas my pathway beyond evangelical Protestantism's rationally conceived and exhaustively described God has been richly sensorial, i.e., encounters with Nature.

8. Whitehead, *Religion in the Making,* 16.

9. Martin Buber, *I and Thou* (New York: Scribner's Sons, 1970), 123.

ing of Scripture and processing of received doctrine. To find a piquant example, one need look no further than Karl Barth's experience of the fecklessness of the liberal Protestant paradigm in the wake of the Great War, and his subsequent encounter with demonic evil in the rise of the Third Reich.

3. The acceptance of these two theses leads directly to a third: faith communities and philosophical worldviews need each other. One implication of this thesis is that individual religious believers and the communities they constitute are at great risk unless their faith convictions are accompanied by a consistent and coherent worldview. Without a plausible worldview to ground their core convictions, no matter how deeply and sincerely these convictions are held, these believers may find that their convictions lack roots in the soil of their own larger lives, and lack credibility and persuasive power outside the core community. The television evangelist who reaches millions by the electronic signals of his chosen medium and communicates with his supporters by computer implicitly accepts modern science and its practical applications as they further his ministry and form his comfortable lifestyle. At the same time he may scornfully denigrate scientific research into human and cosmic origins, call its principles and conclusions into question, and question the integrity of its practitioners. Such inconsistency is fatal in the long run to the persistence of the core religious convictions so nakedly held, within the community of faith as well as in the larger world where there are no in-group loyalties to counter the believers' irrationality. Thus religious communities may become intellectually isolated and impoverished strange bodies in the broader culture; this is one way of understanding the growing lack of credibility of traditional Christianity in large segments of contemporary culture.

Traditional Christian believers have often been accused of fideism: simply accepting the assertions of their faith tradition on the tradition's own authority — scriptural, magisterial, or otherwise, but supposedly, at root, the authority of the self-authenticating self-testimony of the Deity — with no attempt to connect those assertions to independent canons of authority. In my opinion, alleged instances of fideism are normally connected to a covert acceptance of substantial elements of the culture's regnant worldview, which in turn bootlegs into the faith community the weaknesses and inconsistencies connected to that worldview, without accessing that worldview's explanatory value due to the inconsistent and covert nature of the connection. Indeed, the extent to which evangelical Christianity has been hostage to key elements of post-Enlightenment modernism that are in great tension with biblical teaching – including modernism's radical individualism, its elevation of an autonomous reason to a position of arbiter of faith's integrity, and its reading of Scripture as a collection of propositional truths – has been widely discussed in intellectual circles but not sufficiently acknowledged in the life of the church.[10] Explicit consideration of worldview issues in the manner I am proposing will help to expose this "Babylonian captivity" of the church's intellect. For everyone has a worldview, more or less acknowledged, self-conscious, consistent, and adequate to the publicly accessible facts of our common world.

Ironically, many traditional Christians defend their loyalty to antimodern convictions by an appeal to a reality that is not of this world – *super*natural – and therefore inaccessible to normal canons of reality. If the distinction between "natural" and "supernatural" means that God and the world are in some sense qualitatively different kinds of being, then as an evangelical I am not ready to let that distinction go. Elsewhere I have defended what I call a "hybrid" view of God, in which I attempt to think together the ontological ultimacy and self-originating actuality of God in classical theism and widespread religious intuition with the radical mutual immanence and interdependence of God and world in process theism.[11] In this view the self-actual Creator God provides the context in which God-world interactions and world-world interactions occur; all such interactions in so far as they take place in the world are in principle subject to rational analysis. Thus if by the nature/supernature distinction we mean to say that we live straddling two different worlds, and the structures and processes of the latter world

10. See, e.g., Stanley J. Grenz, *A Primer on Postmodernism* (Grand Rapids: Zondervan, 1996), and the critique of Grenz by Millard J. Erickson, who comes across as an unrepentant modernist in *The Evangelical Left: Encountering Postconservative Evangelical Theology* (Grand Rapids: Baker, 1997). See also my "Commending Faith in a Postmodern World," in *Central Thoughts on the Church in the Twenty-First Century,* ed. Thomas E. Clifton (Macon, Ga.: Smyth & Helwys, 1998), 135-52.

11. See David L. Wheeler, *A Relational View of the Atonement: Prolegomenon to a Reconstruction of the Doctrine* (New York: Peter Lang, 1990), 53-55. My thinking on this issue bears some affinity to Clark Pinnock's efforts in "Between Classical and Process Theism," in *Process Theology,* ed. Nash, 316-27.

impinge on the former as strange bodies not subject to the canons of reason; and if we mean to say that supernatural knowledge ("revelation") is a different mode of knowledge not subject to epistemological analysis analogously to other forms of knowledge, I cannot accept this distinction. Faith communities that do accept it will ultimately become irrational and isolated from the flow of human history and culture. "We must have the conviction that our values express the Sacred, that is, reflect the way things really are," says evangelical thinker Stephen Franklin,[12] and this conviction must be defensible.

Laying aside for the moment the extent to which biblical supernaturalism, archaic cosmologies, and mythological narrative forms render biblical texts problematic for the direct production of a single unified worldview in the sense we are discussing, it seems that the persuasive power of key elements of a demonstrably biblical perspective on reality (e.g., God's creative and ordering activity, the power of love, the intrinsic value of all elements of the cosmos) would be greatly amplified by their association with compatible independent perspectives on our common world. While I appreciate the efforts of proponents of "evangelical openness" to produce readings of biblical texts that emphasize God's intimate involvement with the created order and genuine reciprocity with it,[13] I fear that this effort might have limited apologetic value in the long run unless there are independent reasons for believing that this view of the biblical God and God's creation represents a genuinely fruitful perspective on "the way things are." If evangelical Christianity and process-relational theism are both in some profound and important sense "true" – that is, in their own terms they accurately reflect and express the nature of things – and if evangelical Christianity needs a companion worldview, then honest and energetic conversations among evangelicals and process thinkers could be of great profit for all concerned, and for our global culture, which is at such great risk from political, technocratic, and religious imperialisms.

If faith communities risk weakness and fragmentation without

12. Stephen T. Franklin, "The Dying of the Sacred Light: An Essay on Religion and Culture in America" (unpublished, 1996).

13. Cf. Clark Pinnock et al., *The Openness of God: A Biblical Challenge to the Traditional Understanding of God* (Downers Grove, Ill.: InterVarsity Press, 1994).

intentionally addressing the issue of worldview, the converse is no less true. Cosmological schemes, no matter how compelling in terms of scope, coherence, and illuminating power, have only a limited ability to form character and guide behavior. Character is formed in communities of common concern, where protocols of discourse and action are taught, modeled, and reinforced, and where elements of a worldview/conceptual scheme, which may in fact have great truth value and persuasive power in the cognitive domain, are clothed in the community's shared symbols and saga, enacted in the community's sacred rituals, and put in practice in the community's pattern of living. Process theists note proudly that Whitehead has produced a cosmological scheme of great power in which God is a systemic implicate of the scheme and a central explanatory factor within it. I am reminded again of Schleiermacher, who in his own system claimed that human being-in-the-world is inexplicable apart from a universal generic "God-consciousness." But as I maintained above in thesis 1, this God-consciousness flourishes and empowers in specific, historical faith communities. It is no accident that powerful and persuasive religious interpretations of Whitehead have been done by Christian theologians such as Cobb, Griffin, and Suchocki, and have picked up on Whitehead's own evocation of the "brief Galilean vision of humility" through which Jesus of Nazareth embodied God.[14]

It may seem that I have been somewhat lengthy and tedious in laying out what are essentially prolegomena for any concrete dialogue between evangelical Christianity and process theism. But unless participants in such a dialogue share convictions something like those expressed above, then the dialogue cannot be substantive nor will it be carried out in good faith. The believer who understands his or her system of belief as uniquely and exhaustively true will engage in dialogue only out of trivial curiosity or academic courtesy, or with a covert desire to refute and perhaps convert. For me, on the one hand, the presence and persistent call of a mighty *Ur-Person* who is Alpha and Omega and at the same time intimately identified with the broken and poured-out Jesus has been an antidote to idolatry – either a sort of pantheistic idolatry of nature and its vitalities to which I might otherwise be prone or an idolatry of human culture and its successes and competencies.

14. Whitehead, *Process and Reality,* 342. Hereinafter cited in the text as *PR.*

On the other hand, my lifelong immersion in nature and my affinity for beauty and beings other than human have preserved me, I hope, from the worst excesses of extreme anthropocentrism and works righteousness ("I am because I do") to which classical Christianity is so prone. Process relational thought has furnished me an intellectual framework through which to conceptualize this side of my experience, and read it synoptically with my explicitly Christian side. For me, this dialogue of ideologies has been vital; for others, I at least wish to commend it as possible and possibly fruitful.

Locating Evangelicals

It is beyond the scope of this essay to attempt an exhaustive exploration of the theological and cultural roots of American evangelicalism. But there is a distinct value in snapshots as well as in panoramic vistas. Let me expand on the epigrammatic description offered in the previous section by accessing a characteristic and widely circulated self-definition of evangelical faith. The National Association of Evangelicals (NAE) was founded in Wheaton, Illinois, in 1942 as an intentional alternative to the institutions then expressive of global ecumenism (WCC, etc.), which many conservative Christians in the United States perceived as insufficiently committed to the confessional consensus of the historical Christian mainstream and overly involved in an ideologically inspired activism that strays far from the Great Commission.

Member churches and denominations in the United States claim some twenty million individuals. As we examine the NAE's confessional statement below, we will find that it is not explicitly "Baptistic" in nature; indeed, only the first clause on exclusive biblical authority would give pause to a traditional Roman Catholic or Orthodox believer. But communions of a Baptistic type – emphasizing the experience of the new birth, believer's baptism, and the formation of congregations through the voluntary association of believers – predominate in the NAE's membership. Given what Martin Marty calls the "Baptistification" of American communions of every type of polity, and the pervasive presence of a sort of personal, voluntaristic folk Christianity among millions of unchurched or casually churched Americans, it is safe to say that the defining convictions of the NAE are held more or less strongly and consistently by many millions of other Americans beyond those officially associated with the organization.

Here is the statement of faith that is the original basis for membership in the NAE:

1. We believe the Bible to be the inspired, the only infallible authoritative Word of God.
2. We believe that there is one God, eternally existent in three persons: Father, Son and Holy Spirit.
3. We believe in the deity of our Lord Jesus Christ, in His virgin birth, in His sinless life, in His miracles, in His vicarious and atoning death through His shed blood, in His bodily resurrection, in His ascension to the right hand of the Father, and in His personal return in power and glory.
4. We believe that for the salvation of lost and sinful people, regeneration by the Holy Spirit is absolutely essential.
5. We believe in the present ministry of the Holy Spirit, by whose indwelling the Christian is enabled to live a godly life.
6. We believe in the resurrection of both the saved and the lost; they that are saved unto the resurrection of life and they that are lost unto the resurrection of damnation.
7. We believe in the spiritual unity of believers in our Lord Jesus Christ.[15]

How interesting that the first clause of this Christian confession is not about God or Christ but about the Bible. In the Enlightenment, questions of ontology are characteristically preceded in inquiry, superceded in importance, and sometimes even swallowed whole by questions of epistemology. In a world of competing ideologies, how can we know for sure? Characteristically, in post-Enlightenment modernity an autonomous reason posits itself as the arbiter of the meaningfulness of all authorities and sources of evidence, including traditional "sacred"

15. I requested and received this statement directly from the headquarters of the NAE in Wheaton, Illinois, while researching an earlier version of this essay in January 1997.

authorities such as the Bible. In his famous *Meditations,* René Descartes engaged in a rigorous exercise of systematic doubt.

> Rather than take for granted the deliverances of the senses or the existence of God or any of the received wisdom of the race, he found himself able to doubt it all, *except* for the fact that *he,* the thinker/doubter, by the very fact of his thinking and doubting, *was.* The autonomy and self-authenticating nature of human reason thus became the cornerstone of global modernity.[16]

Ironically, then, in much evangelical thought, autonomous reason proceeds to essay a thoroughly modern demonstration of Holy Scripture's intrinsic authority by a demonstration of its superior explanatory and illuminative power vis-à-vis our experience. As John W. Cooper puts it: "The tactic of some apologists has been to adopt modernism's rationalistic standard of truth in order to argue against modernism that reason actually supports rather than undermines Christian truth claims."[17]

But surely Scripture is not self-evidently true in the manner of an a priori proposition? The teachers of my youth applied an interesting gambit to the justification of this foundational claim of biblical authority. "All scripture is given by inspiration of God, and is profitable for doctrine, for reproof, for correction, for instruction in righteousness" (1 Timothy 3:16, KJV). This self-justification escaped the charge of circular reasoning, in their thinking, because the living Christ, introduced to us and described for us in Scripture (a) himself accepts and utilizes the authority of Scripture (Matthew 5:17-20; Luke 4:4-8); and (b) continues to live within and manifest himself to every contemporary believer in an unmistakable, life-transforming manner (Romans

16. Wheeler, "Commending Faith in a Postmodern World," in *Central Thoughts,* ed. Clifton, 138. Descartes did ground his certainty in the accuracy of the self-conscious self's analysis of reality in his belief in God, producing along the way a version of the "ontological argument" first described by Anselm. An all-good, all-knowing God is the guarantor of human reason's deliberations, since he is its creator (see Descartes's "Meditation Three: Concerning God, That He Exists," in *Meditations on First Philosophy*). For later, secular modern thinkers, reason continues its role as autonomous arbiter without the presence of God the guarantor.

17. John W. Cooper, "Reformed Apologetics and the Challenge of Postmodern Relativism," *Calvin Theological Journal* 28/1 (1993): 108.

8:1-11; Galatians 2:20).[18] "Ask me how I know he lives; he lives within my heart!" Do we, at root, then, ground our appeal to scriptural authority in the appeal to experience characteristic of Schleiermacher's romantic response to the Enlightenment? If so, how do we justify this privileging of experience, and whose experience or what type of experience is foundational? Emerging postmodern thought challenges Christian apologists at the point of their implicit assumption of a generic, universal human experience. On the contrary, "experience" is that of specific, concrete persons, of different genders, community statuses, and faith postures. Does God's saving presence "in Christ" (2 Corinthians 5:19) offer the same promise for the Southern Baptist husband and the Southern Baptist wife, for the culturally Christian American and the Iranian Muslim woman living in cloistered *purdah,* for the person of mystical, aesthetic temperament and the person who is temperamentally empiricist?

Returning to the issue of Scripture's inherent truth, we hear conservative Southern Baptist leader R. Albert Mohler proclaim confidently: "The Christian tradition understands truth as established by God and revealed through the self-revelation of God in Scripture. Truth is eternal, fixed and universal."[19] Postmodernism also envisions a fracturing and relativizing of "truth."

> To cite a notorious contemporary instance of this struggle: the "truth" about the football hero, television personality and accused murderer O. J. Simpson has been a shifting will-o'-the-wisp, produced, deconstructed and reconstructed by whatever linguistic community was interpreting him – prosecuting or defense attorneys, the mainstream media, the tabloid press, racially-divided public opinion.[20]

18. Historical-critical questions about who is responsible for the reputed words of Paul and Jesus in these quotations and what constitutes Scripture as referred to in them did not enter into these discussions, nor do they in similar discussions among evangelical laity and many pastors today.

19. R. Albert Mohler, "Ministry Is Stranger Than It Used to Be: The Challenge of Postmodernism," *The Tie* 65/2 (1997): 4.

20. Wheeler, "Commending Faith in a Postmodern World," in *Central Thoughts,* ed. Clifton, 142.

Looking at the Bible itself through postmodern lenses, is its truth value the same for Francis Schaeffer, with his hermeneutical usage of the logical principle of the excluded middle,[21] as it is for a Hegelian exegete? Process-relational thought reminds us that all our data comes to us under perspectival objectifications. Only God's perspective is all-inclusive, and even God's perspective is constantly growing and changing as God weaves the world's cumulative actuality into the divine experience. This picture of God's relationship to the world and "the truth" about the world certainly presents a challenge to Mohler's notion of truth (above).

Be that as it may, for the evangelicals represented by the NAE statement, once the claim of biblical authority is established, the other elements of belief as denominated by the statement are understood to follow from a plain and simple reading of Scripture in its totality. Stephen Franklin describes this hermeneutical conviction/method: "Once we have used the whole of Scripture to get at the meaning of a particular verse, the truth of that verse stands on its own as an independent fact. That is, they believe the Bible reveals as many distinct truths as it contains distinct, declarative sentences."[22] Thus the Bible (as a unit) speaks directly and prescriptively to believers.

The ultimate erudite defense of such a propositional hermeneutic is found in the work of Carl F. H. Henry. According to Henry, "evidence" for Christian faith assertions is not amassed inductively, either from features of generic human experience (Schleiermacher), or from features of our common world analyzed via a realist epistemology (the classic "proofs" tradition of Thomas Aquinas et al.). "Rather, the decisive evidence is inspired Scripture; the Bible is Christian theology's authoritative verifying principle."[23] Henry again: "Christianity contends that revelational truth is intelligible, expressible in valid propositions, and universally communicable."[24] Henry roundly criticizes his bête

21. See, e.g., Francis A. Schaeffer, *How Should We Then Live?* (Old Tappan, N.J.: Revell, 1976), 144ff.

22. Franklin, "Dying," 40.

23. Carl F. H. Henry, *Toward a Recovery of Christian Belief* (New York: Crossway Books, 1990), 16.

24. Carl F. H. Henry, *God, Revelation, and Authority,* 4 vols. (Waco: Word, 1976-79), 1:229. For Henry's comprehensive theological position, see his entire four-volume work. This issue of the propositional nature of biblical revelation is specifically addressed in 1:225-44.

noire Karl Barth, whose alternate view of scriptural revelation as nonpropositional revelatory events "collapses under the weight of inherent contradictions." Yet he seems to miss the irony in his own subsequent statement that "the fact that no theologian has succeeded as yet in fully organizing the truth of revelation in the form of axioms and theorems is no reason to abandon this objective."[25] Perhaps even some evangelicals might be led to question such a hermeneutic if they fully and honestly confronted the futility of squeezing a vast array of narrative, poetry, formulaic folk wisdom, and epistolary advice and counsel into the straitjacket of an axiomatic system.

Though never thinking in terms of axiomatic system, my early teachers – homemakers, insurance agents, mechanics, plumbers, and ordained seminary graduates alike – did assume that the human authors (plural) of Scripture were superintended directly by God the Holy Spirit, thus guaranteeing Scripture's truthfulness and consistency. Apparent inconsistencies in narrative sequence, historical data, or images of the divine character (e.g., the "scorched earth" Lord of Joshua and the compassionate Father of our Lord Jesus Christ) were attributed to the finitude and fallibility of Scripture's interpreters. Sophisticated evangelical scholars have regularly made the same apologetic claim.[26] Furthermore, they looked at the Scriptures through a sort of historical transparency, in which it was taken for granted that the attitudes, issues, and normative social relationships with which we struggle were identical to those obtaining in (uniform) "Bible times." Thus, for example, husbands are husbands and wives are wives and (nuclear) families are families, and the issues of authority and mutuality in marriage as discussed in Ephesians 5:21ff. are identical to those confronting Americans today. But ironically, the conversations and challenges regarding

25. Ibid., 240.

26. "The truthfulness of Scripture is not negated by the appearance in it of irregularities of grammar or spelling, phenomenal descriptions of nature, . . . or seeming discrepancies between one passage and another. . . . Apparent inconsistencies should not be ignored. Solution of them, where this can be convincingly achieved, will encourage our faith, and where for the present no convincing solution is at hand, we shall honor God by trusting His assurance that His Word is true, despite these appearances, and by maintaining our confidence that one day they will be seen to have been illusions" ("The Chicago Statement on Biblical Inerrancy," *Journal of the Evangelical Theological Society* 21/4 [1978]: 295).

the application of these timeless principles, though commonly taking place in the "communal exegesis" of the church school class, were brought to the point of decision – in typical American fashion – in the privacy of the home by the individuals involved.

Parsing the NAE Statement

My own spiritual formation has taken place in that stream of Christian tradition, that part of the body of Christ, that is "evangelical." Begging the question for the moment of how Scripture might most faithfully and fruitfully be read, I affirm that the story of God's interaction with God's creation set out in Holy Scripture, in all of its exuberant and sometimes perplexing variety, is the context in which I process and understand my own story. Jesus of Nazareth, called the Christ, is the primary and normative mediator of my relationship with the Sacred. Yet I have called for an intentional and disciplined dialogue between the speakers of the language of (evangelical) faith and the public worldview architects of the process-relational community, believing for the reasons stated above that this is a crucial enterprise for both camps. If we can accept and utilize the NAE confessional statement as a fair and representative expression of evangelical convictions, then our next question is this: Where are the critical points that might call for and even facilitate the kind of mutually enriching dialogue I have called for? A second, related question follows: Where are the critical points at issue between evangelical faith and process theism? I shall address these questions by looking at each of the seven parts of the NAE statement of faith.

1. "We believe the Bible. . . ." Process thought per se can never give normative value to a text, much less a collection of texts brimming, on some accounts, with internal contradictions. Process thought seeks to inform and guide through the creation of a "philosophical scheme" that should be "coherent, logical," and "applicable and adequate" to the world of public experience (*PR* 3). Evangelical Christians deem the Bible as normative for their common life prior to any independent demonstration of its coherence, logic, adequacy, and so on, and they consider its concrete particularity – the opposite of abstract generality – a source of its strength and a sign of the sovereign freedom of God in his dealings with his creation. "[God] has free control over the wording of Holy Scrip-

ture. He can use it or not use it. He can use it in this way or that way."[27] Furthermore, evangelicals will not make common cause with "Christians" who dilute or question biblical authority. There are, however, some evangelicals working with hermeneutics quite different from that which sees the Scripture as a collection of prescriptive atomic facts. Rather, they understand the Bible as a people-forming narrative, a conversation across the centuries between God and God's people, evolving and cumulative, yet exemplifying certain core principles, for instance, God's redemptive love.[28] This view of Scripture – God's Word – bears striking resemblance to process theism's "dipolar" view of God's reality: constant character and cumulative, evolving self. Further, process thinkers culturally and religiously formed in Christian contexts could readily claim our normative biblical heritage on these terms, with great benefit to the vividness and concreteness of our faith. The good-faith appropriation of biblical content thus construed by process thinkers could keep lines of communication open with evangelicals.

My students listen eagerly to revised understandings of God, Christ, God's action in the world, and so on, if I present them initially not as implications of a philosophical scheme but as attempts to do justice to Scripture. Once the conversation is joined in a manner that respects the primacy of Scripture for evangelicals, the mutually reinforcing nature of insights from religious experience (e.g., answered prayer), the implications of a comprehensive worldview (e.g., radical divine responsiveness), and readings of Scripture newly liberated from alien concepts and paradigms (e.g., divine aseity, hypercalvinism), can bear striking fruit of religious vitality and apologetic vigor. For even evangelicals of a Baptistic stripe operate with some version of Wesley's famous quadrilateral;[29] why not maximize its use?

2. "The Trinity, affirmed in traditional terminology. . . ." This

27. Karl Barth, *Church Dogmatics,* I, 1, trans. G. W. Bromiley, ed. Bromiley and T. F. Torrance, 2nd ed. (Edinburgh: T. & T. Clark, 1975), 139.

28. See, e.g., the work of James William McClendon, *Biography as Theology* (New York: Trinity Press International, 1996); or Stanley J. Grenz, *Theology for the Community of God* (Nashville: Broadman & Holman, 1994); idem, *A Primer on Postmodernism* (Grand Rapids: Eerdmans, 1996).

29. For an explanation of the Wesleyan quadrilateral and its relationship to the authority of Scripture, see John B. Cobb Jr., *Becoming a Thinking Christian* (Nashville: Abingdon, 1993), 61-69.

statement, NAE 1 notwithstanding, goes beyond Scripture and implicitly "canonizes" language and decisions that are part of the conciliar tradition. Process thinkers could point out this inconsistency and probably only generate defensive responses and labored explanations of the Trinity's "implicit" appearance in Scripture. Better we should be glad that Greek and Latin conceptions of divine simplicity and aseity have never completely co-opted Christian faith, because the passionate, interactive God of Scripture begs for a better metaphysical portrait. Conversely, Yahweh filtered through the "brief Galilean vision of humility" (*PR* 342) of Jesus of Nazareth can give vividness, concreteness, and a particular communal setting to the devotees of the God of process theism.

In process theism, divine occasions, like all actual occasions, achieve subjective unity by uniting data from their past actual world. Thus God is dynamic and exhibits diversity in unity. The Christian doctrine of the Trinity is trying to get at the same point, which believers contend is exemplified in God's interaction with humanity and with all of creation as recorded in Scripture. In particular, God, without ceasing to be the Sacred One who creates, sustains, and pervades the whole universe, becomes available to us in the specific, personal history of the Human One, Jesus Christ. The theologians of the conciliar tradition attempted to wed this experience of God's unity and diversity to their own philosophical worldview using the terminology of *hypostasis, prosopon,* and *ousia.* In other words, they were engaged in the sort of process I envision today for biblical believers and process theists. That their project was praiseworthy and the results fruitful and enduring does not necessarily mean that their terminology and formulae must be permanently binding. But nevertheless the threefoldness of God and the associated language of "persons" – whose evolution from *hypostasis* and *prosopon* through *persona* to the very different modern conception of individuated personality is not acknowledged by the brief NAE statement – seems nonnegotiable for evangelicals.

Process theism seems systematically binitarian if we ponder God's "primordial" (mental or ideal) and "consequent" (physical or concrete) natures, but unitarian if we think of God's subjective unity. John Cobb's treatment of God's immanence under the biblical symbol of *Logos,* with "Christ" representing the transformative historical specification of *Logos* ("incarnation"),[30] certainly seems to carry forward a binitarian understanding of God. But Marjorie Suchocki has argued that one can systematically differentiate Christ and Spirit within the general framework of Cobb's process treatment of divine being and acting by correlating Christ with God's immanence as "initial aim" for occasions of experience, and Spirit with "the birth in us of God through our adoption of the aim."[31] Spirit then finally represents the incarnation of God's manifold peace in the world, as God through a complex and utterly open relationship with the world exhibits "an everlastingly deeper complexity that surpasses all number."[32] Regardless of the compatibility or lack thereof of any particular process treatment of the Trinity with confessional orthodoxy, it is not finally unimportant that evangelicals and process theists have multiple reasons, not without some overlap, for rejecting a static and undifferentiated divine simplicity. This is an important sharing that should be explored and promoted in an age in which an impersonal, pantheistic monism is growing in cultural influence.

3. "We believe in the deity of our Lord Jesus Christ . . . in His miracles . . . in His vicarious and atoning death. . . ." In *Christ in a Pluralistic Age,* John Cobb argues that his Christology preserves the intent of the Chalcedonian Christology using process categories of the divine immanence in all actual occasions rather than the substantialist categories of Chalcedon. The immanent divine lure that is a sometimes honored and exemplified factor, a sometimes ignored or thwarted factor, in the self-constitution of all actual occasions is understood by Cobb to be unambiguously present and effective in the self-constitution of Jesus Christ. Now this claim can, to be sure, be attacked from both the left and the

30. See Cobb, *Christ in a Pluralistic Age,* esp. 82-94.

31. Marjorie Hewitt Suchocki, "John Cobb's Trinity," in *Theology and the University: Essays in Honor of John B. Cobb, Jr.,* ed. David Ray Griffin and Joseph C. Hough Jr. (Albany: SUNY Press, 1991), 161.

32. Ibid., 162. Suchocki gives a brief history, with references, of trinitarian speculation by Cobb and other process thinkers in the introduction to Joseph A. Bracken, S.J., and Marjorie Hewitt Suchocki, eds., *Trinity in Process: A Relational History of God* (New York: Continuum, 1997), ix ff. But as Cobb observes in the first essay in the volume, even for Christian process thinkers already confessionally committed to trinitarianism, "there is no one doctrine of the trinity that is dictated by that conceptuality" ("Relativization of the Trinity," 4).

right. From the left would come the call for the historical justification of such an exaltation of Jesus Christ, and Cobb attempts to answer this challenge by adducing evidence from a broad ideological spectrum of biblical scholarship for an extraordinarily consistent picture of a Jesus who, with his associated community, is an unparalleled catalyst of "creative transformation" of the human condition.[33] From the right would come the criticism that this understanding of Christ as a maximal case of the immanence of the divine in all of us robs him of his unique divine identity and makes all of us potential Christs, much in the manner of Schleiermacher's understanding of Christ as the human being with maximal, uninterrupted "God-consciousness."[34]

Cobb replies in essence that a quantitative difference in the effectiveness of the lure of God in subjective experience leads incrementally to a threshold at which there is a qualitative difference in that subject. If the universal divine immanence is understood as maximally effective for the constitution of the self in Jesus as the Christ, then there is a qualitatively unique presence of God in Christ and a genuine unanimity of character and purpose of God and Christ. And since, on a process model, the self consists in continuity of character and purpose in an historical stream of events rather than some enduring "substance," then there is a sort of identity between Christ and God. "The Logos incarnate in Jesus is God himself. Furthermore the presence of the Logos in Jesus is in a genuine way structurally coconstitutive of his selfhood."[35] Outside the parameters of the traditional christological conversation, such claims about Jesus may seem pointless, at least insofar as they entail his alleged uniqueness as a God-bearer. But after all, Christians are the community that confesses "Jesus is Lord"; he is our concrete universal (Paul Tillich). Process christologies can be presented in good faith as attempts to detach confession based on Scripture, tra-

33. Cobb, *Christ in a Pluralistic Age,* 97-110. There are many sophisticated works of evangelical apology for the uniqueness of Christ, such as C. S. Lewis's *Mere Christianity* (New York: Macmillan, 1952) and John R. W. Stott's *Basic Christianity* (London: InterVarsity Press, 1958). Lewis argues that, given the reliability of the Gospel testimony to Jesus, the view of him summarized in orthodox high Christology is more rational than a humanizing reduction of his nature.

34. Schleiermacher, *Christian Faith,* §94, p. 385.

35. Cobb, *Christ in a Pluralistic Age,* 170. For the broader context and development of this argument, see pp. 163-73.

dition, and personal knowledge from necessary connection with particular ontologies. This is a conversation evangelicals need to have; process thinkers can irenically push them toward it.

If belief in "His miracles" means that God suspends or bypasses normal structures and conditions of God-world interaction in these extraordinary deeds of Jesus, then the process God by definition cannot do it. Process theism assumes a uniformity of God-world interaction. "God and the world stand over against each other, expressing the final metaphysical truth that appetitive vision and physical enjoyment have equal claim to priority in creation. . . . Thus each temporal occasion embodies God, and is embodied in God" (*PR* 348). Fundamental differences between process thought and traditional Christianity on the "ultimacy" and ontological independence of God separate the two camps at this point. But if certain societies of occasions have been so guided by God and have so accepted God's luring that they are optimally placed to be *semeia* (sign-events) of God's abiding love and purpose, then process thinkers who are so motivated by confession and tradition can fit these faith-defining sign-events into their worldview. Conversely, evangelicals might be encouraged to think about miracles in ways more congruent with the biblical witness, in which God is immediately responsible for all natural occurrences, not just those we would denominate as miraculous because of their apparent contravening of natural law.

S. V. McCasland defines "miracle" as "an event, whether natural or supernatural, in which one sees an act or revelation of God."[36] Much evangelical thought has been co-opted by a rigid understanding of natural law and strict causality that is now scientifically outdated. The point, I take it, in affirming miracles is the affirmation of God's ability to communicate with us in extraordinary and transformative ways. If the world is an open structure characterized in its entirety, as per process thought, by divine luring, human response, and renewed divine luring, then the miraculous is there all around us for those who have "eyes to see and ears to hear" (Matthew 13:16).

David Basinger takes a less optimistic view of the possibility of dialogue at this point. "The evangelical worldview is fundamentally

36. S. V. McCasland, "Miracle," *Interpreter's Dictionary of the Bible,* ed. G. A. Buttrick (Nashville: Abingdon, 1962), 3:392.

supernaturalistic. That is, evangelicals not only believe that God *can* unilaterally intervene in worldly affairs, they believe that God has often done so. The Whiteheadian worldview, on the other hand, is antisupernaturalistic in this sense."[37] Yet where faith confessions and intellectual loyalties bring contrasting ontologies together, we do best to seek common ground, for the reasons I have continually rehearsed. The key question at issue here is this: What events most powerfully and faithfully represent God's character and intentions to us? If we can move toward agreement on the roster of miracles thus defined, then our apologetic theologies can work both sides of the supernatural/antisupernatural street for the purposes of the new creation/creative transformation (2 Corinthians 5:17) we unanimously desire.

"His vicarious and atoning death . . ." To limit in principle the role of catalyst of creative transformation (Cobb) toward optimal richness and harmony of experience for the world to a single historical strand of occasions deeply contradicts the process-relational worldview. But to locate this creative transformation in concrete personal histories important to individuals and communities – indeed, to make judgments about movements and trends of world-historical importance – this lies within the horizon of every serious believer and thinker. Now Cobb's soteriology concentrates on the *life* of Christ as an exemplification and promotion of God's aims for humanity and the creation; much evangelical thought and the centuries of mainstream Catholic and Protestant soteriology that underlie it seem to be preoccupied with the *death* of Christ, variously construed as payment of an obligation incurred by sinful humanity toward a holy God, exemplification of the limitless depths of the divine love, or overcoming of the power of anti-God forces through deflecting and absorbing their destructiveness.[38]

My thinking at this point is that process thinkers could help evangelicals connect Christ's death to his life, by interpreting his death not as a "transaction" extrinsic to the divine-human relatedness, but as the tragic yet liberative outcome of a life lived in utter obedience to God's aims in a broken world. Liberative because the power and virtue

37. David Basinger, "Process-Relational Christian Soteriology: A Response to Wheeler," *Process Studies* 18/2 (1989): 117.

38. See Gustaf Aulen's classic treatment of three historical types of atonement doctrine in *Christus Victor* (London: SPCK, 1953).

of Christ's unbroken faithfulness and undiluted goodness are lifted up by God, preserved in God, and ever thereafter a factor in subsequent human becoming. Conversely, evangelicals can remind process theists of the centrality of Christ's passion in the original Christian documents and self-understanding, and the pervasiveness and tragic cost of human sin in the divinely promoted process of becoming. In the words of Pierre Teilhard de Chardin, not a Whiteheadian, but very much a "process-" oriented thinker, "Jesus on the Cross is both the symbol and the reality of the immense labour of the centuries which has, little by little, raised up the created spirit and brought it back to the depth of the divine context."[39]

4, 5, and 7. "Regeneration, godly living and the unity of believers through the ministry of the Holy Spirit. . . ." The immanence of God in Jesus as the Christ (= Logos in Cobb's *Christ in a Pluralistic Age*) and the immanence of the Holy Spirit in believers as the basis of sanctification and Christian unity are systematically differentiated in accordance with trinitarian theology in traditional Christianity. In process thought there is no systemic reason for making this differentiation. "Logos" and "Spirit" would simply be two historically attested metaphors for describing divine immanence. But once again, as the interests of the two communities overlap with respect to identifying and describing God's efficacious luring, they could profit from reexamining together the complex and subtle biblical witness to *ruach/pneuma//dabar/logos.* God's creative and transforming presence is sometimes a mighty wind (Genesis 1:2; Ezekiel 37:9), sometimes an intimate breath (Genesis 2:7; Ezekiel 37:4), sometimes a commanding, ordering word (Genesis 1:3, 6, 9, 11, 14, 20, etc.; John 1:1-3), sometimes a gentle whisper (1 Kings 19:12). Paul's marvelous soliloquy in Romans 8:1-11, where God, Christ, and Spirit are used interchangeably to name the divine presence, and the believer is alternately described as *dwelling in* the divine presence and having the divine presence *indwelling,* should deter any sensitive interpreter from trying to squeeze the Poet of the World into or onto an organizational chart. However, process-relational de-

39. Pierre Teilhard de Chardin, *The Divine Milieu* (New York: Harper & Row, 1965), 79. I would refer the reader to my further development of this theme in "Toward a Process-Relational Christian Soteriology," *Process Studies* 18/2 (1989): 102-13; and *A Relational View of the Atonement,* esp. part III, 189-224.

scriptions of the universal and systemic role of the divine immanence in human life and the cosmos offer persuasive apologetic support to the general Christian insight of God's creative and transformative presence and action in the world. "In Whitehead's words, 'The world lives by its incarnation of God.' . . . The implication of this analysis is that God as Logos is effectively, if unconsciously, present and felt in all events. . . . Christ is a reality in the world."[40]

6, 3. "We believe in the resurrection . . ." and "in [Christ's] personal return in power and glory." One can certainly imagine and describe resurrection in process-relational terms,[41] although it has been widely debated in the literature whether there is any systemic reason for – or against – personal survival or subjective immortality in process thought. Whitehead's God exhibits "a tender care that nothing be lost" (*PR* 346), but process thought excludes guaranteed outcomes, either for individuals or for the cosmos, because God's power, while great, is never absolute or uncontested. The ultimate metaphysical fact is not "success" or even progress, but simply "the creative advance into novelty" (*PR* 349). This "creative advance" is an open-ended process that is suffused with hope, since God patiently superintends the world's societies of occasions toward God's own vision of maximal correspondence of depth and breadth of experience, but never invested with certainty. Thus resurrection and personal immortality for certain personal societies could indeed be features of God's preservation and perpetual enjoyment of realized truth and beauty without the necessity of a corresponding enrichment of and "progress" for the God-world togetherness as a whole. This sober admission is a systemic consequence of the radical openness of the cosmic process in process-relational thought.

40. Cobb, *Christ in a Pluralistic Age,* 77; citing Whitehead, *Religion in the Making,* 156.

41. Marjorie Suchocki discusses the possibility of subjective immortality as a systemic implicate of process-relational thought, contrasting her view with that of Charles Hartshorne – who rejected both its possibility and theological appropriateness – in her essay "Charles Hartshorne and Subjective Immortality," *Process Studies* 21/2 (1992): 118-22. See also chap. 8 of her *End of Evil: Process Eschatology in Historical Context* (Albany: SUNY Press, 1988). Granville C. Henry and I both address the topic of subjective immortality in process terms with special emphasis on immortality as bodily resurrection. See Henry's "Does Process Thought Allow Personal Immortality?" *Religious Studies* 31 (1995): 311-21; and my "Here and Hereafter: A Process-Relational Perspective," *Perspectives in Religious Studies* 22/3 (1995): 259-97.

In light of this fact, the stereotypical conservative Christian expectation of "Christ's personal return in power and glory" would seem to bring into stark relief several of the incommensurate features of evangelical thought and process theism that make the dialogue I am promoting seem quixotic. "This Jesus, who has been taken up from you into heaven, will come in the same way as you saw him go . . . ," two angels tell the apostles (Acts 1:11). This account reflects – seemingly in mythical language – the mystical experiences of an ancient faith community; process thought intends to deal with the world of public facts. The account reflects an ancient cosmology; process thought seeks to frame a contemporary scientific cosmology. Christ's return marks the absolute end of history as we know it (1 Corinthians 15:28; 1 Thessalonians 4:16-18); process thought is open-ended. This confession seems, in sum, paradigmatic of the supernatural/antisupernatural antinomy that, according to David Basinger (above) divides evangelicals from process thinkers. Yet I persist in questioning whether things are as hopeless as that. One could argue that the linear cast of process thought in particular ("creative advance") and Western historicized culture in general are rooted in biblical "salvation history," and even in their most secular expressions gain energy from a residual eschatological hope; conversely, the specific, potentially invigorating hope couched in the evangelical profession of Christ's return can only gain in persuasive power by being separated from a deterministic literalism.

Evangelicals and Process Theists: A Call for Mutual Transformation

In the previous section of this essay, I lifted up from the confessional statement of the NAE points of doctrine where evangelical-process dialogue seems to me called for, whether for likely mutual enhancement of the two communities, or because the indicated convictions seemed most defining of the differences between the two. At its most trivial, this sort of exercise could be simply the sort of "compare and contrast" exercise that goes on all the time in religious studies circles, where schools of thought or faith communities are connected by tenuous historical ties or perhaps only by the personal interests of the researcher. But I have maintained from the beginning that this project is more momentous than that. Evangelical faith and thought characterize a vital and growing strand of American and global Christianity, whose peculiar weaknesses can be fruitfully addressed by certain principal concepts in that worldview called process-relational. Conversely, the strikingly persuasive worldview called process-relational could greatly expand its scope and power by extending its working relationship with Christian faith communities in the direction of evangelicals, beyond its traditional home in liberal Protestantism. To that end, I wish to highlight in this concluding section five key doctrinal areas where dialogue would be, in my view, vitally important, and would contain striking possibilities for mutual transformation of the two traditions.[42] I invite the reader to note that I am not going to be talking about the nature of God and God's action in the world, process Christology, or theodicy, except as these topics have been raised en route above or may be implicated incidentally in the five sections below. This turf has been plowed and replowed in our generation; the areas below hold promise, in my judgment, for less thoroughly explored new insights.

Understanding of Scripture

Everyone hears and reads, whether a word of Scripture or any other word, from a more or less self-conscious and intentional point of view. Our generation has seen the tremendous influence that the choice of a hermeneutical viewpoint can have on the reading and hearing of biblical texts, as demonstrated by feminist theologies and theologies of liberation coming from the margins of First World order and affluence. Making that point of view maximally consistent, maximally illuminating, authentically related to the text, and authentically related to one's personal and group experience are among the tasks of hermeneutics.

42. John Cobb gives an example of how this mutual transformation of traditions might work, using Christianity and Buddhism as examples, in "The Perfection of Love," chap. 13 of *Christ in a Pluralistic Age,* 203-20. Another example is the work Jay McDaniel does, also with Christianity and Buddhism, in "Revisioning God," chap. 15 of *Liberating Life: Contemporary Approaches to Ecological Theology,* ed. Charles Birch et al. (Maryknoll, N.Y.: Orbis, 1990), 228-58.

My reader might anticipate that at this point, once again, I would adduce the illuminating power of the process-relational worldview to inform and guide these generic hermeneutical tasks. And so I might. But a "process hermeneutic" lays a challenge before evangelicals that is specific to evangelical understandings of the nature and task of hermeneutics. Process-relational thought insists on the radically perspectival nature of all our putative knowledge. Clark Williamson speaks specifically to the question of Christianity's relationship with Judaism, but with far-reaching implications for all Christian "truth": "Acknowledging that Christianity itself is one perspective (indeed, this is too simple; there are many 'Christianities' . . .) upon what is ultimate, one relative and limited perspective, strikes at the heart of anti-Judaism's exclusivistic universalism and its triumphalism."[43]

In contrast, a lively debate within evangelical circles in recent years has been whether correct exegesis of Scripture will yield a single univocal meaning. Carl Henry's understanding of Scripture as an axiomatic system of propositional truths would seem to imply a positive answer to this question. Walter C. Kaiser Jr. forthrightly locates this conclusion in an inclusive hermeneutical theory as follows: "A literary work like the Bible can have one and only one correct interpretation and that meaning must be determined by the human author's intention."[44] Citing a prominent feature of traditional Christian exegesis, however, other evangelical authors point out that Old Testament authors could have had no explicitly Christian "intention" with respect to prophetic passages later seen as fulfilled through the life of Jesus – for instance, Jeremiah 31:5, "the slaughter of the innocents," as interpreted in Matthew 2:16-18.[45]

Millard J. Erickson, whose survey of evangelical discussion of this issue I am following here, admits that much evangelical hermeneutics,

43. Clark Williamson, "Process Hermeneutics and Christianity's Post-Holocaust Reinterpretation of Itself," *Process Studies* 12/2 (1982): 85.

44. Walter C. Kaiser Jr., "Response to Authorial Intention and Biblical Interpretation," in *Hermeneutics, Inerrancy, and the Bible,* ed. Earl D. Radamacher and Robert D. Preus (Grand Rapids: Zondervan, 1984), 441; cited in Millard J. Erickson, *Evangelical Interpretation: Perspectives on Hermeneutical Issues* (Grand Rapids: Baker, 1993), 13.

45. See Donald Hagner, "The Old Testament in the New Testament," in *Interpreting the Word of God,* ed. Samuel J. Schultz and Marcus A. Inch (Chicago: Moody Press, 1976), 9; cited in Erickson, *Evangelical Interpretation,* 15.

even in the late twentieth century, seems embarrassingly pre-Freudian, as if we could still believe that authors' presuppositions and intentions were all clearly and unambiguously entertained and rationally elucidated and applied in the conscious mind.[46] On the contrary, at this date in history we must all acknowledge multiple presuppositions and multiple tracks of experience wending in and out of the conscious awareness of both authors and their interpreters. Furthermore, today's philosophers are teaching us that the very coinage of our communication, language itself, does not bear fixed meanings in the sense assumed by traditional Christian interpreters. Susan Brooks Thistlethwaite explains: "In addition to the [modern] view that human subjectivity is constructed by language, poststructuralists believed that language itself is not fixed but 'built,' as words acquire meanings in specific historical locations. These locations are always the site of competing meanings, and, hence, of struggle."[47] Mark C. Taylor speaks of our words as "an unending play of signification" and adds: "There seems to be no exit from this labyrinth of interpretation."[48]

One might respond to this "deconstructive" side of postmodern intellectual culture by unleashing a jeremiad against the "relativism" and "nihilism" of its linguistic theory, and insisting that texts and their correct interpretations are true descriptions of reality – what David J. Lull calls an "objectivist hermeneutic."[49] This has been the dominant evangelical hermeneutic, but will have, I believe, for the reasons adduced, less and less apologetic validity in contemporary culture. Or one might continue to defend a "subjectivist" hermeneutic, in the manner of Bultmann, which privileges "the interpreter's own created 'world'" as the criterion of meaning for the text. But in truth, objective data and imaginative construction are both always part of the understanding of author and interpreter, and are brought together in the work of interpretation to create working proposals about reality.[50] Which brings us

46. Erickson, *Evangelical Interpretation,* 21-22.

47. Susan Brooks Thistlethwaite, "Christology and Postmodernism," *Interpretation* 69/3 (1995): 270.

48. Mark C. Taylor, *Erring: A Postmodern A/Theology* (Chicago: University of Chicago Press, 1984), 172.

49. David J. Lull, "What Is Process Hermeneutics?" *Process Studies* 13/3 (1983): 191.

50. Ibid.

to the unique contribution that process-relational thought can make to the appropriation and use of Christianity's sacred text.

David Griffin has proposed and described in numerous writings a "constructive" postmodern project, which does not give in to the relativism and the endless ungrounded signification of deconstructive postmodernism, but rather advocates the systematic engagement of reality through the formation and testing of "propositions" in the Whiteheadian sense.[51] It is the central role of the "proposition" that distinguishes process hermeneutics as such. For Whitehead, a proposition was not, as for evangelicals like Carl Henry and for many secular philosophers of language, a verifiable linguistic transcript of a state of affairs in the world. Rather it was a "lure to creative emergence in the transcendent future" (*PR* 263). In other words, it is oriented toward the free subject's self-creation in the reality and possibility of its own situation – not so different, really, from the "call to faithful discipleship" endemic to classical Christianity, particularly when that call is interpreted eschatologically (cf. "the transcendent future") as has been done increasingly by contemporary Protestant thinkers such as Jürgen Moltmann, Wolfhart Pannenburg, and Marjorie Suchocki.

Hermeneutics done out of this understanding of propositions in the text will guide us in engagement with the world's systems and powers. For the bottom line will not be "Can this proposition be proved true?" (objectivist hermeneutic) or "Can I live authentically by this proposition in the unique world of my interiority?" (subjectivist hermeneutic), but rather "Will I live faithfully in our common world, with *this* end in view?" Process thought recognizes that we are embodied persons, living in specific communities. The aesthetic dimension in Whitehead's thought ties our ideals to our embodied nature. Thus a process-influenced hermeneutics will be collaborative, like the best American Academy of Religion/Society of Biblical Literature seminars and working groups or the best local church Bible classes. For the teachers of my youth, the hermeneutical key unlocking the mysteries of the Scriptures and weaving together diverse scriptural characters and their fates was God's "plan of salvation," intended for all but accessed only by that individual "whosoever" who would believe. For evangelicals today, en-

51. See David Ray Griffin, *God and Religion in the Postmodern World* (Albany: SUNY Press, 1989); idem, *Varieties of Postmodern Theology* (Albany: SUNY Press, 1989).

counter with process thinkers can remind them that scriptural accounts of God's redemptive intentions and activity are not entirely or even primarily about the destinies of individuals. Rather, from the creation narratives in which humanity is set in the midst of a rich tapestry of divinely ordered nature (Genesis 1–2), through the various covenant traditions in which the nations, the beasts of the field, and even the land are among the beneficiaries (Genesis 9:8-11; 12:1-3; Leviticus 25:1-7; Isaiah 60:1-3), right through to the central motif in the ministry and teaching of Jesus, the universal reign of God (Matthew 6:9-13; Mark 1:14-15), the actualization of the individual is a function of the apotheosis of the entire created order, "so that God may be all in all" (1 Corinthians 15:28). "[God] saves *the world* as it passes into the immediacy of his own life" (*PR* 346, my emphasis).

Process thinkers understand the cosmic adventure as "creative advance into novelty" (*PR* 349). This process understanding can be concretely exhibited and illustrated by reference to this collection of texts that has functioned as the *Ur*-Story or master narrative for a significant portion of the human race. Clark Williamson again: We admit "that while *a* perspective can be transcended, the reality of having *some* perspective cannot."[52] The emergence of humanity from "dreaming innocence" (Tillich) into culpable responsibility, the journey of self-dissolution and self-definition "into the far country" (Luke 15:3), the vision of the as yet unattained city, "the city whose builder and maker is God" (Hebrews 11:10) – these themes resonate with the life journeys of self-conscious individuals and the collective journeys of the Western, historically conditioned communities that were birthed in the womb of these primal narratives. These themes are propositions par excellence, "lures for feeling" in the sense we have been discussing. The process vision of the world has great affinities for these motifs – they *are* motifs of process – and will gain in power by tapping into them.

Reexamining the Self

Certainly a major benefit that evangelicals can receive through dialogue with process thinkers is critical perspective on their normally

52. Williamson, "Process Hermeneutics," 85.

uncritical acceptance of Enlightenment views of the autonomous, substantial self. I need to say at this point that this phenomenon is not entirely a capitulation of evangelical thinkers to an alien cultural norm. In addition to Homeric, Platonic, and Aristotelian traditions of the autonomous self that are influential parts of our Western cultural heritage before the Enlightenment, and the characteristic Enlightenment doctrines of the self – especially Descartes's doctrine of thinking substance and the Kantian teaching of the self as the creator and shaper of our experience – there is an important strand of biblical teaching that singles out and values the individual on its own terms. From the tribal sagas of Abraham, Isaac, and Jacob and his twelve sons (Genesis 12–50), through the Mosaic covenant uniting the "tribes of Yahweh" (Norman Gottwald), on through the historical epic of the Davidic dynasty (the four books of Samuel-Kings) and into the literature of the Diaspora, there is certainly the unifying theme in Scripture of God's choice of a people, who are blessed and cursed collectively, and who collectively will be a conduit of blessing to all humanity (Genesis 12:1-3; Isaiah 40:3-5). On the other hand, individual heroes and heroines, their stories marked by varying degrees of probability in the eyes of critical historians, emerge to the light of day as more than archetypes, but rather as individually accountable respondents to God's call. From Abram in Haran (Genesis 11:27-32) to the boy Samuel in the sanctuary at Shiloh (1 Samuel 3:1-21) to David to the colorful roster of characters Jesus of Nazareth confronted one by one, one can see in the Hebrew-Christian Scriptures an independent source of the historical strain of individuation.

> The word of the Lord came to me: What do you mean by repeating this proverb concerning the land of Israel, "The parents have eaten sour grapes, and the children's teeth are set on edge"? As I live, says the Lord God, this proverb shall no more be used by you in Israel . . . it is only the person who sins that shall die. (Ezekiel 18:1-4, NRSV)

The biblical individual is not an enduring substance, characterized by a roster of privileged attributes: rationality, aesthetic sense, moral obligation, and so on. Contemporary field observation of our fellow creatures shows us chimpanzees using tools, ravens calculating, and elephants mourning their dead. Indeed, the biblical individual is constituted by the creative call of God, as we were reminded a generation ago by the neoorthodox theologians.[53]

> For it was you who formed my inward parts; you knit me together in my mother's womb. . . . In your book were written all the days that were formed for me, when none of them existed. (Psalm 139:13, 16)

With appropriate recognition of the relatively stronger role the Bible grants to divine causative power vis-à-vis creaturely power than does process thought, the process picture of God's role as "principle of concretion" for every actual occasion, seeking to guide that occasion toward the most valuable self-actualization possible in its environment of origin, is highly congruent with the biblical picture of God's role in the promotion of selfhood (*PR* 244).

> The word is very near to you; it is in your mouth and in your heart for you to observe. See, I have set before you today life and prosperity, death and adversity. (Deuteronomy 30:14-15, NRSV)

> For the gate is narrow and the road is hard that leads to life, and there are few who find it. (Matthew 7:14, NRSV)

> The initial aim is the best for that *impasse*. . . . What is inexorable in God, is valuation towards 'order.' (*PR* 244)

Having said all this, however, I would again maintain that the central motif in the ministry and teaching of Jesus – especially the Jesus of the Synoptic Gospels – is not the individual self-perfection ("salvation") so highly valued and so exclusively sought by much evangelical piety. Instead, it is the reign of God (Mark 1:14-15; Luke 4:18-19; cf. Isaiah 11:1-9; 61:1-4), a new state of wholeness, harmony, and well-being (Hebrew *shalom*), comprising liberation from sin and injustice and achievement of God's original creative intent. The self-actualization and well-being of the individual here and hereafter is presented in the New Testament as a function of this "new world or-

53. See, e.g., Emil Brunner, *Dogmatics,* vol. 2: *The Christian Doctrine of Creation and Redemption,* trans. Olive Wyon (Philadelphia: Westminster, 1952), esp. 55-61.

der" being instituted by God through Christ (Ephesians 1:5-19; Colossians 1:15-20; Revelation 22:1-5). Further, the "spiritual unity of believers" (NAE 7) defines and fulfills those individuals, whose ultimate destiny is attained as members of the glorified "body of Christ" (1 Corinthians 12:27; Colossians 1:16-17). In a process metaphysic, the individual occasion catches up in itself, theoretically, its entire past actual world. Its self-formation is a function of that past actual world *and* a contribution to the future. That is, in so far as the process cosmology is accurate and illuminating of the nature of things, all "self-actualization" is thoroughly social. Truly the cosmos describes a total creative advance, and that totality is preserved and cherished by God, becoming "the perfected actuality [that] passes back into the temporal world. . . . For the kingdom of heaven is with us today" (*PR* 351). Process theists can and should challenge evangelicals to claim their own (biblical) heritage at this point.

On the other hand, the evangelical tradition carries potential learnings for process thought on the vexing issue of the nature of the self and identity. If complex realities such as human beings are not, as per Aristotle and the dominant Western tradition, enduring substances, but rather – as process thought has it – patterns sustained through the appearing and disappearing of myriad "perpetually perishing" energetic events, then the question of the nature and identity of the self becomes problematic.[54] Evangelicals, to the extent that they are genuinely responsive to their biblical heritage, can transcend Enlightenment definitions of the self and recast the *imago dei,* as I suggested above, in terms of a divine calling/naming/equipping that brings the individual into being and endows the individual with standing and purpose in God's plan (cf. Jeremiah 1:5; John 1:13-17).[55] Thinking genetically about acts of becoming: does the actual occasion arise in just such a locus in the extensive continuum because God anticipates, desires, and directs becoming there? With respect to past actual occasions, especially those routes of occasions with personal order, located optimally in animal bodies, which for Whitehead constitute "the en-

54. For an examination of the problem of the self in process thought as it applies to human beings and, by extension, to God, see Rem B. Edwards, "The Human Self: An Actual Entity or a Society?" *Process Studies* 5/3 (1975): 195-203.

55. See Brunner, *Christian Doctrine,* 75-78.

during personality" (*PR* 119): is it not God who gives them their ultimate identity and location in God's everlastingness? The answers to the questions of the self, its identity, its destiny, and its ultimate importance might be fruitfully pursued by process thinkers using the biblical understanding of God's identity-constituting call as a heuristic tool to probe the Whiteheadian corpus for insight, especially the enigmatic part 5 of *Process and Reality.*

The Body of Christ

Examining the key New Testament image of "the body of Christ" is one way of getting at a cluster of associated issues that bristles with difficulties between evangelical thought and process-relational theism, but where the two might nevertheless interact with great vigor. What is the nature of God's presence in the world? Is that presence differentially located in specific societies of occasions? With what degree of freedom does God act in the world, and to what ends?

It seems a natural step for Christian theology steeped in process-relational thought to connect the process doctrine of God's universal immanence in the world's occasions to biblical images of divine embodiedness (John 1:14; 1 Corinthians 12:12-27; Colossians 1:15-20), and conclude by accepting Sallie McFague's challenge: "What if we dared to think of our planet and indeed the whole universe as the body of God?"[56] In Whitehead's cosmology,

> God and the World are the contrasted opposites in terms of which Creativity achieves its supreme task of transforming disjointed multiplicity, with its diversities in opposition, into concrescent unity, with its diversities in contrast. . . . For God the conceptual is prior to the physical, for the World the physical poles are prior to the conceptual poles. (*PR* 348)

God and the world exist simultaneously and interdependently. God's conceptual vision of the possible is (partially) embodied in every

56. Sallie McFague, *The Body of God: An Ecological Theology* (Minneapolis: Fortress, 1993), 19.

worldly occasion; the world, for its part, is permeated by God's ideals and yields God concrete actuality. This radical divine immanence is central to process cosmology; God seeds novelty and preserves order in the world while the world embodies God's aims. Is the "body of Christ," then, a specific historical exemplar of God's essential and universal immanence in the world? Or, going somewhat further, to the extent that this history of divine embodiment supremely mirrors God's character and purposes – for example, "the brief Galilean vision of humility" (*PR* 342) – does it become a "leading shoot" of cosmic evolution, to use Teilhard's phrase?

By contrast, evangelical thought emphasizes God's infinite prior actuality vis-à-vis the world and God's transcendence of the world and absolute freedom over against it. Karl Barth puts it thus: "God could be alone; the world cannot. The world would not exist at all if God did not exist and if it were not from Him. . . . And God is before the world in the strictest sense that He is its absolute origin, its purpose, the power which rules it, its Lord."[57] In this conversation we revisit the concerns about God's ultimacy I mentioned above. For the theology of evangelical openness, God would embody, as per Scripture, at once the universal relatedness and responsiveness of the process God, the self-actuality of the God-world togetherness in process thought, and the ultimacy of the process category of Creativity. Thus there are key questions of fundamental ontology that will continue to divide the two traditions, further consequence of the naturalism/supernaturalism gap (Basinger). But there are important areas of common concern as well. The God of the Bible may indeed be radically transcendent. But this God, having created the world and its creatures through the divine Word (Genesis 1:3, 6, 9, etc.; John 1:1-3), the metaphor of Order, or alternately through the divine Spirit (Genesis 1:1-2; 2:7; Psalm 104:29-30), the metaphor of Energy and Life, is pleased to work indefatigably for the renewal and perfection of the creation, notwithstanding the brokenness introduced into it by God-dishonoring decisions and actions (sin). In so working, God's immanence in the creation is radicalized; this redemptive presence is represented in Scripture by the same two metaphors that characterize God's creative presence.

57. Karl Barth, *Church Dogmatics* III, 1, trans. J. W. Edwards et al., ed. G. W. Bromiley and T. F. Torrance (Edinburgh: T. & T. Clark, 1958), 7.

> And the Word became flesh and lived among us. (John 1:14, NRSV)

> Very truly I tell you, no one can enter the kingdom of God without being born of water and Spirit. What is born of the flesh is flesh, and what is born of the Spirit is spirit. (John 3:5-6, NRSV)

> But you are not in the flesh; you are in the Spirit, since the Spirit of God dwells in you. (Romans 8:9, NRSV)

The result of this renewal and intensification of divine immanence in the world is a progressive conformation of the world to God's aims, which is historically represented and exemplified by the church, understood as the spiritual body of Christ (1 Corinthians 12:27). "The church constantly *re-presents Christ* to the world, and insofar as it is faithful to him, multiplies his influence manyfold."[58] Teilhard described in *Phenomenon of Man* a universal movement of the world toward and by means of its ultimate point of attraction and unifying principle, the immanent-transcendent Christ.[59] This image implies a classic Roman Catholic treatment of the relationship between "nature" and "grace" that is more easily conjoined with process-relational thought than the typical Reformation understanding. In process thought, God's love is universal, constitutive of every becoming, and characterized by a formal unity of the divine interaction with every worldly occasion. Returning to the theological language, we might say that grace fulfills nature, for humanity and cosmos are oriented toward God as telos.[60]

Evangelical thought emphasizes the discontinuity between nature and an "unexacted" redemptive grace. "Has the potter no right over the clay, to make out of the same lump one object for special use and another for ordinary use?" (Romans 9:21, NRSV). Again I refer to Barth: "The subject matter, origin and content of the message received and proclaimed by the Christian community is at heart the free act of

58. David L. Wheeler, "Toward a Process-Relational Christian Soteriology," *Process Studies* 18/2 (1989): 108.

59. Pierre Teilhard de Chardin, *The Phenomenon of Man* (New York: Harper & Row, 1954).

60. See the classic treatment of this theme by Thomas Aquinas, *Summa Theologia,* "Treatise on Grace," II I III, QQ. 109-14.

the faithfulness of God."[61] But in sharply distinguishing nature and grace and protecting the freedom of God, evangelicals have often ended up with "A lists" and "B lists" of saved and lost individuals, whose togetherness, if any, is voluntaristic and aggregate. God's lure in process theism is not differentiated in the sense that God wishes anything less than blessedness for any occasion, but God's lure is differentiated in terms of the richer aims that God can offer to certain occasions in light of their history and social location, the antecedents of such occasions having responded to God's previous luring in such a way as to enrich and multiply subsequent possibilities for their successors – a sort of Arminian reading of the issue of nature and grace. In the nature of things, according to process thought, the fulfillment of worldly occasions is social in nature, and achieved levels of rich and harmonious togetherness open up richer possible futures for their successors.

This is a truth the evangelical church affirms in theory (cf. NAE 7) but often heeds little in its piety and practice. Process-relational cosmology could thus serve at this point as a heuristic device to guide the reading of Scripture with respect to the progressive and social nature of redemption. Agreeing on the subject of the faithfulness of God – it is Whitehead himself who emphasizes "God's tender care that nothing be lost" (*PR* 346) – both schools can utilize the imagery of the body of Christ and God's gathering and equipping of it through the divine Spirit as a powerful and inspirational portrayal of the realization in the world of God's purposes. Christian imagery of the body of Christ, and Christian faith experience of mutuality and common cause transcending divisions of age, gender, race, and culture (Acts 2:40-47; 11:1-18; Galatians 3:28) can serve as a vivid concrete instantiation of the process-relational vision of becoming in togetherness. "The church in its expansive self-realization moves toward the exemplification *par excellence* of the Whiteheadian notion of a society – a togetherness of actual occasions characterized by their mutual positive apprehension of a common element of form."[62]

61. Karl Barth, *Church Dogmatics* IV, 1, trans. G. W. Bromiley, ed. Bromiley and T. F. Torrance (Edinburgh: T. & T. Clark, 1956), 3.

62. Wheeler, *Process Studies* 18/2 (1989): 109. See my further development of this topic in the cited article. Also, for a process-relational development of the doctrine of the church, see Marjorie Hewitt Suchocki, *God, Christ, Church: A Practical Guide to Process Theology* (New York: Crossroad, 1982), esp. 125-60.

Earth Community

If we rethink the notion of "church" under the influence of process-relational thought, understanding it not as an arbitrary aggregate of saved individuals but as a prototype of the world healed and harmonized by Christ's spiritual presence, this raises further questions. Scripture is clear that not only human beings but also the nonhuman creation suffers as a result of human sin. A broken creation waits with longing for the eschatological hope symbolized by Jesus as "the kingdom of God" or "the kingdom of heaven." "For the creation waits with eager longing for the revealing of the children of God; for the creation was subjected to futility, not of its own will but by the will of the one who subjected it, in hope that the creation itself will be set free from its bondage to decay and will obtain the freedom of the glory of the children of God" (Romans 8:19-21, NRSV).

On the other hand, the church is the "body of Christ," the Human One in whom God was, according to traditional Christian teaching, uniquely incarnate. Its members as well are human beings. When the NAE confessional statement speaks of sin and salvation, it speaks uniquely of human beings (NAE 4, 6); indeed, nothing in this brief statement indicates that denizens of the natural world are subjects before God in their own right or special objects of our or God's concern. This is also true of much longer and more detailed evangelical statements of faith, for instance the 1963 "Baptist Faith and Message" statement of Southern Baptists. In all fairness, this omission is not unique to evangelical Christianity. I recently perused the seven hundred pages of John Leith's *Creeds of the Churches,* which journeys from the second century through the great creedal statements of the ecumenical councils, the Reformation and the Counter-Reformation, straight through to the founding statements of twentieth-century ecumenism, looking in vain for a single reference to the natural world as the subject of a point of doctrine.[63] It is simply a historical fact that "the Christian message was initially a gospel of personal salvation"[64] in its original

63. John H. Leith, ed., *Creeds of the Churches: A Reader in Christian Doctrine from the Bible to the Present,* 3rd ed. (Atlanta: John Knox, 1982).

64. John Austin Baker, "Biblical Views of Nature," in *Liberating Life,* ed. Birch et al., 21.

Greco-Roman setting of missionary expansion, and with few exceptions (e.g., St. Francis of Assisi, Hildegaard of Bingen) has continued thus to the present day. The natural world in this view becomes a sort of stage setting for the real focus of the biblical narrative, the playing out of the divine-human drama of creation, fall, and redemption. Nonhuman creatures are "natural resources" (Genesis 1:29; Psalm 104:14-15), whose value is always instrumental, never intrinsic. Barth expresses it this way: "Like man himself, the beasts have a *proprius nutus*. . . . But in contrast to man they have no independent dignity and function even within the creaturely world. They belong to man."[65]

Sinful human beings will inevitably take their "central status" in God's creative and redemptive plan as a rationale for unholy pride and its harvest of destruction. Pioneering ecological theologian Wesley Granberg-Michaelson describes the cultural shadow side of such a theology: "Modern humanity has become too confident in its own power and has trusted far too deeply in its dominance over the creation. It has constructed a worldview that places human power and glory at the center of the universe."[66] Ironically, it is only the unraveling of the web of life under the pressure of human dominance and the subsequent threat to human life and well-being that has led some Christians to question the reading of Scripture and resulting theological construction that form at least part of the superstructure for a radically anthropocentric modern Western culture. We are concerned about the nonhuman creation because we find ourselves in danger along with it; we cannot get to heaven if we cannot survive to the "age of accountability" and accept Christ! But what evangelicals really need at this point is at least to consider the application of a radically different hermeneutic to Scripture that would decenter humanity in a manner analogous to James Gustafson's project of "*theo*centric ethics."[67]

65. Barth, *Church Dogmatics* III, 1, 205. The title of the section from which this quote is taken is itself illuminating: "Creation as the External Basis of the Covenant" (§41.2). For according to the biblical witness to creation, "the purpose and therefore the meaning of creation is to make possible the history of God's covenant with man which has its beginning, its centre and its culmination in Jesus Christ" (p. 42).

66. Wesley Granberg-Michaelson, "Covenant and Creation," in *Liberating Life,* ed. Birch et al., 29.

67. James M. Gustafson, *Ethics from a Theocentric Perspective,* 2 vols. (Chicago: University of Chicago Press, 1981-84).

From God's more inclusive point of view one might claim that:

> Though the Genesis creation accounts are constructed from the point of view of the humans who experience earth as their created home, God testifies to the goodness of the entire creation, prior to and independently of the creation of humanity (Genesis 1:4, 10, 12, 18, 21, 25, 31); God's covenant after the universal deluge is with "every living creature" (Genesis 9:8-17); the Sabbatical Year and the Year of Jubilee are for the livestock, the wild animal, and the land itself as well as for the humans in the land (Leviticus 25); humanity and nature alike ("heavens" and "Torah") testify to the greatness and providential care of God (Psalms 8, 19, 24, 104, 148, 150); God delights in the denizens of nature, and testifies to their value quite apart from their utility for human beings – indeed, in some cases, in spite of the danger they pose for humans (Job 38–41); Jesus takes delight in nature and teaches key lessons of faith based on God's care for it (Matthew 6:25-34; 10:28-31 and parallels); God's promises of redemption are cosmic in scope (Isaiah 11:1-9; Romans 8:18-25; Ephesians 1:8-11; Colossians 1:15-20; Revelation 22:1-5); there is continuity as well as discontinuity between this age and the age to come (1 Corinthians 3:10-15).[68]

Precisely at this point I would again invoke insights from process-relational cosmology as an ideologically neutral worldview in confirmation for the exegetical insights to which I have alluded above. In process thought, every occasion of experience receives an ideal aim from God (speaking "evangelically," God has a purpose for it), is the subject of its experience, and a collaborator with God, as it constructs itself in response to God's purpose for it and the exigencies of the world in which it finds itself, and is preserved everlastingly as a source of value to the God who, again, exercises "a tender care that nothing be

68. See, for comparison, the ecologically-revisionist readings of Scripture by the Anglican John Baker, "Biblical Views," 9-26; and the Orthodox Paulos Mar Gregorios, "New Testament Foundations for Understanding the Creation," in *Liberating Life,* ed. Birch et al., 37-45. See also the hermeneutical essays by Theodore Hiebert, Gene McAfee, Diane Jacobson, and Eilon Schwarz in part 1, "Biblical Roots and Modern Interpretation," in *Theology for Earth Community: A Field Guide,* ed. Dieter T. Hessel (Maryknoll, N.Y.: Orbis, 1996).

lost" (*PR* 346). This "pan-psychism" or "panexperientialism" of process thought meets intuitive resistance from we humans whose experiences and worldviews are both myopic and self-centered. But if we make the mental and emotional effort that the paradigm shift to this worldview takes, we will find it both compelling as a philosophical construct and marvelously illuminating of Scripture.

> The salmon fights through obstacles in response to the ancient imperative of the spawning; the human gazes in wonder on the night sky or the beloved's face: each is utilizing the measure of subjectivity that is its own.

> The heavens declare the glory of God . . . (Psalm 19:1); the conies are a feeble folk, yet they make their homes in the rocks; the locusts have no king, yet all of them march in rank . . . (Proverbs 30:26-27); whoever becomes humble like this child is the greatest in the kingdom of heaven (Matthew 18:4).

John Cobb and David Griffin, in their classic "Introductory Exposition" to process theology, evoke a vision of the theological-ethical outcome of this paradigm shift: "The belief that all levels of actuality can enjoy some degree of experience provides the basis for a feeling of responsibility directly to them. . . . Since God's purpose is the evocation of enjoyment, and since all levels of enjoyment are seen as valued by God, reverence for the neighbor becomes reverence for all creatures."[69]

Theologies of liberation in our generation, coming from the margins of dominant culture, have rediscovered the ancient biblical and catholic theme of the presence of Christ in the poor and in the suffering. This is a direct implication of the theology of the incarnation. Who is suffering more today than the nonhuman denizens of the earth? "We know that the whole creation has been groaning in labor pains until now" (Romans 8:22). We also know that the least powerful in the human family are most directly bound to the creation in its groaning. Finally, we know – when we decline to oversentimentalize and become self-indulgent in our guilt – that nature itself is riven with suffering

69. John B. Cobb Jr. and David Ray Griffin, *Process Theology: An Introductory Exposition* (Philadelphia: Westminster, 1976), 77.

quite apart from destructive human intervention. Thus we are confronted with Jay McDaniel's unforgettable image of the "backup" pelican chick, which enters this world carrying a 90 percent probability of an early and gruesome mortality, simply to insure the species a healthy margin of survival.[70] Joining this sort of unblinking knowledge to an expanded confession of the presence of God, a reformed incarnational theology if you will, must we follow McDaniel to his conclusion?: "This means that as we humans watch a starving pelican chick, we are watching God."[71] What would this new sensitivity to the presence and passion of God do for an evangelical theology that has, to be sure, been strong on zeal and passion, but has directed much of it in selfish and self-serving ways while God's creation groans? What must the words of Christ mean in these days of ecologically opened eyes: "Truly I tell you, just as you did not do it to one of the least of these, you did not do it to me" (Matthew 25:45, NRSV)?

Eschatology

Vivid eschatological thinking has been a key feature of evangelical thought in the United States, particularly in its dramatic premillennial form, correlated text by key text with predictive readings of current events.[72] The positive side of evangelical renderings of biblical eschatology lies in their championing of a robust faith in a just, merciful, and sovereign God who moves human and cosmic affairs to an appropriate outcome. This faith can create hope in the midst of trials and suffering ("We shall overcome!"), principled resistance to evil against all odds, and courageous perseverance in the life of discipleship. "If you conquer, I will make you a pillar in the temple of my God; you will never go out

70. Jay B. McDaniel, *Of God and Pelicans: A Theology of Reverence for Life* (Louisville: Westminster/John Knox, 1989), 19-21.

71. Ibid., 29-30.

72. This interest has generated myriad writings from the most popular and imaginative (cf. Hal Lindsey, *The Late Great Planet Earth* [Grand Rapids: Zondervan, 1970] to the most painstakingly erudite (cf. J. Dwight Pentecost, *Things to Come* [Grand Rapids: Zondervan, 1964]), but characteristically sharing a literalistic hermeneutic that reads discrete biblical texts, from both testaments, and various literary forms, as interchangeable pieces of chronological mosaic.

of it" (Revelation 3:12, NRSV). The negative side has consisted in the promulgation of a rigidly deterministic view of history – nothing we do hastens, delays, or alters the playing out of a detailed, divinely ordained end-time script – and the alternately passive or self-serving behavior that goes along with waiting for the end-time Godot. (Think of James Watt, the Reagan-era secretary of the interior who advocated unrestrained exploitation of natural resources, since God was soon to destroy this earth and everything in it by fire anyway.)

Here, perhaps more than at any point in this essay, process theism might seem an unlikely source for constructive theological insights for evangelicals. Traditional eschatology speaks of "God's final acts toward his creation."[73] Conversely, process thought, says John Cobb, manifests "an inability to participate in this confident expectation of a consummation of the historical process. Indeed, history is really open."[74] Carl Henry concurs archly: "Process theology can offer no final guarantee of victory; the ultimate outcome remains in doubt."[75] Yet the vexing temptation toward an eschatological determinism must be engaged from some quarter. The evangelical mantra is always "Address the text," meaning Scripture; the often suppressed subtext, as I claimed above in my autobiographical musings, is "Consult experience." Both of these strategies have been followed in the last century with notable power and originality by biblically oriented thinkers outside the camp of both process thought and American evangelicalism, namely the German exegetes of the concept of hope, Ernst Bloch and Jürgen Moltmann. Bloch criticizes traditional eschatological and futurist schemes, both religious and secular. "Because in the whole of Judeo-Christian philosophy, from Philo and Augustine to Hegel, the Ultimum relates exclusively to a Primum and not to a Novum; consequently the Last Thing appears simply as the attained return of an already completed First Thing which has been lost or relinquished."[76]

73. Val J. Sauer, *The Eschatology Handbook: The Bible Speaks to Us Today About Endtimes* (Atlanta: John Knox, 1981), 3.

74. John B. Cobb Jr., *Process Theology as Political Theology* (Philadelphia: Westminster, 1982), 77.

75. Carl F. H. Henry, "The Stunted God of Process Theology," in *Process Theology,* ed. Nash, 374.

76. Ernst Bloch, *The Principle of Hope,* trans. Neville Plaice et al., 3 vols. (Cambridge: MIT Press, 1986), 1:203.

The preaching, teaching, and speculation I heard about the future – God's future – in my youth and young adult years was certainly dominated by thoughts of return – return to Eden, to the sinless perfection of our first parents, to the original relationship of intimacy and integrity that the original pair enjoyed with their Creator. My original teachers did not contrast what Tillich characterizes as the mythical "dreaming innocence" of primordial humanity[77] with the possibility of a new humanity drawn ever forward by the not yet – a life combining the intimacy and integrity of our Lord and elder brother Christ's relationship with Abba, the hard-won lessons of the "journey into the far country" (Luke 15:13-16), and the festive life in community prefigured by the infant Christian community in the wake of Pentecost. In the words of Moltmann, "The feast of eternal joy [Matthew 25:21] is prepared by the fulness of God and the rejoicing of all created being."[78] This vision is quite literally a never-realized ideal, presented to human hope, so Christian faith might claim, by Christ and his Spirit working through his body the church, as a "lure for feeling" in precisely the Whiteheadian sense. Bloch's exploration of the role that the "not-yet-conscious" plays in the drama of human actualization,[79] and Moltmann's readings of Scripture in which God is the "power of the future,"[80] mount a dramatic challenge to habitual evangelical eschatology.

> I am about to do a new thing [God says through the prophet Isaiah]. (Isaiah 43:19, NRSV)
>
> So if anyone is in Christ, there is a new creation. (2 Corinthians 5:17, NRSV)
>
> Beloved, we are God's children now: what we will be has not yet been revealed. (1 John 3:2, NRSV)

77. See Paul Tillich, *Systematic Theology,* 3 vols. (Chicago: University of Chicago Press, 1951-63), 2:33-36.

78. Jürgen Moltmann, *The Coming of God: Christian Eschatology,* trans. Margaret Kohl (Minneapolis: Fortress, 1996), 338.

79. Bloch, 1:114-78.

80. See "Introduction: Meditation on Hope," in Jürgen Moltmann, *Theology of Hope: On the Ground and the Implications of a Christian Eschatology,* trans. James W. Leitch (New York: Harper & Row, 1967), 15-36.

On this reading of Scripture, God is drawing the creation toward a genuine *novum,* and Christ and Christ-community are the prototype. "Christian eschatology does not speak of the future as such. It sets out from a definite reality in history and announces the future of that reality, its future possibilities and its power over the future. Christian eschatology speaks of Jesus Christ and *his* future."[81] For Moltmann, it is evident from Scripture that this world is not a matter of indifference to God, an *addendum ad extra* to God's eternal, self-generated, and self-sustained beatitude. On the contrary, in direct consequence of the communion and mutuality of God's trinitarian life, God creates, sustains, and draws toward optimal actualization human and all created being. In his high priestly prayer in John's Gospel, Jesus says to his heavenly Abba, "I glorified you on earth by finishing the work that you gave me to do. So now, Father, glorify me in your own presence" (John 17:4-5, NRSV). Moltmann comments: "The fellowship between Christ and God in the process of mutual glorification is so wide open that the community of Christ's people can find a place in it."[82] From this understanding of the triune (e.g., fundamentally social) God's eschatological motivations and goals, Moltmann develops a case for privileging biblical images of the eschatological future as a transformation of the present and future created order rather than an annihilation and replacement of it as per some texts (and a great deal of evangelical tradition).[83]

This fundamental exegetical choice has tremendous ramifications for our theological and ethical stance toward our embodied existence in this present life, the value and ethical standing of the earth and its abundance of living beings other than humans, and the relationship of this earthly life to the life to come. On an exegetical basis Moltmann has persuasively made the case for an eschatology that is: (a) oriented toward the future as a genuine *novum;* (b) fundamentally social and pancosmic rather than exclusively concerned with aggregates of human individuals; (c) transformative rather than annihilating; (d) a process or project in which we are invited to participate rather than passively await. Philosophically such an eschatology finds strong confirmation

81. Ibid., 17.
82. Moltmann, *Coming of God,* 334-35.
83. Ibid., 267-80.

in process-relational thought, whereas its opposite is radically at odds with this cosmology.

For Whitehead, the actual occasion is not only "subject," creating its own moment of experience out of the data of the past actual world, but it is also "superject," aiming toward an intended future. That future already exerts a power on the occasion's self-constitution, beginning with the optimal "initial aim" presented to each occasion by God: "the future has *objective* reality in the present, but no *formal* actuality. For it is inherent in the constitution of the immediate, present actuality that a future will supercede it" (*PR* 215). This future is a genuine *novum,* which God and the world build collaboratively. It is never a private dream or project, for the actual occasion "arises from the publicity which it finds and it adds itself to the publicity which it transmits" (*PR* 289). Indeed, it would seem that God's own "kingdom of heaven" vision is a work in progress, as God's ideal aims "resident in" the primordial nature are adjusted to the world's ongoing realization of them in the enigmatic "fourth phase" of the universe's accomplishment of its actuality, "in which the perfected [in God, to this point] actuality passes back into the world and qualifies this world" (*PR* 351).

We are not talking abstract metaphysics here; in the field of eschatology evangelical theology and process theism are charged to ponder and to act with respect to humanity's most cherished aspirations and their ultimate outcome. Evangelical theology's vivid expectation of a God-ordered end – in the sense of both *finis* and *telos* – to the human and cosmic adventure, with specific expectations concerning the justification of God's righteousness (Isaiah 11:1-5), the renovation of all creation (Isaiah 11:6-9), and the overcoming of suffering and death (Revelation 21:1-4), should challenge evangelicals and process thinkers alike to move beyond analysis to specific hopes and commitments and specific commitments to communities of hope and justice making. At the same time, process thought's insistence on the radical openness of the God-world interaction can challenge traditional Christianity's inherent tendency toward determinism and its implicates, quietism and acquiescence to injustice. To imagine, as traditional Christians do, the eschaton "as a radical change of state of the cosmos might imply *finis* to this 'cosmic epoch,' . . . but not necessarily imply any sort of ultimate *finis.* Rather, it could simply represent cosmic/human openness to some now unimaginable newness on 'the other side.'"[84]

Conclusion

Evangelical Christianity and process-relational thought, for all their differences, share manifold common themes and a common rootedness in the vision of a purposive Intelligence both present to and in the world of our common experience and transcendent of it. This vision is rooted in the vivid experiences of ancient Hebrews and – in its christianized form – has been spread around the globe by adherents of myriad times and cultures indwelt, as they believe, by the presence of this One, as that presence has been mediated by the crucified and risen Christ.

Evangelical Christianity is flourishing in these United States, and in various forms both indigenous and inherited from North American forms, is multiplying explosively in Southern Hemisphere cultures around the globe. This latest wave of global Christian expansion is characterized by a vivid awareness of the presence and power of God, typically symbolized by Holy Spirit imagery often neglected in North American evangelical piety, NAE 2, 4, 5, and 7 notwithstanding. Such power for good must not be enfeebled now or in times to come by its ignoring or misreading of worldview questions. By the same token, a comprehensive and persuasive cosmology, already steeped in biblical themes, at home with evolutionary theory and the quantum, and powerfully illuminating of vexing perennial issues for both philosophy and theology, such as the mind/body problem and the freedom/causal determinism problem, must not be left only to the professional scribes and scholars. Rather, let it break out into lay communities of faith, both to enrich and to be enriched.

I began this essay with autobiographical reflections. These reflections were offered precisely as a hopeful example of how these two contrasting traditions, if they are experienced with open mind and heart and thoroughly absorbed, can be mutually informing and empowering

84. David L. Wheeler, "Toward a Process-Relational Christian Eschatology," *Process Studies* 22/4 (1993): 236. See my further development of the topic in the cited article.

in the very way I have anticipated in the previous section of this essay. I absorbed evangelical piety and tried and proved evangelical values from my youth, and the beauty and power of that experience has been for me, at least, not easily vulnerable to skeptical debunking. The narrative and evaluative explanations in my faith tradition of humanity's and the world's ultimate origin and destiny, and the accompanying call to a life of loving identification with my neighbors on the way, shine with manifest truth. At the same time, the scientific explanations of the world's temporal origin, continuing connections and processes, and anticipated temporal destiny bear their own manifest truth, for they illuminate and explain the natural world whose beauty and complexity I also absorbed and relished from my youth. Process thought came later, but it came naturally and powerfully as the best and most comprehensive explanation I had encountered of the truth and beauty I had experienced in nature. And it came laden with God. When systems of symbolic representation are in important ways true to our experience, and that experience is constitutive of our selves, it is the most natural and useful thing imaginable to seek to think and live those representational systems together. I offer up my own experience as testimony it can be done. Let the dialogue continue.

In Response to David L. Wheeler

NANCY R. HOWELL

David Wheeler's "Confessional Communities and Public Worldviews: A Case Study" is an ambitious essay. After setting the autobiographical context of his theology, Wheeler defines both evangelical Christianity and process relational theism, posits three theses to guide dialogue, enters dialogue between process theology and the National Association of Evangelicals' statement of faith, and sets the agenda for mutual transformation of evangelical and process thinkers in terms of five doctrinal projects. Because of the scope of Wheeler's paper and because of the compatibility between our views, my response is necessarily selective. In particular, I organize my response in relation to a key statement in Wheeler's paper: "Cosmological schemes, no matter how compelling in terms of scope, coherence, and illuminating power, have only a limited ability to form character and guide behavior."

Wheeler's statement that philosophy has limited power to evoke character and behavior is set in his discussion of three guiding theses for dialogue. Wheeler's first thesis is that faith is experienced in the *communitas* of living faith traditions. Religious experience is socially constructed in the rituals, relationships, worship, and actions of the community. The second thesis is that particular faith communities are limited in the extent of their encounters with the Real, with the divine, and do not exclude the possibilities of encounter with the Real in other faith communities or traditions. Faith communities are contextual and their encounters with the Real are shaped in concrete circumstances.

Wheeler's third thesis is that "faith communities and philosophical worldviews need each other." There are two corollaries of this thesis. The first is that "individual religious believers and the communities they constitute are at great risk unless their faith convictions are accompanied by a consistent and coherent worldview." Wheeler asserts that all persons and communities have worldviews, which are more or less acknowledged and which are more or less adequate. Agreeing with Stephen Franklin, Wheeler believes that faith convictions and values should relate to reality and express the way things are. The second corollary is the key statement informing this response. This corollary asserts that cosmologies on their own are insufficient to form character and guide behavior. Character and behavior are shaped in community, which teaches formative discourse, actions, and rituals. Thus it is just as true to say that cosmologies need faith communities as it is to say that faith communities need worldviews.

My interpretation of these three theses is that they set the tone and the method for the remainder of Wheeler's paper in two ways. The first two theses establish the perspectival limits of faith claims and communities. Without diminishing the importance and truth of faith claims, Wheeler implicitly makes a case for humility in faith communities. The third thesis sets the method for the dialogue that Wheeler engages. The main points of the essay triangulate among evangelical theology, process theology, and process cosmology. My judgment is that process cosmology and theology are treated very generously in this dialogue. While Wheeler mentions some points where process theology could learn from evangelical theology, more often Wheeler addresses challenges to evangelical theology from the worldview of process theology and philosophy.

My stake in the discussion has to do with the third thesis that worldviews and faith communities reciprocally enhance each other. As Wheeler's discussion stands, I have no quarrel with the points that he wishes to make. I, too, have found Whitehead's cosmology to be extraordinarily helpful in giving coherence and meaning to the multiplicity of the world from faith to science, joy to suffering, individuality to community, and God to the world. Like other feminist relational theologians, I consult with process philosophy because it rings true to my experience of the world and satisfies my desire to express the coherence of the world. Further, I agree with Wheeler that values and character entail more than intellectual satisfaction. Communities, which may be nations, churches, schools, neighborhoods, or families, create in us the integrity and behaviors that fit their moral constructs. Often without saying a word or formulating an argument, communities by means of raised eyebrows, cold shoulders, warm embraces, and gold stars employ rituals and models that form us into solid citizens or force us into social ostracism.

The dialogue between the open view and process theism so far concerns the consonance between the two views and the challenges that each presents to the other. Some larger issues are not addressed, however, if consonance and challenges exhaust the dialogue. Wheeler's essay suggests to me that some common thought experiments could expand the horizons of evangelical theology and of process theology and cosmology. One common thought experiment might lead evangelical theology and process theology and cosmology to depart from their diverse abstractions to focus on experience in broader terms.

Both evangelical theology and process thought could do more, for example, to incorporate the experience of the Other into their worldviews. Wheeler raises this issue for me when he writes, "Emerging postmodern thought challenges Christian apologists at the point of their implicit assumption of generic, universal human experience. On the contrary, 'experience' is that of specific, concrete persons, of different genders, community statuses, and faith postures." Wheeler raises this point in discussing the National Association of Evangelicals' statement of faith and its first article about the status of scriptural authority and biblical interpretation. In spite of its appeal to relationality and experience, however, process thought falls victim to abstractions about experience. As Richard Rice charges, process thought speaks very well of generic and universal experience, but it does not consistently succeed in addressing concrete, historical experience. Like evangelical theology, philosophy, including Whiteheadian and Hartshornean philosophy and derivative contemporary philosophies, turns to categories and schema to describe experience and rarely engages the messy complexities of the lived experience of others. Process philosophy may be postmodern, but postmodernism as it raises the question of "the Other" often manages to support the status quo, to draw a faceless and voiceless other, and to isolate self and other by erecting boundaries that create a neo-individualism, not too different from post-Enlightenment autonomy. This postmodernism differs from the social postmodernism of womanist or Latin American theology, which engages particular struggles and historical contexts and rages at unjust relationships.

In some regard, the interdependence between faith communities and worldviews, to which Wheeler calls our attention and with which I agree, is also a danger. As Wheeler notes, worldviews can connect faith claims with reality as it can be known publicly, and faith communities can advance character and behavior. But faith communities and worldviews can collude to support injustices, such as sexism, which has been sustained by theology that once denied souls to women and by science that attempted to prove women less evolved and less rational than European men. Nancy Tuana traces the history of philosophy and religion in establishing that woman was neither possessed of a soul nor endowed with rationality like that of her male counterpart. From Plato and Aristotle to Augustine to Descartes, the inferiority of woman's rationality, often ideologically connected with reproduction, was asserted to support claims that woman was soulless and immoral, and thus not fully made in the image of God.[1] Science likewise supported the inferiority of women's rationality. For example, Darwin argued from natural selection that women's intellect was and would remain inferior to men's intellect on the grounds that protecting the family requires greater intellect than bearing and caring for children.[2] Similarly, craniologists in the nineteenth century sought to document size and structure differences in the brain, but they often compromised measurements and altered data rather than give up the thesis that the size of women's and non-European men's brains or skulls demonstrated intellectual inferiority.[3] Sometimes, the collaboration of faith communities and worldviews puts two foxes in the henhouse. The danger in interdependence of worldviews and faith communities is that the common culture inhabited and shaped by both can carry grave injustices. Faith communities and philosophical worldviews can mask and support injustices in dogmas and abstractions that claim absolute status.

With high regard for the few theologians and philosophers in

1. Nancy Tuana, *The Less Noble Sex: Scientific, Religious, and Philosophical Conceptions of Woman's Nature* (Bloomington: Indiana University Press, 1993), 53-64.

2. Ibid., 66.

3. Ibid., 69-74.

both evangelical and process thought who do engage human particularity, I join David Wheeler in calling for transformation. But the mutual transformation of evangelical and process perspectives, however relational they may be, is not likely to address particularities as long as the two views conduct a dialogue. For us to engage historical and living realities, such as violence toward women and children, economic exploitation of the Southern Hemisphere, evolving forms of racism, war against ethnic or religious communities, or destruction of ecological relationships, the dialogue must move from speech to listening.

The life and death of Jesus Christ model this kind of transformation. The incarnation of God in Christ tells us that our relational God was transformed in the person of Jesus, taking on human joy and suffering as God's own. God's desire for relationship entailed willingness to become human and to undertake a life and ministry with particular folks. Incarnation is the first sign of God's openness to the world, because God received the human condition as God's being. The cross is the second profound act of God's willingness to receive humanity in Godself. At the cross, God invited an unrestricted experience of all human suffering and sin into the divine being. What I am describing is very much like Gustavo Gutiérrez's concept of "conversion to the neighbor."[4] Gutiérrez advocates a preferential option for the poor that transforms theology by a conscious decision to let go the hegemony supported by theological abstractions. The relational views of God require attention to human relations that mirrors God's openness to humanity and meets Christ through the neighbor.

How might God's model of openness invite us to transformation or to conversion to the neighbor? Wheeler hints directly at ways that the dialogue must become a conversation with colleagues who have more theological success in responding to historical contexts. First, he calls us to consider the perspectival nature of knowledge and specifically of hermeneutics, which is demonstrated by feminist and liberation theologies. Second, he calls us to reflect inclusively on the body of Christ, with openness to the cosmos as part of the body of God, as we consider the social nature of redemption affirmed by the evangelical church. This reflection brings us to dialogue with the theologies of Sal-

4. Gustavo Gutiérrez, *A Theology of Liberation: History, Politics, and Salvation,* trans. Sister Caridad Inda and John Eagleson (Maryknoll, N.Y.: Orbis, 1973), 173.

lie McFague and others whom Wheeler consults. Third, Wheeler encourages us to undertake dialogue concerning reverence for all creatures in such a way that we see that suffering in nature is akin to the preferential option for the poor of liberation theology and the biblical theme of the presence of Christ in the poor and suffering. Wheeler opens the way for dialogue with liberation theologians such as Leonardo Boff, who calls us to widen the option for the poor to include an option for other threatened beings and species and to see that poor humans and threatened species are not-so-distant relatives.[5] Fourth, Wheeler's dialogue with Moltmann emphasizes the transformation of the present and future toward the reign of God and the importance of an eschatological future built collaboratively between God and the world. Gutiérrez's theology, which calls for Christians to work for political liberation even as we depend on God for the ultimate liberation in the kingdom of God, likewise might enter the conversation to call us to participate in the divine work of salvation.

My point underscores a subtlety in Wheeler's essay. Wheeler states that cosmological schemes have limited ability to form character and guide behavior. I agree and add that the truth of the statement applies to philosophical, religious, and cultural cosmological schemes. The communities within which we are shaped profoundly form us in character and behavior. What Wheeler quietly advocates is that those in the dialogue between process theology and open view evangelical theology follow their relational perspectives to a logical conclusion, opening the dialogue into a conversation with the global Christian community and its neighbors.

5. Leonardo Boff, *Ecology and Liberation: A New Paradigm,* trans. John Cumming (Maryknoll, N.Y.: Orbis, 1995), 89.

In Response to David L. Wheeler

RICHARD RICE

> *"When systems of symbolic representation are in important ways true to our experience, and that experience is constitutive of our selves, it is the most natural and useful thing imaginable to seek to think and live those representational systems together."*

It is a pleasure to read a theological proposal that reflects so clearly a deep personal concern. From beginning to end, David Wheeler's essay shows that he has a significant stake in the effort to bring evangelical Protestantism and process thought together. He not only wants the marriage to succeed, he strongly believes it can, because it has worked so well for him. A childhood filled with religious fervor and intellectual curiosity led to an apparently seamless union of personal commitment to Christ and a process perspective on reality. His early religious convictions have remained with him ever since.

Although he does not tell us just how he happened onto Whitehead's writings, they quickly persuaded him that process philosophy provides a coherent, integrated account of our complex world. The blending of the intellectual and the spiritual in his own life convinced him that all truth is one, whether religious or scientific in nature. Thus he hopes that his comments here will promote a dialogue between "two important contemporary intellectual and cultural movements." Evangelical Christianity and process thought form a balance in his life, he asserts, each protecting him from "the potential excesses of the other." Beyond that he believes that the two have the capacity to transform each other in mutually beneficial ways.

One of the reasons I appreciated Wheeler's essay is that my experience parallels his in several ways. I too was raised in a devout Christian home, entered fully into the life of a conservative Protestant denomination (like Wheeler, from "cradle roll" on up), and carry with me to this day the deepest religious convictions of my early years. Moreover, as soon as I became acquainted with process thought, though this did not occur until I was in graduate school, I saw its potential contribution to Christian theology. And I have worked over the years, though less extensively than Wheeler has, to bring the perspectives of evangelical theology and process thought together.

It is not easy to criticize a piece like Wheeler's, given its narrative nature. Indeed, it almost seems inappropriate. After all, one does not reply to a story by offering a critique; one tells another story. Nevertheless, Wheeler's essay makes a number of important claims, and several of them call for particular scrutiny.

Does theology need philosophy? Wheeler's answer is clearly yes, and by training and inclination, so is mine. But in recent years the theological climate has changed in ways that require us to explain this relation with considerable care. I emerged from graduate school twenty-five years ago with a clear conception of the theological task. It consisted of showing that the essential claims of the gospel are intelligible to the modern mind, that they satisfy contemporary criteria of meaning and truth. As Schubert M. Ogden expressed it in a 1972 essay, theological understanding is correlative in structure, bringing together witness and existence. Accordingly, theology "is subject to assessment by dual criteria of adequacy," namely, "appropriateness and credibility." A theological statement is "appropriate" when it reflects the same understanding of faith found in the normative Christian witness to faith, the New Testament. It is "credible" when it "meets the relevant conditions of truth universally established with human existence."[1] As thus conceived, the task of theology is to mediate between the Christian message and the modern

1. Schubert M. Ogden, "What Is Theology?" repr. in *On Theology* (San Francisco: Harper & Row, 1986), 4-5.

world. Thus we have the contents of Christian faith on the one hand, the modern world on the other, and the rational mind that brings them together.

Such a conception of theology gives philosophy an important role to play. Philosophy helps to determine the meaning and establish the truth of Christian claims. It shows that Christian beliefs apply to all experience and help to illuminate all of reality. In this vein, Wheeler insists that "religious believers and communities need a plausible worldview to ground their core convictions." Without it, he asserts, they may find "that their convictions lack roots in the soil of their own larger lives, and lack credibility and persuasive power outside the core community." Conversely, key elements in the biblical perspective on reality "would be greatly amplified by their association with compatible independent perspectives on our common world." Process thought, of course, provides just such a perspective.

Although I am drawn to such a view of philosophy's theological role, my confidence has been tempered by two factors. One is the changing intellectual climate in recent decades. For the most part, the subtleties of postmodern and postliberal thinkers elude me, but the general impact of their work on the task just outlined is clear. It calls into question each element in this conception of theology.

First, as many people now see it, the notion of the Christian faith, or the essential claims of the gospel, is an abstraction from the rich blend of ambiguous and provocative narratives, metaphors, and symbols that constitute the Bible. We cannot fold the gospel, the Christian message, into a package of propositions to be intellectually assessed. Second, the modern world, a vision of reality produced by unqualified confidence in scientific inquiry and unqualified optimism for the fruits of technology, is also an abstraction. We can embrace it only by ignoring the vast sweep of human experience past and present, which has always been open to ranges of meaning inaccessible to mere rational inquiry, and by overlooking the effects of our ceaseless manipulation of the environment.

Finally, the rational mind is an abstraction. There is no one way of looking at reality, no integrated program of intellectual operations, no "value-neutral or publicly accessible objective truth," no "universally accessible foundation for public discourse."[2] We privilege one perspec-

2. Timothy R. Phillips and Dennis L. Okholm, "The Nature of Confession: Evangelicals and Postliberals," in *The Nature of Confession: Evangelicals and Postliberals in Conver-*

tive, the critique goes, only by ignoring others, specifically those outside the stream of thinkers who are Western, white, male, and straight. The very idea of the rational mind, critics charge, seems to ignore that there are various ways of thinking.

This widespread disaffection with Enlightenment rationality opens the door to other approaches to theology. For postliberals, it means that contemporary culture is no longer the norm for Christian thought. Accordingly, the primary concern of Christian theology is not to find other language with which to express the Christian message, but to employ the narrative form of Scripture. In doing so, it reverses the tendency of modern theology to accommodate itself to culture. Instead of letting the world absorb the gospel, its goal is for the gospel to absorb the world. "Rather than translating Scripture into an external and alien frame of reference, which devalues and undermines its normative position and eventually produces an accommodation to culture, the postliberals call for an intratextual theology that finds the meaning of the Christian language within the text."[3]

Evangelical theologians who share the conviction that theology's primary concern lies within the text will have reservations about Wheeler's call to employ process philosophy in hopes of getting a larger hearing. In particular, they will question the very idea of an independent perspective that corroborates the biblical perspective. As they see it, our most important concern should not be to find conceptual, philosophical ways of expressing the Christian message, but to let the primary symbols and narratives of Christian faith speak with their own power. To make the case he wants to for process thought, Wheeler needs to take into account the shifting theological scene.

In addition to recent changes on the theological horizon, Wheeler should note the complexities of the philosophical landscape. Process thought is an impressive philosophical system, but it is not the only system around, and theologians have made extensive use of others. To make the case for an evangelical process theology, therefore, one would need to take into account philosophical as well as theological alternatives to his position. In the past twenty years or so, there has been a re-

---

sation, ed. Timothy R. Phillips and Dennis L. Okholm (Downers Grove, Ill.: InterVarsity Press, 1996), 18.

3. Ibid., 13.

markable resurgence of interest in the perennial questions that have occupied philosophers of religion – ancient, medieval, and modern. "Christian philosophy," as its participants call it, is alive and well, and many believe that it offers a significant resource for dealing with contemporary theological issues.[4] In addition, Christian theologians in recent decades have variously employed the insights of analytic philosophy, phenomenology, and existentialism, to mention a few. What does process thought provide that cannot be found elsewhere? To flesh out the case for the theological value of process thought, we need to compare it to some of the alternatives.

Besides taking into account some recent theological and philosophical developments, Wheeler could also clarify his position by identifying the participants in the dialogue he wants to promote. He speaks of "two important contemporary intellectual and cultural movements," but who belongs to these movements? Do the evangelicals he has in mind include those who subscribe to the 1942 NAE statement? I wonder, since he makes some pertinent criticisms of the statement. Does it include Calvinists as well as Arminians? If so, some issues will need to be sorted out along with the topics he touches on in the paper. Who represents the process tradition Wheeler wishes to engage? Process theologians are already deeply involved in the attempt to integrate process insights within Christian faith, and process philosophers are not likely to view Wheeler's call as relevant to their work. Furthermore, I am not sure that process thought and Christian theology can engage each other in quite the way Wheeler has in mind. Process philosophy is a metaphysical theory, Christianity is a concrete religion. They operate on logically different levels. Their interests coincide on certain issues, surely, notably on the topic of God, but I do not think the intersection between them is as broad as Wheeler thinks it is.

Something else that gives me pause when it comes to a dialogue between evangelical theology and process thought is the tendency for philosophy to take over the theological landscape. This is a tricky issue, because Wheeler wants to show how helpful process thought can be to

4. For numerous examples, see the articles in *Faith and Philosophy: Journal of the Society of Christian Philosophers.* Philosophers of religion like Alvin Plantinga and Richard Swinburne draw on resources other than process thought to articulate versions of Christianity to which many evangelical theologians are sympathetic.

us in understanding Christian faith, and this naturally leads him to apply it to a broad range of theological issues. But some process theologians seem to shape the language of the gospel to the language of the system, and let process terms and categories take over the discussion. They invoke the special vocabulary of process thought to explain various elements of Christian faith – words like "concrescence," "ideal aims," and "the primordial and consequent natures of God."

Looking at the final, most important section of his essay, we see that Wheeler generally avoids this tendency. He works hard to show that process thought and evangelical theology can be "mutually informative and corrective." He finds a number of ways in which process thought can contribute to Christian ideas, from church and community to eschatology. Indeed, he finds it both "compelling as a philosophical construct and marvelously illuminating of Scripture." Yet, as much as he wants to combine the insights of the two traditions, he is aware that they are distinct, and there are abiding tensions between them.

Wheeler deserves credit for extending the discussion between process thought and evangelical Christianity into new doctrinal areas. I appreciate, for example, his insights into the impact of the biblical notion of divine call on our understanding of self and identity, and the way biblical eschatological images challenge us to embrace specific hopes and commitments. These are ideas that enrich the thinking of both sides of the discussion. As an Adventist, I particularly appreciate his creative approach to eschatology, although, as he notes, the content of Christian hope is a topic on which evangelicals and process thinkers will probably never see eye to eye. Perhaps the most important contribution process thought can make to an evangelical perspective is to help it develop a vision of community that encompasses the entire cosmos within God's love and care. This provides a helpful corrective to the anthropocentrism that often afflicts our view of nature and the individualistic tendencies in our views of salvation and human destiny.

While I welcome Wheeler's proposals, I am concerned about the areas he elects to pass over in this discussion, such as the nature of God and God's action in the world, Christology, and theodicy. We could use more from him on these themes. It is true that a good deal has been written on these topics, but they involve the most fundamental differences between the perspectives he wants to bring together, and they generate the most persistent objections that process thinkers make to evangelical Christianity, as we see from David Griffin's contribution to this volume (chapter 1 above). Unless we meet them effectively, or at least respond to them carefully, our attempts to achieve a serious dialogue may be thwarted. More important, these topics constitute the epicenter of Christian faith. The christological understanding of God, more fundamentally, the christological experience of God, defines Christian faith. It is basic to all the talking points that Wheeler raises in the constructive concluding section of his essay.

I am also interested in Wheeler's thoughts on these themes because he seems to side with the open view of God on crucial issues like God's ontological priority to the world and God's capacity to act unilaterally in the world. As an evangelical, he says, he retains the distinction between God and the world as "qualitatively different kinds of being." In addition, he defends a "hybrid" view of God, which "thinks together" the "ontological ultimacy and self-originating actuality" that classical theism attributes to God and the "radical mutual immanence and interdependence of God and world" characteristic of process theism. Thus he apparently applies only to God the ontological priority that process thought attributes to God-and-world.[5]

Wheeler also notes that the Bible grants to divine causative power vis-à-vis creaturely power a "relatively stronger role" than does process thought. He comes close to affirming divine intervention, or least unilateral divine action, in a couple of places, particularly when he comments on evangelical eschatology. But just how he correlates these ideas with his commitments to naturalism elsewhere in the paper is not entirely clear.

While I believe that the differences between the two positions are just as important as their similarities, I appreciate Wheeler's quest for common ground and mutual interaction. He concludes rightly that process thought and evangelical theology, particularly as expressed in open theism, share a profound vision of God's radical immanence and pervasive activity within the world. I welcome his conviction that such a God works "indefatigably for the renewal and perfection of the cre-

5. He maintains that God "would embody" the relatedness and responsiveness of the process God, along with the self-actuality of the God-world togetherness in process thought and the process category of creativity.

ation," and I am moved by his summons to both evangelical and process theists to work with the divine for the benefit of all creation. For emphasizing that common vision and issuing that call, I applaud his contribution to this volume.

4 *Process Theism and the Open View of God: The Crucial Difference*

RICHARD RICE

What is the relation between process theism and the open view of God? Process theologians draw on the writings of Alfred North Whitehead and others like Charles Hartshorne as major philosophical resources for interpreting Christian faith. The open view of God is a perspective on God's relation to the world embraced by a growing number of evangelical theologians over the past twenty years or so. They believe that the biblical evidence indicates that God enjoys an interactive, dynamic experience of the world. The two groups have important similarities, but they are also different in significant ways, and the time has come to compare them more closely.

Anyone contributing to a symposium on topics as rich and suggestive as "process thought" and "evangelical theology" will be tempted to spend a good deal of time defining terms. After all, each expression encompasses a wide range of possible meanings. Readers deserve to know, it seems, just what stream of process thinking one espouses or rejects and just what brand of evangelicalism one subscribes to. I shall resist that temptation here. I do not wish to enter into debate with process thinkers over which figure(s) and what writings best represent their position. Nor do I want to split hairs with other conservative Christians over the precise meaning of "evangelical." These are certainly worthy issues. But my purposes here are better served, I believe, if

I simply "tell my story," as it were, and let others decide whether and in what ways the relevant expressions apply to it.

In addition, I shall not repeat here what conservative Christian theologians have done elsewhere as they consider alternatives to the general position known as "classical theism." I shall not seek to show that a dynamic (or "relational" or "interactive") view of God is more faithful to the biblical portrait than "classical theism" and preferable to it for philosophical, theological, and practical reasons, too. Other works pursue that objective.[1] There are also works that note the various differences between the doctrinal convictions of evangelical Christianity and the tenets of process philosophy.[2] These are not difficult to find, since evangelical and process theologians stand at different ends of the theological spectrum. But I do not think a catalogue of doctrinal differences would advance the discussion. Instead, my objective here is to locate the place where two visions of God – process theism and open theism – diverge. Their similarities are significant, but the differences between them are profound, and in fairness to all sides of the discussion they need to be clearly identified.

A Personal Journey

Theology is biography, we often hear today, and that is certainly true in my case. I pursued the study of theology as an extension of my own religious experience, and my attraction to and reservations about process philosophy are a part of that spiritual journey.

If Horace Bushnell is right, then my experience is close to the ideal of Christian education – "that a child is to grow up a Christian, and never know himself as being otherwise." I am a fourth- or fifth-generation Seventh-Day Adventist, and I was born into a deeply religious family. My grandparents on both sides left the United States for overseas mission work. My mother was born to missionary parents in Seoul, Korea.

1. See Clark Pinnock et al., *The Openness of God* (Downers Grove, Ill.: InterVarsity Press, 1994); Richard Rice, *God's Foreknowledge and Man's Free Will* (Minneapolis: Bethany House, 1985); John Sanders, *The God Who Risks: A Theology of Providence* (Downers Grove, Ill.: InterVarsity Press, 1998).

2. Ronald H. Nash, ed., *Process Theology* (Grand Rapids: Baker, 1987).

My religious roots grew strong during a protracted family crisis fairly early in my childhood. My parents' marriage disintegrated over a period of six years or so, and as things became more difficult at home I found personal support in the close-knit and caring community of our small church and the church school I attended. Caring teachers, church leaders, and friends were always there for me. The community they provided helped to compensate for the deteriorating situation at home.

These experiences had a lasting effect on my religious outlook. Our family's problems made me sensitive to life's larger issues at an early age. The solace my religious beliefs provided along with the reassurance I drew from my religious community confirmed the value of my convictions on a deeply personal level. At the same time, the difficulties we faced left me unconvinced by facile assurances about "God's protecting care" and "God's perfect plan." Thus I felt God's presence in my life, but the feeling did not provide easy answers to some important questions.

In many ways the rest is history. At the age of ten I requested baptism. Three years later I enjoyed the most intensely religious phase of my life. God became a vivid presence in my daily life. My later decisions to study for the ministry and to attend graduate school in theology seemed the natural outgrowth of those early experiences. When the placement officer at the University of Chicago looked over my transcripts and saw majors in systematic theology in college, seminary, and graduate school, she said, "Well, Mr. Rice, you've certainly been consistent!"

I took a leave of absence from pastoral ministry to pursue graduate work in theology at the University of Chicago Divinity School. Conservative as my background was, I was drawn to a place like Chicago because I wanted to see how people dealt with the sorts of issues that are unlikely to get much attention at a denominational seminary or church-related college. I wanted to see how first-rate thinkers respond to the most serious challenges confronting Christian faith in the modern world. Graduate school led me to look at a lot of things differently, but on the whole it turned out to be a faith-confirming experience. I discovered that the claims of Christianity – the central ones, certainly – could measure up to searching rational scrutiny.

Process thought did not occupy the position at Chicago in the

1970s that it had in the 1950s (from what I was told), but you could still get a healthy dose of it. I studied the thought of Whitehead in seminars taught by Schubert M. Ogden and Langdon Gilkey. But it was Hartshorne's philosophical theology that particularly attracted me. There were several reasons for this. On the most basic level, I was impressed that a powerful mind, determined to follow reason to the end in matters of religion, found abundant evidence for God and developed impressive arguments for God's existence. I also felt that Hartshorne's particular conception of natural theology could benefit theologians in a number of important ways.

Most important, I found what growing numbers of conservative Christian thinkers have also discovered in recent years. If we accept a version of Hartshorne's dipolar theism, we can formulate a doctrine of God that is superior by every relevant criterion to the God of classical theism. The notion that a perfect being can change is not only conceptually coherent – a point Hartshorne argues at great length – but it gives us an idea of God that is more faithful to the biblical portrait than is classical theism and more helpful to us on the level of personal religion as well. The idea that God's relation to the world is interactive, or dynamic, makes it possible for us to develop coherent concepts of divine love and creaturely freedom. In so doing it helps us to overcome some of the problems that have perplexed Christian thinkers for centuries, such as the relation of human freedom and divine foreknowledge.

While I developed a strong appreciation for Hartshorne's philosophical theism, I also realized that his view of God not only diverges sharply from classical theism but also conflicts with the biblical portrait of God in several important ways. Indeed, the differences are so fundamental that what we variously call "the open view of God," "free will theism," or "open theism" is just as distant from neoclassical theism as it is from classical theism. The burden of those supporting the open view of God has typically been to show its advantages over the traditional or classical view of God. But we also need to clarify its differences from process, or neoclassical, theism.

It is not difficult to find things that process thinkers and "open theists" disagree on. Such a list would include many of the issues that divide liberal and conservative theologians. Process thinkers embrace a view of reality that renders problematic many things that conservative

Christians believe. What we need is to find the fundamental difference in their perspective on God's relation to the world. A close look at the views of an influential process thinker will get us started.

From Metaphysics to God

In numerous articles and books – the most recent published during the tenth decade of his life – Hartshorne develops his understanding of God as part of an elaborate metaphysical vision. In contrast to Whitehead, who introduces God into *Process and Reality* as a "derivative notion," Hartshorne makes God the center of his metaphysics. In fact, he sees a reciprocal relation between metaphysics and philosophical theism. Start with metaphysics, and one comes inevitably to the question of God. Or, start with the idea of God, and one can unpack an entire metaphysical system. To appreciate Hartshorne's thought, therefore, we need to note what doctrine of God flows from his metaphysics, and what sort of metaphysics flows from his doctrine of God.

As Hartshorne describes it, the object of metaphysical reflection is sheer generality, or universality. Metaphysics concerns the necessary and permanent aspects of reality, the qualities that apply to everything that is, from quarks and electrons at one end of the scale to the universe as a whole at the other.[3]

Because of their unlimited applicability, metaphysical ideas are highly abstract, so Hartshorne describes them as "empty though important truths."[4] The ideas are empty because they convey no knowledge of anything factual. But they are important because no fact whatever can fail to exemplify or illustrate them. Thus metaphysics does not tell us what the facts are, it tells us what it means to be a fact.[5] Because metaphysics concerns the ultimate features of reality, the ultimate explanation for everything else, there is nothing beyond these principles that explains *them*. Thus the only way to verify metaphysical ideas is to

3. *Man's Vision of God and the Logic of Theism* (Chicago: Willett, Clark, 1941), 72-73.

4. *The Logic of Perfection and Other Essays in Neoclassical Metaphysics* (La Salle, Ill.: Open Court, 1962), 280.

5. Cf. ibid., 297.

show that they are conceivable and mutually consistent. Taken together, they must be self-explanatory.[6]

But where do we find such principles? The answer, in a word, is "experience," the fundamental category for all process thought, the key to understanding reality. For Hartshorne, however, experience "is not merely a bridge which we may cross to reach reality; it is a paradigm case of reality." Accordingly, experience provides our model of reality.[7] We can define metaphysics as the study of "the universal traits of experience."[8]

If experience is the paradigm of reality, human experience is the paradigm of experience. After all, human beings are part of all that is, so the principles that explain "the whole show" also apply to us, and the ultimate features of the universe lie somewhere within our own experience. The basic metaphysical task, as Hartshorne sees it, is therefore to find those aspects of human experience that we can apply without restriction to everything that exists.

Hartshorne finds four basic features in human experience that are capable of unrestricted application. One is its momentary character. Our experience is not a smooth, uninterrupted continuum, but a succession of finite experiences. It consists of discrete units of definite temporal and spatial scope.[9] The other three qualities – memory, sociality, and freedom or creativity – all refer to these momentary experiences.

As ordinarily understood, memory is the recollection of past experience. But on a more basic level, memory imports the past into the present. It makes the past a factor in present experience. Every momentary experience is connected to previous moments of experience. Each moment of experience is also social. It is inherently connected to other moments of experience, and each moment of experience is free. Although it is connected to the past and thereby to other moments of experience, it is never wholly determined by them. Its final unity is a "self-created" actuality.[10]

6. *Reality as Social Process: Studies in Metaphysics and Religion* (New York: Free Press, 1953), 29.

7. *Whitehead's Philosophy: Selected Essays, 1935-1970* (Lincoln: University of Nebraska Press, 1972), 173, 163.

8. *Reality as Social Process,* 130.

9. *Whitehead's Philosophy,* 173.

10. *Creative Synthesis and Philosophic Method* (La Salle, Ill.: Open Court, 1970), 2-3.

Since these four qualities are sufficiently flexible to apply to the entire range of reality, they lead to the conclusion that becoming, or process, is the basic form of reality.[11] In contrast to classical philosophy, process thought holds that the least units of reality are not enduring substances like the objects of ordinary experience, such as tables, trees, and human bodies. Instead, the ultimate constituents of reality are events, occasions of experience. Each event has a definite temporal and spatial scope, and each one contains a free response to preceding events and remains forever as a datum for future events to deal with.

On this view of things, to be real is in some way to experience, to be both partly free and partly determined, both internally related to the past and externally related to the future. Both society and process are ultimate. Process is ultimate in the sense that new experiences are constantly taking place. It does not mean that things pass out of existence. Thus process is sheer addition, not addition *and* subtraction.[12] Since experiences occur constantly, there can never be a timeless totality of all past and future events.[13] Thus expressions such as "the universe," "the real," or "reality-as-a-whole" refer to something different every time we use them. Like the word *now,* their precise meaning varies from moment to moment.[14]

The same principle applies to each object of ordinary experience, the "things" and "persons" we encounter in daily life. We must clearly distinguish the momentary event from the enduring object. For process thought, the locus of reality, the truly concrete, is the event here and now, not the qualities and characteristics that endure through time. An enduring object, like a desk, a car, an animal, or a human being, is a linear succession of experiences, not a single thing.

The priority of event to object reverses the conventional understanding of the things we experience, including persons. As we generally think of it, the real "you" is what stays more or less the same from day to day, like certain physical features and personality traits, while the "you" here and now, with all the particular thoughts and feelings

11. *Reality as Social Process,* 18-19.

12. "Process Philosophy as a Resource for Christian Theology," in *Philosophical Resources for Christian Theology,* ed. Perry LeFevre (Nashville: Abingdon, 1968), 47-48.

13. "The Development of Process Philosophy," introduction to *Philosophers of Process,* ed. Douglas Browning (New York: Random House, 1965), vi.

14. *Whitehead's Philosophy,* 117.

you have at this precise moment, is somewhat less real. But for Hartshorne, it is the other way around. The real you is the concrete momentary experiencing subject. The enduring qualities that give you identity over time – your "individuality" – are an abstraction from the succession of concrete experiences that make up your life. To use his words, "beings are finally in happenings, not happenings in beings."[15]

On this view, a personal self is essentially "dipolar" in nature. It represents a succession of momentary concrete experiences that include the abstract characteristics that form its "identity." Individuality and actuality are related like part and whole. The real person is the whole person, the actually experiencing human being. A person's individuality is a part of the whole, the abstract part that stays more or less the same over time.

Putting all this together we can see the essential features of Hartshorne's philosophy of creative synthesis, or social process. It is monistic: it takes creativity as the metaphysical ultimate. It is pluralistic: it conceives of a multiplicity of occasions, events, or instances of creativity. It is social, or relativistic: it holds that every unit of reality is sensitive or responsive to others. It is temporalistic: it denies that any existent is purely timeless. And it is indeterministic: it denies that an effect is wholly accounted for by its causes.[16]

Hartshorne's philosophy is also something else: it is theistic. God plays an essential role in this metaphysical scheme. A philosophy of social process, or creative synthesis, needs a supreme being for two major reasons – to account for cosmic order and to account for the permanence of the past. Since freedom is universal and creaturely choices can conflict with each other, the world society needs a dominant member to set limits on potential disorder. Since ordinary experience is partial and fragmentary, reality needs a comprehensive experience, or a succession of actual experiences, that is cosmic in scope and perfectly adequate to its objects. Accordingly, process thought attributes two principal functions to God. His initial function is to establish the laws of nature, and his ultimate function is "to enable the passing moment to have abiding significance."[17]

15. Ibid., 120.
16. *Reality as Social Process,* 134-35.
17. "Process Philosophy as a Resource," 55.

Most people wonder why there is disorder in the world, but for Hartshorne it is order that requires an explanation. It is no surprise that a universe consisting of a multiplicity of self-creative occasions of experience should exhibit disorder. But why isn't the disorder greater than it is? What keeps it from disintegrating into sheer chaos? The reality of God provides the best answer. Without a radically dominant member in the universe, setting limits to the chaotic possibilities of freedom, there is nothing to prevent things from dissolving in a chaos of unmitigated conflict. Process thought thus requires God as the ultimate ruler of the world society.[18]

Of course, this order could never be absolute. Because creativity is a universal principle, the creatures are always partly self-determined. Thus God's function is not to rule out disorder entirely, but to keep it within tolerable limits, to keep the risks and opportunities that freedom entails in some sort of rough balance. God allows freedom but prevents chaos.

The basic principles of process thought not only require a supreme ordering entity but also show what it must be and how it must work. If creative freedom is the ultimate principle of reality, then God can only be a superior form of the same sort of freedom that characterizes everything else. Thus God acts on the creatures much as they act on each other. He responds to other entities, and they in turn respond to him.

But because each instance of reality is inherently free, God cannot determine absolutely just how it will respond to his influence. Thus when he exerts an attraction on others, he "persuades" or "lures," but does not coerce them to follow his directive. They cannot ignore his influence, but just how they respond is to some degree, however small, their own decision.[19] God does not accomplish anything by sheer fiat, by unilateral action. He cannot, in principle, override creaturely freedom.

The second reason Hartshorne introduces God into his philosophical system is the need for a perfect or cosmic case of memory. Process thought needs a way to explain how events that become and instantly lose their subjective immediacy continue to exert an influence

18. *Reality as Social Process,* 38-39.

19. "Development of Process Philosophy," xvii-xviii.

on subsequent events. We know from our own experience that the past endures in memory, so there must be a complete or cosmic memory, a divine consciousness, that preserves the totality of past events.

Our intuitive sense of moral value also argues for a case of all-inclusive memory. To reject moral nihilism is to insist that something matters, to insist that our actions "make a difference" in the scheme of things. Moreover, this difference must be permanent; it must last forever. Events have permanent value because they remain forever in the mind of God. God, then, is the all-inclusive and permanent receptacle of creaturely events. The divine consciousness is completely aware of all that has occurred.[20]

The two reasons for introducing God into the process scheme show what qualities must be attributed to God. God must be the supreme, but not the sole, case of creative decision, and God's reality must be endlessly enriched by data.[21] As we see from the title of one of Hartshorne's books, *The Divine Relativity: A Social Conception of God,*[22] process thought leads to the view that God is a social and temporal individual.[23] Because creative becoming is the supreme principle in reality, the supreme form of reality must itself exemplify creative becoming. Like everything else, God freely responds to the free decisions of others. Thus his own reality requires the existence of other creative agents, which he synthesizes in his own experience. God is a socially receptive being, who takes within himself the very being of others, and thus depends on others for the content of his own reality.[24]

For traditional theology, God is distinguished from everything because nothing affects him, because he is impervious to creaturely influence. But for process thought, God is distinguished by the fact that *everything* affects him. The scope and intensity of his experience are unrivalled. God responds to all others. He comprehends each instance of creativity in all its detail, not just for the moment but forever. Thus

20. *Whitehead's Philosophy,* 135.

21. Ibid., 164.

22. *The Divine Relativity: A Social Conception of God* (New Haven: Yale University Press, 1948).

23. *Man's Vision of God,* 230.

24. *Reality as Social Process,* 144.

God is the one individual who at all times embraces the fullness of all other individuals, in complete vividness, forever.[25]

For process thought, the words *God* and *world,* or *reality* and *divine reality,* are merely different ways of talking about the same thing.[26] God is what makes the cosmos a cosmos.[27] He is the "self-identical individuality of the world."[28]

We can summarize Hartshorne's metaphysics by using three of his favorite philosophical expressions. One is *social process.* For Hartshorne, the ultimate principle in reality is "process," "becoming," or "creativity," rather than "being" or "substance." Reality is dynamic rather than static. Becoming is more basic than being. Change is fundamental to changelessness, not the other way around.

A second metaphysical principle is *event pluralism.* The ultimate constituents of reality are momentary, self-creative occasions of experience, not the enduring objects of ordinary experience. The locus of concrete reality is therefore the momentary event, not the object that endures through time. The qualities that give ordinary objects, and persons, their identity over time are really abstractions from the concrete events that embody them moment by moment as long as they last. An enduring object is therefore not a single thing but a linear society of occasions, each of which includes many of the same characteristics.

A third metaphysical principle in Hartshorne's scheme is *creative synthesis.* Each momentary occasion or event, each ultimate constituent of reality, is a response to preceding occasions of experience. It synthesizes other events that have occurred before, and it does so in a way that is to some degree self-determined, or free. There is a wide range of freedom in the way events are synthesized, according to Hartshorne. For example, the events that make up a rock have relatively little freedom. The range of options available to each mineral event is extremely limited. In contrast, the freedom available to higher animals is comparatively vast. In the case of personal beings, it is literally enormous. Human beings have great freedom to determine what role the past will play in their present experience. What is necessarily true of all events is that they take into account

25. *Whitehead's Philosophy,* 60; idem, *Reality as Social Process,* 42.

26. *Logic of Perfection,* 100.

27. *Man's Vision of God,* 51.

28. Ibid., 230.

preceding events and that they do so with some degree of freedom or self-determination. Just how much freedom varies from one level of reality to another. Thus the present is always conditioned by the past, yet the past never wholly determines the present.

As an instance of concrete reality, of course, all the metaphysical principles just mentioned apply to God. God is essentially social. He requires a world of nondivine creative events to which he responds. God is a plurality of events. Literally speaking, he is a succession of occasions of experience – a linear society of such occasions – all of which include the essential divine qualities. Finally, God creatively synthesizes other events in his own experience. God's range of freedom is conceivably larger than that enjoyed by anything else, and his experience is literally cosmic in scope. It includes the entire universe. Every creaturely event is a datum in God's experience. Indeed, for Hartshorne, an experience of cosmic scope is required to make sense of the world.

Taking human experience as the paradigm case of reality, Hartshorne thus formulates a metaphysical system in which experience, discreteness, freedom, society, and memory constitute the ultimate categories. Such a system requires supreme instances of creativity and memory, and these are embodied in a supreme individual, who is God. Thus conceived, God is the universal individual, whose reality is coextensive with all reality and therefore includes the world.

From God to Metaphysics

Hartshorne argues that we can take the same path in the opposite direction. We can start with God and come up with the same metaphysical system – the view that reality is a temporal, social process, and its supreme instance is an all-inclusive conscious experience, an integrated experience. This integrated, integrative experience gives reality its essential structure and makes sense of all the basic features of thought and experience.

Hartshorne's understanding of God emerges clearly from the ways he characterizes his position. One is *dipolar theism.*[29] This designa-

29. The clearest expression of dipolar theism is found in Hartshorne, *Divine Relativity.*

tion underscores the idea that God has both concrete and abstract dimensions, like every other instance of reality. Hartshorne employs four principles to explain divine dipolarity. One is the "law of polarity." This means that concepts of ultimate generality come in pairs. Think, for example, of cause and effect, absolute and relative, simplicity and complexity, eternity and temporality, necessity and contingency. Each term in a pair of metaphysical concepts acquires its meaning from the other. None stands alone.

Furthermore, both elements in each pair admit of supreme exemplification. Hartshorne calls this the "principle of dual transcendence." This means that there is a supreme effect as well as a supreme cause, a supreme case of relativity as well as of absoluteness, and so on. Thus God is supremely dependent as well as supremely independent, supremely complex as well as supremely simple, and supremely changing as well as supremely changeless.

According to Hartshorne, the supreme example of each element in a metaphysical pair is something positive because the categoreal contrasts are "non-invidious." In other words, they are good. Classical philosophy made the mistake of regarding one side of these pairs "good" and the other "bad" – a practice Hartshorne calls a "monopolar prejudice." But it is not better to be independent than dependent; there are positive as well as negative forms of both. Relativity is not worse than absoluteness, it is just different. The only invidious contrast we need to worry about is the contrast between good and evil.

But how can we apply stark contrasts to the same reality? Can the same thing be absolute and relative, eternal and temporal, changeless and changing? It can if we accept the principle that the concrete includes the abstract. We can apply contrasting qualities to the same object if we apply them to different aspects of that object. For example, when a car pool driver picks up another rider, the totality of people in the car changes, but the identity of the previous occupants remains the same. If something changes, its overall reality is different, but some of its parts can remain the same. Thus one element in each categorical contrast applies to God's total reality, while the other applies to something within God. God's totality, then, God's concrete actuality, is relative, changing, temporal, and so one; and God's abstract individuality is absolute, changeless, and eternal.

But can a perfect being change without compromising its perfection? If it is perfect, it seems, change could only make it worse. And if God is somehow growing toward perfection, then he cannot be perfect already. Hartshorne solves this problem with his notion of *surrelativism,* the concept that certain dimensions of value allow for and require self-surpassing. The essential idea of perfection, Hartshorne argues, is superiority. The perfect being is superior to all others. But suppose it remained superior to all others, while it became superior to itself in a previous state. Would it still be perfect? Hartshorne says yes. As long as God is superior to all others, God is perfect in the relevant sense of the word.

Hartshorne observes that there are different dimensions of value. Some of them are open; others are closed. An open dimension of value does not admit of maximum realization. Consider happiness, for example. Could one ever be so happy that one could not conceivably be happier? No. The continuation of the same experience would add to one's happiness. In contrast, there are dimensions of value that do admit of a supreme exemplification. These are ethical values, such as knowledge, goodness, and power. If we think of perfect knowledge as knowing everything there is to know, for example, we have identified a closed dimension of value. Perfect knowledge perfectly reflects its object. But notice, the adequacy of the knowledge may remain the same, while the content of the knowledge changes. Suppose I remember everything on page one of a book while I read and remember everything on page two. The content of my knowledge has increased, but the adequacy of my knowledge has remained the same. Hartshorne argues along these lines to show that a changing God is by no means an imperfect God. God's relativity and temporality do not compromise his generic excellence.

To describe his concept of God's relation to the world Hartshorne uses the well-known expression *panentheism.*[30] It avoids the pitfalls, he argues, of both classical alternatives. Theism and pantheism share the view that God is wholly necessary and proceed to different, but equally unacceptable, conclusions. For theism, the world is wholly contingent, and since God is wholly necessary, the world can have no effect on God. This presents classical theism with some vexing problems. For how can

30. The most extensive discussion of panentheism, in comparison with other models of the divine reality, appears in Charles Hartshorne and William Reese, *Philosophers Speak of God* (Chicago: University of Chicago Press, 1953).

a wholly necessary being have any relation to a wholly contingent world? If God is completely unaffected by the world, what are we to make of the biblical narratives, which are filled with accounts of God interacting with his creatures? Another dilemma arises from the question of whether the creaturely world has any value. On the one hand, if the world is outside God, then the total value of God and the world must be greater than God. But this undermines the grandeur of God. On the other hand, if nothing is greater than God, and the world is wholly external to him, then the world must have no value at all.

For classical pantheism, God includes the world, but since everything about God is necessary, the world must be wholly necessary, too. Consequently, nothing is contingent. Nothing could be other than it is. There is no such thing as freedom.

Panentheism overcomes these various problems by holding that God is not, contrary to theism and pantheism, entirely necessary. Instead, God is partly necessary and partly contingent. This dipolar view of God enables us to affirm the theistic insight that God is distinct from the world *and* the pantheistic insight that God is inclusive of the world. In his contingent pole, God includes the world, so his reality incorporates all the value of the creaturely existence. But in his necessary pole God is distinct from the world, so God would be God no matter what world actually existed. For panentheism, there must be some creaturely world or other, not necessarily *this* world. Any world will do. There is nothing greater than God, because God includes the entire value of the creaturely world. God can enjoy genuine relations with his creatures, because his concrete experience is contingent, just as theirs is.

Some Conservative Misunderstandings of Process Thought

It is worthwhile to get the basic features of process thought well in hand. For one thing, it represents an impressive metaphysical proposal. Though I do not have the time to spell them out here, this pluralistic, temporalistic, indeterministic interpretation of reality provides helpful answers to a great many of the classic questions of philosophy. Another reason to view process thought as a whole is the fact that the process view of God is part and parcel of its metaphysical vision. We cannot understand the process view of God without appreciating the comprehensive system to which it belongs.

Looking carefully at process theism can also help us to avoid the sorts of mistakes conservative theologians sometimes make in reacting to process thought. For example, Ronald Nash argues that process thought provides no explanation for actuality, no explanation for "these particulars that happen to exist." "Whitehead and other process thinkers develop a metaphysical system that leaves unanswered the most fundamental of all metaphysical questions, why is there anything at all?"[31]

The problem here is the classical assumption that ultimate reality can be conceived only in terms of a wholly necessary or absolute being. Otherwise, the thinking goes, we have no explanation for the world's existence. But there is plenty of necessity in process theism. The point of dipolar theism is not that God is less than necessary, but that God is more than mere necessity. Process thought agrees with the tradition that ultimate reality must be necessary, but insists that ultimate reality must be contingent, too. Put simply, the ultimate metaphysical principle for process thought is this: contingent reality necessarily exists.

A failure to grasp dipolarity lies behind other misunderstandings of process theism. We see it when Nash questions God's continuity over time. "It is difficult," he asserts, "to see how the God of process thought can retain any identity." "Since in process thought God is totally subject to the vicissitudes of change, nothing can possibly ground His identity."[32] But dipolar theism shows clearly that God is not totally subject to the vicissitudes of change. True, in one pole of the divine reality, God changes constantly in response to events in the creaturely world. But in the other pole, God is utterly unchanging. Indeed, in this aspect of his being God is absolute, necessary, and immutable. This is the pole that individuates or identifies God. Contrary to Nash, then, in the abstract pole of his being, God is as unchanging as classical theism insists God must be.

The genius of dipolar theism also eludes another critic, who concludes that process thought does not provide a view of God after all.

31. Ronald H. Nash, *The Concept of God* (Grand Rapids: Zondervan, 1983), 33.

32. Ibid., 35.

According to Bruce Demarest, "The primordial pole of God, which possesses no actuality, in fact possesses no reality."[33] It is nothing but "a desperate attempt to forestall the system's collapse into radical immanentism and pantheism." Demarest concludes that process thought does not need a God after all, and the God it offers is no better than no God at all. "Having created from naturalistic premises a relatively consistent non-theistic vision of the universe, process theology should lay all its cards out on the table and eliminate God entirely."[34]

But Demarest underestimates the importance of both divine natures. From the perspective of Whitehead's thought, God's primordial nature is not only real but seems to play a more important metaphysical role than the consequent nature.[35] The role of the consequent nature is somewhat different in Hartshorne, but as we saw above, it is indispensable to his vision of things. Thus it is a mistake to construe the process view of God as a last-ditch effort to save a traditional idea. After all, Whitehead and Hartshorne were philosophers, not theologians. They were not scrambling for ways to keep God in the scheme of things. They were led to theistic conclusions by metaphysical concerns.

Theological Misgivings about Philosophy

This is not to say, of course, that there is no reason to be concerned about process philosophy. From a conservative theological perspective, process thought and its use by process theologians raise a number of perplexing questions.

The first concerns any reliance of theology on philosophy. From a careful study of eighteenth-century religious thought, Michael J. Buckley draws the sobering conclusion that modern atheism origi-

33. Bruce A. Demarest, "Process Trinitarianism," in *Perspectives on Evangelical Theology: Papers from the Thirtieth Annual Meeting of the Evangelical Theological Society,* ed. Kenneth S. Kantzer and Stanley N. Gundry (Grand Rapids: Baker, 1979), 31.

34. Ibid., 32.

35. According to Whitehead's thought, the ongoing advance of the creative order requires a principle of novelty, and the primordial nature serves this essential purpose. The purpose of the consequent nature, in contrast, is primarily to provide the primordial nature a basis in reality.

nated when theologians turned the question of God's existence over to philosophy. Consequently, they had nothing to say when philosophy's answer was no. "In failing to assert its own competence," Buckley concludes, "in commissioning philosophy with its defense, religion shaped its own eventual negative."[36] When theology lets philosophy do its work, the moral seems to be, it runs the risk of losing its central vision. But theologians should take Buckley's work as a methodological caveat, not a summary condemnation of philosophy. I do not think we can flatly assert that every notion of God that originates in philosophical reflection is irrelevant, let alone inimical, to religion. Instead, we need to "test all things and hold fast what is good."

Nevertheless, the expression "process theology" does raise some questions. If it is a synonym for process philosophy, or for the process view of God, there is no problem. But if it represents a synonym for Christian theology, then it confuses two disciplines. Process thought and Christian theology belong to different realms of discourse. Process thought is a philosophy, more specifically a metaphysics, an attempt to interpret reality as such by appealing to our common human experience. By contrast, theology is the interpretation of religion, of a particular religion, to be precise. Its primary appeal is not to common human experience, but to the specific vision and the specific experience of a particular religious tradition. The two have different concerns and operate on different levels.

It was Schubert Ogden who introduced me to both Whitehead and Hartshorne. Though he makes extensive use of process philosophy, and his name often is, or used to be, linked with John B. Cobb's as an influential process theologian, he had reservations about the expression "process theology." According to Ogden, theology's one task is to be theology, period. While theology is accountable to many of the same criteria incumbent on philosophy, such as conceptual adequacy, its essential concern is to interpret the gospel of Jesus Christ, and its primary objective is appropriateness to the Christian witness of faith. Process thought may provide a resource to theology in its attempt to express this witness, but it should not be the determining factor in giving this expression its final shape.

36. Michael J. Buckley, *At the Origins of Modern Atheism* (New Haven: Yale University Press, 1987), 357.

Some people object to the "ethos" they find in process theology.[37] They are bothered by the enthusiasm with which certain theologians embrace Whiteheadian terms and concepts. Such thinkers, they feel, seem to "know too much" and subordinate theology to a specific philosophical vision. They articulate process ideas in the name of theology, and they construe Christian themes as the symbolic representations of philosophical categories.

Such a reaction to process thought is ill formed, to say the least. Further, it leaves us wondering, what exactly is supposed to be wrong with process theology? Is it the metaphysical system itself? Is it the way theologians use, or misuse, it? Or, is it that for some people process thought tends to move from philosophical conceptuality to religious vision?

From my perspective, process thought helps Christian theology in certain ways as theology attempts to express the contents of faith. It supports the conviction that ultimate reality is personal, and it provides a conceptually coherent way of attributing relational qualities to God. But I do not think that process thought and Christian theology engage each other in the way that the expression "process theology" suggests. They are about different things and they operate on different levels. If process thought is metaphysics, then it is useful as a description of what always happens, but not particularly helpful in explaining what only sometimes happens. As evangelicals construe it, the central claims of Christianity concern historical events, things that happened once, and to understand them, metaphysical categories are of limited value. It is like applying physics to Michael Jordan's jump shot, or diagramming Hemingway's sentences. It might tell you something about its object, but not the most interesting things. My belief is that process thought helps on the level of the universal and the categorical – in other words, on the level of God's relation to the cosmos – but becomes less helpful as it moves into attempts to describe the more particular, historical aspects of Christian faith.

Recent discussions of the nature and purpose of theology raise

37. See Jay McDaniel's paper, "The Ethos of Process Theology: Repenting from the Enlightenment," Conference on "The Enlightenment in Evangelical and Process Perspectives," Center for Process Studies, Claremont Graduate University, Claremont, CA, March 20-22, 1997.

sweeping questions about any theological use of philosophical thought. I left graduate school with the general idea that theology's task is to translate the basic symbols of Christian faith into contemporary conceptual languages. The assumption was that modern men and women can believe the gospel because the essential claims of faith make sense when they are extracted from their original, archaic expressions and appropriately reformulated. As thus conceived, the task of theology is to show that the gospel satisfies contemporary criteria of meaning and truth. Thus we have the contents of Christian faith on the one hand, the modern world on the other, and the rational mind that brings them together.

Recent critics of the Enlightenment challenge each element in this threefold configuration of theology. As they see it, the notion of the Christian faith, or the essential claim of the gospel, is an abstraction from the rich blend of ambiguous and provocative narratives, metaphors, and symbols that constitute the Bible as it reads. We cannot wrap Christianity in a package of propositions to be intellectually assessed.

Likewise, the modern world, a vision of reality produced by unqualified confidence in scientific inquiry and unqualified optimism for the fruits of technology, is also an abstraction – an abstraction with deadening and deadly consequences. We can embrace it only by ignoring the vast sweep of human experience past and present, which has always been open to ranges of meaning inaccessible to mere rational inquiry, and by overlooking the devastating effects of our ceaseless manipulation of the environment.

Finally and most emphatically, the rational mind is an abstraction. There is no one way of looking at reality, no integrated program of intellectual operations, no single set of solid assumptions, that gives humanity access to truth, or Truth. We privilege one perspective only by ignoring, if not dehumanizing, others, specifically those who stand outside the stream of thinkers who are Western, white, male, and straight. The very idea of the rational mind seems to ignore that there are other ways of thinking, that there are others who think, indeed, that there are others at all.

These criticisms create a climate in which any theological use of philosophy is suspect. There is a decisive turn, or return, to the view that Christian faith is understood most clearly when we attend closely to the elements of the biblical symbols and narratives and best articulated within its own terms – a position variously characterized as postmodern, confessional, unapologetic, or even "Barthian."

Appeals to adopt a more Bible-centered approach to theology naturally stir the emotions of someone with conservative religious convictions. They have led me to reshape my understanding of the theological task in several important ways. But I still think that philosophical reflection has an important role to play in Christian thought. Christianity has always been a missionary religion. From the beginning, its adherents faced the task of communicating their convictions to the world around them. To be faithful to our heritage we must look for ways to give our beliefs serious intellectual expression.

I do not think we should rule out the importance of philosophy to the theological task. Philosophy may no longer be the handmaid of theology, but it still has a contribution to make. At the same time, open theists believe that we must avoid making theology subservient to any philosophical system. Thus while we appreciate some of the insights of process thought, we have major reservations about it, too, and we need to spell these out.

Where Process Thought and the Open View of God Converge

For the most part, proponents of the open view of God accept process philosophy's critique of traditional, or classical, theism. They, too, oppose the concept of a divine absolute, utterly unaffected by the world, whose ultimate goal is its own glory. Instead of sovereignty and majesty, open and process theists alike emphasize the divine attributes of love, sensitivity, and compassion. They do not view divine power as the exercise of absolute control. They do not believe that God unilaterally determines the entire course of creaturely events, and they do not believe that divine knowledge includes future free decisions. Both embrace a highly interactive view of God's relation to the world. Not only does God affect the creatures, but the creatures also have an effect on God.

Love and power are the prominent elements in this shared vision of God. Indeed, process thought is often described as a metaphysics of love, an attempt to develop a full-fledged metaphysical system from the fundamental insight that God is love. The open view of God shares this emphasis on the priority of love.

For both perspectives, love involves sensitivity to the other. Because God loves the creatures, he is open to their experiences. What happens to them makes a real difference to him. Love also involves affirming and valuing the other. God relates to the creatures in ways that respect and preserve their integrity. Consequently, God cannot prevent, negate, or undo their decisions and actions. In a world of genuine freedom, then, actions have consequences, and not even God – or should we say, especially not God – can cancel or reverse the decisions others make. Thus in a universe where love is God's fundamental nature, the creatures make a permanent contribution to the scheme of things. Indeed, God "cherishes" the creatures. Everything they do is preserved perfectly in God's memory, its value retained forever.

This understanding of divine love has important implications for divine power. If love is God's primary attribute, then God cannot have a monopoly on power. Perfect power is not "all the power there is," "power to do anything," or even "power to bring about any logically possible state of affairs."[38] Thus there are significant limits to what God can do. God cannot decide what the creatures shall decide. If their choices are genuinely theirs, they cannot be the product of the divine will. Process and open theism alike reject divine determinism.

Love also determines the essential form God's power takes in the universe. It is persuasive rather than coercive. God achieves his purposes by influencing or "luring" creatures toward the best of the options available to them. He never exerts his influence in ways that violate the integrity of their choices.

It is clear, then, that process and open theists hold views of God that are similar in a number of important ways. For both, love is the supreme divine attribute, the essential nature of God. For both, God's experience exhibits relationality, temporality, and contingency. And for both, the world has significance for the inner life of God.

38. It may sound strange to say that there are possible states of affairs that God cannot bring about, but this is a corollary of the view that creatures have genuine freedom. Some perfectly conceivable states of affairs presuppose creaturely decisions. In such cases, only God *and* the creatures can bring them about, not God alone.

Where Process Theism and the Open View of God Diverge

In spite of their similarities, these two positions have some profound differences. One of them concerns the freedom and sovereignty of love. As we saw in our review of process philosophy, the ultimate metaphysical fact is God-and-world. Without a creaturely world, God would have no actuality and hence no existence. Consequently, God needs the world as much as the world needs God.

For the open view of God, the situation is radically different. The ultimate metaphysical fact is not God-and-world, but God, period. God could exist without the creatures, but he chooses not to. Thus the world owes its existence to God's free choice, not to metaphysical necessity.

Ironically, perhaps, each position appeals to the logic of love to make its case. For process theists, love is inherently social, or relational. Since a loving being requires others to love, we cannot think of God without the company of creatures to care for. The idea of God without world is anomalous.

But if process thinkers maintain that divine love *entails* a necessary world, open theists insist that divine love *excludes* a necessary world. From their perspective, love requires a degree of divine independence that process thought denies. Unless the world owes its existence to God's free choice, divine love is a vacuous concept. Open theism affirms the process insight that love involves profound sensitivity, but it insists that love is a voluntary commitment.

Thus open theism agrees with process thought, against the tradition, that God is not the only factor that accounts for the way things are. There exists a realm of nondivine beings whose decisions, actions, and experiences are not the direct product of the divine will. Their decisions are truly their own. But open theism agrees with the tradition against process thought in holding that the mere existence of such a world is due to God's free decision.

Another important difference between process theism and the open view of God concerns the nature of God's activity in the world. According to process thought, God never acts unilaterally. Or, to put it another way, God never intervenes in creaturely affairs. He is a constant influence in the decisions creatures make, but he never acts directly, brings about, or prevents the occurrence of specific creaturely events.

The contrast between "coercive" and "persuasive" power is fundamental to process thought. In one of his later books, *Omnipotence and Other Theological Mistakes,* Hartshorne distinguishes emphatically "two meanings of 'all-powerful.'" One is "the power to determine every detail of what happens in the world," which he calls "the *tyrant* ideal of power." The other is the power "to significantly influence the happenings."[39] This, he insists, is the only kind of power that makes sense, and the only kind of power worth admiring. "The only livable doctrine of divine power is that it influences all that happens but determines nothing in its concrete particularity." Moreover, the content of "God's power simply is the appeal of unsurpassable love." Or to quote Whitehead, "God's power is the worship he inspires."[40] Thus Hartshorne presents to us, as the only alternative to a power that determines everything, a power that influences everything but actually determines nothing.

For David Griffin, coercive power is central to the traditional concept of creation. Thus rejecting coercion means rejecting the "speculative hypothesis" of *creatio ex nihilo.* "If God created this world out of absolutely nothing, then, the beings of this world are *absolutely* dependent upon God. Any power they have is not at all inherent, but is totally a gift of God, and as such can be overridden (or, which amounts to the same thing, withdrawn) at any time."[41]

This makes the problem of evil utterly intractable, Griffin argues, because it makes God directly and unilaterally responsible for all that is wrong in the world. After all, a being who possesses "omnipotence" could immediately produce any state of affairs it desired. Nothing stands in the way. Thus the only way to solve the problem of evil is to "dissolve" it by rejecting the notion of power that lies behind it.[42]

Since all power is shared power, "the power possessed by the nondivine actualities is inherent to them and cannot be cancelled out or

39. Charles Hartshorne, *Omnipotence and Other Theological Mistakes* (Albany: SUNY Press, 1984), 11.

40. Ibid., 25, 14.

41. David Griffin, "Creation Out of Chaos and the Problem of Evil," in *Encountering Evil: Live Options in Theodicy,* ed. Stephen T. Davis (Atlanta: John Knox, 1981), 104.

42. For an extensive development of Griffin's views on the subject, see his *God, Power, and Evil: A Process Theodicy* (Philadelphia: Westminster, 1976).

overridden by God."[43] God lacks the inherent capacity to control the self-determining power of others. God "can only persuade what we become and how we affect others." The alternatives, then, are creation out of nothing (ex nihilo) and creation out of chaos — the power of control and the power of persuasion.

For open theists, the process critique of classical omnipotence goes too far. There are concepts of divine power that need to be corrected, of course. The idea that God directly wills everything, that he determines and controls the course of creaturely events down to the last detail, has to go. It is incompatible with the biblical portrait of a God who engages in dynamic interaction with his creatures, who suffers when they suffer, rejoices when they rejoice, and modifies his plans in response to their decisions.

But process thought not only denies that God controls everything, it denies that God actually controls anything, for God never acts unilaterally. Nothing ever happens just because God wants it to. God acts only by persuading or influencing his creatures to act, and they must play their part in order for him to achieve his objectives.

God decides the general features of reality. He sets the conditions that are necessary for good things to happen and sketches a broad outline for creation to follow. But the actual course the universe takes always depends on the decisions of others. Thus God cannot by his willing and doing alone bring about any specific state of affairs. Nothing in the actual world exists or happens solely because God wants it to.

This relieves God of responsibility for all the specific ills in the world. As Griffin states emphatically, "God can move a living human body by persuading the soul to move. . . . But there is no corresponding means by which God can directly move a rock." God has literally no way to do things like stop a speeding bullet, hold up the cracking timbers in a mine shaft, keep an airborne automobile from crashing into other cars, prevent a hurricane from destroying the towns in its path.[44] Because God lacks the power to do such things, he cannot be blamed for failing to do them.

It is clear from Griffin's view of divine power just how far the process view of God departs from traditional Christianity. Since anything

43. Ibid., 105.
44. Ibid., 113.

resembling the traditional notion of divine intervention is rejected, it has dramatic consequences not only for creation but also for providence, revelation, incarnation, and eschatology – both individual and cosmic. Of course, it also excludes the possibility of anything like miracles – extraordinary manifestations of divine power to benefit human beings. In short, process thought leaves us with a thoroughly transformed view of the world and God's relation to it.

For open theists, the process view of God provides a valuable critique of traditional theism and a helpful way of conceiving of God's interaction with the creaturely world. But they reject the notion that God requires a world. They believe that the conviction that God is the sole fundamental reality, the one and only ultimate explanatory principle, is essential to the Christian vision of things.

Process thinkers are mistaken in framing theistic options in stark, either-or terms – either coercion or persuasion, either divine tyranny or a necessary world. It is perfectly possible to combine an interactive view of God and the world with a strong concept of divine sovereignty, and to affirm divine persuasion but allow for other forms of divine activity as well. It is even possible to attribute relativity, contingency, and temporality to God without compromising the full freedom of God's love for the world.

A Theology of Divine Restraint

A number of theologians share the process conviction that God interacts with the creaturely world, but reject the idea that the world exists necessarily. In a recent attempt to unify theology, cosmology, and ethics, Nancey Murphy and George F. R. Ellis espouse a "kenotic" or "non-interventionist" view of God. They apply the "emptying" attributed to Jesus in the great hymn of Philippians 2:5-11 to the nature of God and the nature of the cosmos in order to support an ethic of self-renunciation and nonviolent social interaction.[45] Since God's nature is essentially "kenotic,"[46] God refuses to do violence to creation, whatever the cost to himself. God

45. Nancey Murphy and George F. R. Ellis, *On the Moral Nature of the Universe: Theology, Cosmology, and Ethics* (Minneapolis: Fortress, 1996), 173. Compare their thesis, "kenosis is the underlying law of the cosmos" (251).

46. Ibid., 194.

works "in concert with nature, never overriding or violating the very processes that God has created."[47]

This noninterventionist mode of divine activity applies not only to rational beings but to "all levels of reality," "all the way through the hierarchy of complexity within the created world. Hence God cooperates with, but does not overrule, natural entities." Accordingly, natural processes express not only God's will, but the limitations imposed by the nature of the creaturely entities with which God "cooperates." In the case of humans, of course, God encounters not only the limitations of creatures in general but their free choices in rebelling against God.

This "kenotic answer to the problem of evil" explains why it takes such a long time for God to achieve his purposes for creation. The ultimate goal is to achieve creatures in God's own image, "creatures enough like God to relate to God." But "noncoercive, persuasive, painstaking love" works "slowly and indirectly and painfully."

In their words, "God has apparently decided not to violate the 'natural rights' of created entities to be what they are." This means that "God voluntarily withholds divine power, out of respect for the freedom and integrity of creatures," and "God takes the risk and suffers the cost of cooperating with creatures whose activity violates or fails to measure up to God's purposes."[48]

For Murphy and Ellis, then, as for process thinkers like Griffin and Hartshorne, God does not act in history in the conventional sense of that expression. He never overrides the will of the creatures to accomplish his purposes. Divine action is "divine restraint."[49] But there is a major difference between their positions nonetheless. For unlike Griffin and Hartshorne, Murphy and Ellis view God's nonintervention as a matter of divine policy rather than metaphysical necessity. God does not intervene, because he chooses not to, not because it lies beyond his capacity to do so.

Like Murphy and Ellis, Keith Ward endorses an interactive view of God based on divine choice. He appreciates process thought's dipolar,

47. Ibid., xv. For Murphy and Ellis, this view of God "has direct implications for human morality; it implies a 'kenotic' or self-renunciatory ethic, according to which one must renounce self-interest for the sake of the other, *no matter what the cost to oneself*" (ibid.).

48. Ibid., 246-47.

49. Ibid., 248.

or "dual aspect," theism, as a "distinctive reworking" of the idea of God. It presents us with a God who "creatively changes in willing fellowship with creation, and is responsively changed by uniting creation with the divine life. But in another and deeper aspect God remains the unchanging source of this dynamic . . . life."[50]

Ward shares the process convictions that time is real, the future is open, and omniscience does not include future creaturely decisions. He also draws on Hartshorne's thought to develop an interesting account of the divine imagination.[51] But he shares with Murphy and Ellis the belief that God is involved with creation because he wills to be. God commits himself to its welfare voluntarily.

Another theologian who affirms process insights yet rejects process thought's denial that God is the world's origin is Wolfhart Pannenberg. Pannenberg explicitly embraces the formula *creatio ex nihilo* because it expresses the distinctive view of God that appears in Genesis 1.[52] This creation account is unique in emphasizing the "unlimited freedom" or "unrestricted nature of God's power in creation."[53] For Pannenberg, "The unique character of the biblical concept of God's creative action rules out . . . any dualistic view of the origin of the world. The world is not the result of any working of God with another principle." It specifically excludes process philosophy. "Whitehead's God works by 'persuasion,' not by mighty creative action." By thus limiting God's power, process philosophy removes God as the sole object of faith. Creatures "cannot put full trust in God alone for the overcoming of evil in the world." They must rely on other powers.[54]

Although it is inadequate to the biblical view of God's power and freedom, Pannenberg argues, process thought nonetheless contains valuable insights. The notion that God works by persuasion rather than sheer power is a good way to describe God's relation to the crea-

50. Keith Ward, *Religion and Creation* (Oxford: Clarendon, 1996), 284.

51. Instead of passively contemplating all possibilities at once, Ward argues, God envisions new possibilities as the world develops. Over time God's interaction with the world generates new imaginations (ibid., 280-81).

52. Pannenberg acknowledges that there are other biblical accounts of creation, as well as other ancient accounts of creation by word.

53. Wolfhart Pannenberg, *Systematic Theology,* trans. Geoffrey W. Bromiley, 3 vols. (Grand Rapids: Eerdmans, 1991-98), 2:12-13.

54. Ibid., 15.

tures. "Once having called them into existence," he states, "the biblical God then respects their independence in a way that is analogous to Whitehead's description." "To attain his ends in creation, and especially in the end of the creatures' own fulfillment, God works by persuasion and not by force."[55]

Omnipotence versus Determinism

These positions point to a distinct alternative to both classical and process views of divine power. Classical and process theists share the conviction that omnipotence entails determinism. If one being possesses supreme power, they agree, then that being determines everything else. Classical theists accept this concept and conclude that God's will determines everything that happens, even evil, or what appears to be evil. For process theists, this concept of omnipotence is incoherent. Universal power is not concentrated in God but distributed between God and the creatures, so God does not have the power to prevent or eliminate suffering.

But if we reject the equation of omnipotence with divine determinism, we are not forced to choose between "God determines everything" and "God determines nothing." We have the option that an omnipotent God voluntarily decides to share his power with his creatures and henceforth cooperates with them in reaching his objectives for the universe. This means that God's power involves different ways of acting. God manifests majestic power in bringing the world into existence and persuasive power in directing it toward its destiny.

This seems to be the position Keith Ward takes. "Omnipotence theists" agree with process theists that God cannot determine the actions of free, partly self-determining moral agents, but they view the existence of such agents as a matter of divine choice rather than metaphysical necessity. "God has the power to determine everything if God so wills," says Ward. "But if God wills to give some beings a limited degree of autonomy, then God can do so."[56] Thus God is "omnipotent in the sense that God could determine everything," but he may also decide

55. Ibid., 16.

56. Ward, *Religion and Creation,* 259.

not to. "As Creator, it is within God's power of free decision to create a universe containing partly self-determining beings or not."[57]

Besides deciding whether to share power, God also decides just how much power to share. Process thinkers like Griffin argue that God in effect determines everything if he actually determines anything, but Ward disagrees. "Just because God does not determine everything, it does not follow that God cannot determine anything." Indeed, God may determine a great many particular things, including human actions, without "thereby destroying all significant human freedom." "God can easily set up real possibilities so that such an element of choice remains for everyone."[58]

On a view such as Ward's, genuine creaturely freedom is perfectly compatible with a strong concept of divine direction, and this provides a basis for hope that God's purposes will ultimately be fulfilled. "God can foresee that the divine purpose will be fulfilled, and can foresee some details of its fulfillment, since God determines these things to be. But the particular way in which it is fulfilled is left to creatures to decide, within fairly definite limits."[59] By responding creatively and resourcefully to creaturely choices, God directs the course of history to its predetermined outcome.

As Ward conceives it, "omnipotent love" requires two things: a genuine respect for creaturely freedom and the certain achievement of good goals for the universe. Accordingly, "the divine purpose can be frustrated in many particulars, since divine love will not compel. But it cannot be frustrated in its final outcome, since God's power . . . will not suffer love to be defeated." Such a view of providence "gives creatures genuine freedom and yet does not subject God to the possibility that the divine purpose in creation might finally be defeated."[60]

The strength of process philosophy is often thought to lie in its interactive view of God's relation to the world, but an open view of God seems to require, if anything, a higher degree of interaction. For open theism, God formulates specific plans and intentions, establishes the framework or boundaries for creaturely activity, and then works toward

57. Ibid., 170.
58. Ibid., 260.
59. Ibid., 260-61.
60. Ibid., 265.

his objectives by responding resourcefully to every creaturely decision. At every moment along the way, God must intricately adjust his actions in response to the creatures' decisions.

Another Look at Divine Persuasion

For process thinkers a position like Ward's gives God more control over creaturely affairs than logic permits or the facts of experience warrant. For if God has the kind of power that can grant creaturely freedom and still guarantee the ultimate fulfillment of his purposes, we have to wonder why he does not use this power to lessen or eliminate the world's suffering. Why can't he put the universe on a path that does not contain so much destruction and heartache? Why can't he reach his goals in less than billions of years' time?

On this point the arguments of certain process thinkers seem inconsistent. On one hand, they defend the notion of persuasive power on both metaphysical and ethical grounds. Persuasion is not merely the only form of power logically attributable to God, but the only sort of power worthy of God. Divine coercion is morally offensive.

At the same time, process thinkers sometimes argue that God is morally culpable if he has coercive power but fails to use it. Griffin asserts that contemporary theologians who accept both the hypothesis of divine omnipotence and the evolutionary hypothesis "have a lot of explaining to do." They must show "why a God whose power is essentially unlimited would use such a long, pain-filled method, with all its blind alleys, to create a world."[61]

Well, which is it? Is coercive power good or bad? On the one hand, if coercive power is inherently wrong, God is hardly to be blamed for not using it even if he can. On the other hand, if there are times when God *should* employ coercive power, how can its exercise be inherently immoral? As David Basinger argues in *Divine Power in Process Theism,* the moral status of coercive power is not clear within the process system.[62]

61. Griffin, "Creation Out of Chaos and the Problem of Evil," 106.

62. At times, process thinkers "appear to believe that any divine coercive activity would be morally wrong or at least morally inferior." And at times, they "appear to believe that the God of process theism would coerce if this were possible or at least that co-

Basinger also maintains that process theists fail to demonstrate that a God who has the kind of powers process thought accords him is unable to coerce. More is required to establish this than the mere assertion that God cannot unilaterally bring about any actual state of affairs.[63] As process thinkers employ it, the persuasion-coercion contrast seems to dichotomize what is better thought of as a continuum. The mere notion of persuasion allows for tremendous range, so the belief that God's power is the power of influence allows for the possibility that God's influence could be highly effective in achieving God's purposes.

For open theists, logic, the Bible, and human experience all point us to something we might call "directive power." This need not be thought of as a different type of power from persuasion, but as another way of exerting persuasive power, or the application of a certain amount of persuasive power. God can be more involved in certain creaturely decisions than others, depending on God's own choices. After all, if the creatures have genuine freedom, and a range of options to select from, then God must have genuine freedom, too; and the range of options available to him would be correspondingly great. The idea that God acts interactively in some cases and unilaterally in others, that his persuasion is stronger at certain times than at others, is a perfectly coherent position.

Turning, then, from divine determinism to divine persuasion as the preferred description of God's mode of activity does not per se exclude the idea of divine direction, or even divine "intervention." It simply means that we have to construe divine persuasion very carefully. However God manifests his power, open theists agree with process thinkers that love is the ultimate impulse of God's life; thus God's care for the creatures and his respect for their freedom and integrity never vary.

These contrasting views of divine power have profound implications for cosmic destiny. Process thought does not envision an escha-

---

ercion is morally superior to noncoercion in some cases. Many contend, for instance [as we see in Griffin's case], that a being who could coercively remove more evil ought to do so" (David Basinger, *Divine Power in Process Theism: A Philosophical Critique* [Albany: SUNY Press, 1988], 114).

63. Ibid., 113. See also David Basinger, "Divine Persuasion: Could the Process God Do More?" *Journal of Religion* 64 (1984): 332-47.

ton, a final fulfillment of the creative process. We have Whitehead's famous assertion that there is no far-off divine event to which all creation moves. Nor, for Hartshorne certainly, is there any future for our conscious existence after death. Human beings enjoy "objective immortality" in the mind of God, because he retains forever the value of creaturely experiences. But our conscious experience ceases when we die.[64]

The process view of divine persuasion means that God cannot guarantee the fulfillment of specific plans for the world, if indeed God has any.[65] Process thinkers generally account for God's objectives in very general terms. But for open theism, God's loving sovereignty means that God has specific plans for the universe and possesses the means to achieve them. God retains sufficient power to guarantee their fulfillment. While the creatures are genuinely free and God's power is the persuasive power of love, the range of creaturely freedom and the efficacy of divine persuasion are such that God will eventually bring the world to the fulfillment of his purposes.

Love and the Life of God

While the more obvious differences between process theism and the open view of God involve divine power, their more important differences involve divine love. Both process thought and open theism place love at the center of the divine reality. Both believe that God's love comes to expression in God's relation to the world, and both maintain that love involves genuine sensitivity to its objects. Consequently, both believe that ultimate reality is inherently social or relational. Love requires an "other." This is where the two divide. What is the "other" that divine love requires?

For process thought, the answer is "the world." Divine love makes sense only if there are nondivine objects of God's affection. For open theists, the other that love presupposes lies within God's own reality.

64. There are process theologians who believe that Whitehead's thought allows for a concept of human immortality. John B. Cobb and David Griffin believe that it does.

65. There is considerable variation among process thinkers as to what sort of decisions God makes concerning the cosmos.

God's inner life is social and relational; it pulsates with affection. This, of course, is the essential insight of the Trinity. For open theists, a proper understanding of the Trinity allows us to attribute to God sociality, sensitivity, relativity – in short, the essential elements of the process view of God – while preserving the central insight that God alone is creator and lord of all.

Over the past twenty-five years or so, Christian theologians have devoted considerable attention to the doctrine of the Trinity.[66] I cannot review the intricacies of the discussion here, of course, but a few themes in recent trinitarian thought are important for our present concern.

First, the Trinity is a portrait of God that arises from salvation history. Nearly all the major problems in the history of trinitarian thought result when people abstract from this history and treat God as an independent object of speculation.[67] At the same time, God's saving actions are a display of God's very being, a portrait of God's inner reality. In Karl Rahner's famous dictum, "The 'economic' Trinity is the 'immanent' Trinity and the 'immanent' Trinity is the 'economic' Trinity."[68] This means that the revelation of God in salvation history is a genuine *self*-revelation, not a temporary expedient or a public relations ploy, but a portrait of what God is really like. To quote Catherine LaCugna, "The very nature of God who is self-communicating love is expressed in what God does in the events of redemptive history. There is no hidden God . . . behind the God of revelation history, no possibility that God is in God's eternal mystery other than what God reveals Godself to be."[69]

Rahner's dictum also means that this revelation is a genuine self-

66. So many studies have accumulated that there are now books discussing all the books on the topic. See, e.g., John Thompson, *Modern Trinitarian Perspectives* (New York: Oxford University Press, 1994); and Ted Peters, *God as Trinity: Relationality and Temporality in Divine Life* (Louisville: Westminster/John Knox, 1993).

67. Catherine Mowry LaCugna emphasizes this point: "the quest for knowledge of God or of God's *ousia* 'in itself' or 'by itself' is doomed to fail" (*God for Us: The Trinity and Christian Life* [San Francisco: HarperCollins, 1991], 193).

68. Karl Rahner, *The Trinity,* trans. Joseph Donceel (New York: Herder and Herder, 1970), 22.

69. LaCugna, *God for Us,* 322. Cf. the assertion of Robert W. Jenson: "Each of the inner-trinitarian relations is then an affirmation that as God works creatively among us, so he is in himself" (*The Triune Identity: God According to the Gospel* [Philadelphia: Fortress, 1982], 107).

giving. God's true self, God's innermost reality, comes to expression in God's dealings with creation. Consequently, God's saving actions become central to God's identity. In creating and saving a world, he commits himself to the world in such a way that his own destiny and his own identity are forever linked to that of his creatures. Like British generals who acquired titles from their battlefield triumphs, God's name derives from his saving activity. For Christians the Trinity *names* God – as Father, Son, and Spirit – identifying God by the definitive moments in salvation history: the mission of the Son and the sending of the Spirit.[70]

Now, if salvation history is a revelation of God's inner reality, we must think of God in a way that is consistent with what we find in this history. Since the qualities of sensitivity, care, commitment, self-giving, and self-sacrifice are prominent in salvation history, as the cross supremely testified, these are the qualities that characterize God's essential reality. Accordingly, we attribute complexity to the inner life of God. God is not sheer, undifferentiated unity. God is a dynamic, living reality. Indeed, as process thought insists, God is relational. The expressions "Father," "Son," and "Spirit" point to relations that constitute God's being. We cannot go beyond the relations of Father, Son, and Spirit to a divine essence that precedes them, because there is no such essence. The relations constitute the being of God.[71]

70. Jenson explores at length the significance of the designation "Father, Son and Spirit" as a "naming-formula" for God. The expression is "appropriate to name the gospel's God because the phrase immediately summarizes the primal Christian interpretation of God" (*Triune Identity,* 18). Other theologians are equally insistent that the Trinity is a name, and the reality it names is not merely one among several versions of "theism." Says Stanley Hauerwas, "I do not believe that the trinitarian Father, Son, and Holy Spirit is an image. Rather Trinity is a name. Christians do not believe that we first come to know something called God and only then further learn to identify God as Trinity. Rather, the only God Christians have come to know is Trinity: Father, Son, and Holy Spirit" (*Wilderness Wanderings: Probing Twentieth-Century Theology and Philosophy* [Boulder: Westview, 1997], 29). In a similar vein, L. Gregory Jones asserts, "Christians are not concerned primarily with theism (i.e., the notion that there is a general object of ultimate concern, a divinity); we are concerned, rather, to narrate the doctrine of God's Trinity. The Christian affirmation of the Trinity is not a notion 'added to' a theistic affirmation; it *is* the primary affirmation about the God Christians worship" (*Embodying Forgiveness: A Theological Analysis* [Grand Rapids: Eerdmans, 1995], 84).

71. As Clark Pinnock says, "God's nature is that of a communion of three Persons who exist in mutual relations with one another. Each is distinct from the others, but

Along with relationality, the doctrine of the Trinity also applies temporality to the inner being of God. In Keith Ward's words, it stresses "the creative, relational, and unitive involvement of God in the temporal structure of the created universe" and "the importance of that temporal structure to the self-expression of the divine being."[72] Robert Jenson is more emphatic: "The three derive from God's reality in time, from time's past/present/future. . . . The relations are either *temporal* relations or empty verbiage."[73]

The doctrine of the Trinity also allows us to attribute contingency to the inner reality of God. Process thinkers insist that the existence of a contingent world is necessary because ultimate reality must be both necessary and contingent. Open theists can accept the principle that ultimate reality is both necessary and contingent without requiring the premise that the world has always existed. The process position is that God would have nothing to experience, and would therefore lack actuality, unless a nondivine creaturely world also existed. But on a trinitarian concept, God does not need the world in order to enjoy contingent experiences. There is relationality and contingency within God's total reality with or without the world.[74]

---

each is what it is in relation to the others. God exists in a dynamic of love, an economy of giving and receiving" (*Flame of Love: A Theology of the Holy Spirit* [Downers Grove, Ill.: InterVarsity Press, 1996], 30). Or, to quote LaCugna once again, "The point of the doctrine of the Trinity is that God's *ousia* exists only in persons who are toward another, with another, through another" (LaCugna, *God for Us,* 193). Elizabeth A. Johnson makes the same point: "Trinitarian communion itself is primordial, not something to be added after the one God is described, for there is no God who is not relational through and through." "For God as God, divine nature is fundamentally relational" (*She Who Is: The Mystery of God in Feminist Theological Discourse* [New York: Crossroad, 1994], 227, 228).

72. Ward, *Religion and Creation,* 345.

73. Jenson, *Triune Identity,* 125-26.

74. Without the world, God's experience would be significantly different, of course, but that doesn't mean he wouldn't have any experience at all. My retired parents occasionally looked after my young nephew when my sister and her husband left town. During his visits they devoted themselves entirely to his needs – they transported him, fed him, entertained him, bathed him, and storied him at the end of the day. One afternoon during such a visit, Jed turned to his busy grandparents with a quizzical look on his face. "Grandma and Grandpa," he asked, "what do you do all day when I'm not here?" At his age, he was unable to comprehend their lives apart from their involvement with him. Our inability to conceive of God without a world is the result of limited insight or imagination. It is not an indication of metaphysical necessity.

According to process thought the world loses value unless it exists necessarily, but the doctrine of the Trinity shows that the contingent world has profound significance for the inner life of God. As Pannenberg argues, God's decision to create is entirely free; but having chosen to create, God commits himself so profoundly to the world that his very existence is bound up with what he has made.[75] God willingly links his own destiny to the destiny of the world, and henceforth God's dealings with the world both express and fulfill the divine reality.

The Son brings into existence a creation distinct from God out of his own eternal self-distinction from the Father.[76] Through the Spirit the Son brings the creatures into his own fellowship with the Father.[77] The goal of creation is thus "the participation of creatures in the trinitarian fellowship of the Son with the Father."[78] The future of the world is nothing other than God's own future.

These ideas only hint at the richness of recent trinitarian reflection, but they show that the trinitarian view of God affirms many of the essential insights of process theism. On the trinitarian account of God, the divine reality is essentially relational and temporal, and the world has intradivine significance – all concerns that are central to process thought. But whereas process philosophy regards the existence of the world as a matter of divine necessity, trinitarian theism attributes the world's existence to the freedom of divine love. God is under no compulsion to create; he chooses to create. Having chosen to create, God commits himself unconditionally and sacrificially to the world he loves. He devotes himself to its welfare, expresses his innermost life in his care for it, and finds his own fulfillment in bringing it into the fellowship of his own life.

A Permanent Divide

Process thinkers and open theists are united by a commitment to the principle that God is love. But a profound difference in their respective

75. Pannenberg, *Systematic Theology,* 1:447.
76. Ibid., 2:63; cf. 30, 58.
77. Ibid., 2:32.
78. Ibid., 2:75.

conceptions of love makes the division between them wide, and in my opinion, unbridgeable. Each group feels that the other denies something essential to its own concept of love.

For process thought, divine love consists in God's sensitivity to something other than God, to a world for whose sheer existence he is not responsible, though he shapes and guides it. Without relation-to-world, the concept of God is meaningless, indeed, oxymoronic. By contrast, for open theists divine love requires that creation be a choice. Only then can the existence of the world express the freedom that love entails. On the premise that creation is the freely chosen act of God, God's relation to the world becomes a display of God's inner reality, and God's costly commitment to the world has a profound effect on God's inner experience. Without the glorious freedom of love, our view of God is unacceptably diminished.

For proponents of the open view of God, then, process thought is a powerful philosophical vision and a valuable resource in developing biblical insights into God's experience. The process concept of divine power provides a helpful corrective to the view that God is directly responsible for everything that happens. With its concepts of divine dipolarity, creaturely self-determination, and divine persuasion, process thought contributes much to a genuinely interactive view of God's relation to the world. It shows clearly how a perfect being changes.

At the same time, the process insistence on the world's necessity conflicts with God's free and sovereign love. For process thought God's love is a pervasive influence within the world, but not a power over it. It consists in God's sensitivity to the creatures, but not a freely chosen commitment. If the world is just as fundamental, just as basic, as God is, then it does not originate in God's free decision. It cannot be the expression, the outpouring or overflow, of the love that God is. If God literally needs the world, if God could not be God without it, then God's relation to the world is not the free expression of divine generosity, and something important to God's love is lost.

In Response to Richard Rice

NANCY R. HOWELL

Dialogue between theologians is meaningful when two things occur. First, when there are discernible tensions between their theological positions, the theologians are in a conversation where creative contrasts have the potential to produce interesting questions and constructions. Second, when each theologian has made a serious effort to understand and engage the theology of the other, then each has earned the privilege of participating in genuine dialogue and offering significant criticism. The striking quality of "Process Theism and the Open View of God: The Crucial Difference" is the success with which Richard Rice engages in meaningful dialogue with process theism from the perspective of one who positions himself with the open view of God.

Rice's competence with Hartshorne's process metaphysics is the result of an empathetic reading of the philosopher. Rice writes with more than a general understanding and appreciation of Hartshorne's neoclassical, process theism. His knowledge of Hartshorne's philosophy and his openness to dialogue are evidenced in his detailed descriptions of the centrality of God in Hartshorne's metaphysics, of experience as paradigm, of freedom and determinism in relationships, and of the dipolar theism giving coherence to Hartshorne's metaphysics. Rice's understanding and openness are likewise present in his rebuttal of criticisms of process thought posed by Ronald Nash and Bruce Demarest. What Rice draws from his dialogue with Hartshorne is some commonality between the relational views of process theism and open, free will theism. The commonality of the two views is rooted, first, in rejection of classical theism and, second, in focus on the divine attributes of love and power.

Because of Rice's care in summarizing Hartshorne's neoclassical theism, my response is largely one of appreciation, and I have only one slight clarification for his description of Hartshorne's metaphysics. Using Hartshorne's language at points, Rice reports that God is the "self-identical individuality of the world,"[1] which means that the words *God* and *world* "are merely different ways of talking about the same thing." To avoid making Hartshorne's theism indistinguishable from pantheism, this point needs to be read in conjunction with the whole of Rice's discussion of Hartshorne's God. Rice characterizes Hartshorne's God as one who is clearly distinguishable from the world in the divine ability to suffer inclusively the affects of the world, to synthesize a world of events into divine experience, and to enjoy a range of freedom beyond human experience. The divine character is not limited to the world in Hartshorne's philosophy so that talking about God and the world are simply the same thing. As Rice rightly points out, however, Hartshorne's ultimate categories – experience, discreteness, freedom, society, and memory – are exemplified in both God and the world.

Comfortable that Rice understands neoclassical theism in the ways that I do, I want to concentrate the remainder of this response on dialogue between our differing perspectives. Rice invites dialogue on at least five points: (1) the reliance of theology on philosophy, (2) the relationship of God and the world, (3) the power of God and divine intervention, (4) the sociality of God, and (5) the freedom of God's creativity. If I understand his argument correctly, the relationship of God and the world is the locus of the crucial difference between process thought and the open view of God, and the last four points for dialogue concern this crucial difference.

With regard to the first point, the reliance of theology on philosophy, Rice defends process theism from conservative theological perspectives that criticize its use of philosophy. He credits process thought for assisting Christian theology in expressing the relational and personal na-

1. Rice cites Charles Hartshorne, *Man's Vision of God and the Logic of Theism* (Chicago: Willett, Clark, 1941), 230.

ture of God. Given that the Gospels and Epistles use philosophy to express witness to Christ in the early church, I conclude that philosophy is not the enemy of theology but one resource or tool for theological construction and reflection, one that has been present since the earliest Christian thought. Rice agrees that philosophy has an important role to play in theology. I think that Rice and I would agree that the issue is not whether philosophy can inform theology, but how.

Nevertheless, Rice contends that "process thought helps on the level of the universal and the categorical – in other words, on the level of God's relation to the cosmos – but becomes less helpful as it moves into attempts to describe the more particular, historical aspects of Christian faith." I offer three responses to Rice's assessment. First, I suggest that we be very clear about both the relationship and the difference between process philosophy and process theology. On the one hand, like John B. Cobb Jr., I believe that it is difficult, if not impossible, to write theology free from the influences of a worldview or vision of reality. If this is true, then most or all Christian theology is informed by philosophy simply because of the contextual nature of human thought and expression. Likewise, it is hard to imagine that Hartshorne or Whitehead would have generated their metaphysics in quite the same ways apart from the influences of Christianity in their personal and historical contexts. On the other hand, I acknowledge that there are different intents in writing metaphysics and in constructing theology. Metaphysics, as Rice says, is concerned with universal and categorical matters, while Christian theology addresses the particular experience and historical claims of Christian communities. Second, given that metaphysics and theology can be distinguished (even as they can be related), I observe that proponents of the open view of theism more often choose process philosophers and metaphysics for its dialogue partners than Christian process theologians and their theologies. For example, Rice has chosen Hartshorne to represent process thought rather than its most notable theologians, such as John Cobb, Bernard Loomer, Marjorie Suchocki, or Bernard Lee. Finally, I would contend that process theology rather than process metaphysics addresses the historical Christian church and its particular events and experiences. For example, Cobb and Suchocki have written within the Wesleyan tradition as process theologians whose intent is to support the historical identity of the United Methodist Church and to challenge and enrich Christianity as a whole. Further, process metaphysics assists process theology in explaining not just "what always happens" but "what sometimes happens." For example, the relational power of God is the explanation for novelty in the world. The novelty that enters the world through God, for example, gives us an explanation for the good that we see in a world that reasonably leads us to expect evil.[2] Saying this, I simultaneously see that process theology, as a more recent option in theology, has work to do. A number of theological doctrines and questions have not been addressed well or at all, but the unfinished tasks are not sufficient to discredit the potential of process theology to support contemporary faith and meaningful Christian experience.

The second point concerns what Rice calls the crucial difference between process theology and the open view. Rice contends that "the ultimate metaphysical fact is God-and-world" for process theology and that "the ultimate metaphysical fact is not God-and-world, but God, period" for the open view of God. The importance of this distinction, in Rice's estimation, is that process theism requires a world in relation to divine love and the open view excludes a necessary world for the sake of divine love. Rice asserts, "Unless the world owes its existence to God's free choice, divine love is a vacuous concept." If I may, I interpret Rice to mean that the contingency of the world preserves the independence of God as well as the absolute dependence of the world.

My interpretation of Rice's concern is that it sets up a false dichotomy from which, Rice contends, process thought has chosen the option of a necessary world, while the open view has chosen the option of a contingent world. My view is that the world is in a sense both necessary and contingent. Rice is correct that *a* world is necessary, but this particular world is not necessary. With respect to this particular world, God had the freedom not to act persuasively upon events and relationships to enable its existence. This means that this particular world depends on God for its very existence. Process philosophy and theology provide a way for me to express both God's freedom and my dependence without compromising creaturely freedom or minimizing God's identity as Creator, which I express in terms of panentheism. My sense is not that I am driving Christian theology with process philosophy, but that process thought pro-

2. John B. Cobb Jr., "The Problem of Evil and the Task of Ministry," in *Encountering Evil: Live Options in Theodicy*, ed. Stephen T. Davis (Atlanta: John Knox, 1981), 175.

vides a tool that supports my prior Christian commitments to God's creativity, freedom, love, and power – divine attributes grounded in biblical tradition and central to my understanding of God.

A third point concerns the power of God and divine intervention. Rice charges process thought with the view that God never acts unilaterally. His understanding is that process thought sets up a dichotomy between coercive and persuasive power). Rice cites both Hartshorne and David Griffin as persons who reject coercive power in such a way that God influences everything and determines nothing). Griffin derives his view of creation out of chaos and his view of the problem of evil from this critical choice between divine persuasive and coercive power. Rice claims that "process thinkers are mistaken in framing theistic options in stark, either-or terms – either coercion or persuasion, either divine tyranny or a necessary world." God's nonintervention is not the issue for Rice; he is more comfortable with Nancey Murphy and George Ellis's kenotic view of God: God's nonintervention is a policy rather than a necessity. For Rice the issue is actually the necessity of the world.

In response to Rice's concern about God's power and intervention, I make two comments. First, it is not the case that persuasion and coercion are mutually exclusive for all process thought. Indeed, I think that I was at one point disappointed to learn that process thought had not eliminated coercive power from God. It might be more accurate to say that the primary mode of God's power is persuasive rather than coercive. While God's interaction with the world occurs primarily by relational, persuasive power, for example, it is also the case that God determines how the multiplicity of the world will be unified in God's being. Second, God's persuasive, relational power heightens the intervention of God rather than diminishing it. Divine intervention is maximized in process theology and philosophy, which understand God's power as continually and pervasively intervening in the world by influence on every creature and moment. The continual influence of God on the world is significant in process thought, because "apart from the intervention of God, there could be nothing new in the world, and no order in the world."[3]

3. Alfred North Whitehead, *Process and Reality* (1929), corrected ed., ed. David Ray Griffin and Donald W. Sherburne (New York: Free Press, 1978), 247.

The fourth point for dialogue is the sociality of God. Rice poses the question, "What is the 'other' that divine love requires?" For process thought, Rice answers "the world." For the open view of God, the answer is that divine love is first self-referential and is manifest within the divine life itself. The Trinity itself is the fundamental, internal expression of divine love in the social, relational inner life of God. My interpretation of divine sociality in process thought differs somewhat from Rice's. Again, I think that Rice constructs a dichotomy that requires theology to choose between the external and internal sociality in God. I do not agree that the choice between God's interaction with the world and God's interaction within the Godhead is mutually exclusive. I find panentheism to be a helpful way to give coherence to both modes of God's sociality. I most certainly see that the Trinity is complexly relational, dynamic, contingent, and lively, but I simultaneously affirm God's loving, dynamic, living relationship with the world. The Genesis creation stories and the Gospel testimonies to God, Christ, and Holy Spirit are equally compelling to me as givens in the Christian tradition. The biblical texts do not speak to me of either a world without God or God without the world; thus as a theologian, my task is to account for both God's interior relationality and God's relation with the world, both of which are internal to God in process thought. God is not "thinkable" to me without Trinity, incarnation, and creation as ways of naming God's relationality.

The final point for dialogue concerns God's freedom to create. Rice brings the argument full circle by asserting that God is and was under no compulsion to create the world. Rice's conclusion reminds the reader that the existence of the world is a result of God's freedom exercised in consistency with divine love, which cares for the world and brings the world "into the fellowship of [God's] own life." As a process theologian, I could not agree more with Rice's view of God. First, as I wrote earlier, God was not compelled to create *this* world. Our world is a result of God's free creative action in relation to emerging creative and created beings. Second, I agree with Rice that God's fulfillment is connected with the divine relationship with the world. Third, I affirm that God's creative work is the kingdom of heaven. Whitehead describes how the kingdom of heaven is present with us: "What is done in the world is transformed into a reality in heaven, and the reality in heaven passes back into the world. By reason of this reciprocal relation, the love in the world passes into the love in heaven, and floods back again into the world."[4] Fourth, the Christian and biblical traditions compel me to understand God as Creator, and my task as theologian is concerned with who God is as Creator. Whether God was and is compelled to create is less central to my theology than the essential attribute of divine creativity.

In the end, the dialogue confirms that there are differences, perhaps even crucial differences, between process theology and open view theism. My conclusion is that perhaps the truly crucial difference among the authors in this volume has to do with the status of our differences for theology. What difference do our differences make? The answer to this question does not neatly divide us into process theologians or open view theists. My understanding of theology welcomes the differences as a sign of health in Christian theology. On the one hand, the contrasts between our theological worldviews encourages creative discourse. We are raising questions for each other and ourselves that we are not likely to have asked without this dialogue. On the other hand, I believe that Christian faith is enhanced by different theological worldviews. One task of theology is to be evocative. Easy resolution or dismissal of difference risks losing the forms of expression that call us back to the tradition and forward to the new creation. Living with the differences is an act of grace that preserves the diverse metaphors and concepts that affirm our dependence on God and our relationship with God.

4. Ibid., 351.

In Response to Richard Rice

DAVID L. WHEELER

As I read Richard Rice's contribution to our conversation, I am struck, as I was in reading Nancy Howell's, at the importance of our personal journeys in forming our convictions and commitments. This is especially striking given that Rice, Howell, and I all understand our roots to be "evangelical," and whatever that controverted term might be taken to mean, it certainly includes an understanding of God's self-revelation in Holy Scripture as foundational to both our conceptualizing and our living out of our faith. Holy Scripture, though it is itself full of narrated journeys, now exists as a fixed canon, a fact that can easily yield the inference that there is a univocal, objective truth content to Christian faith that transcends and relativizes the novel contents of our various journeys.

This inference has been incarnated in evangelical circles in forms as varied as "one size fits all" evangelistic tracts ("The Four Spiritual Laws") and attempts to construe the theological task as a Scripture-based deductive exercise.[1] But when we share our personal journeys, and connect them to and contrast them with others' journeys, we imply that there is something truly contingent and different about our experience of the Holy in contrast with other (perhaps) equally profound and true experiences. This is why I have preferred to "compare and con-

1. See, e.g., Carl F. H. Henry's explication and defense of such a method in *Toward a Recovery of Christian Belief* (Wheaton, Ill.: Crossway Books, 1990).

trast" theological insights, concepts, and models, moving intentionally and self-consciously along the boundaries of schools of thought and confessional positions, rather than staking out defined positions. This personal predilection is evident both in my contribution to this volume (chapter 3 above) and in my writing in general. It also shapes my response to Rice.

Rice's treatment of process-relational thought is appreciative and well informed; the tone of his writing is every bit as irenic and supportive of genuine dialogue as my work or Howell's. Indeed, I would go further and say that his explication of the thought of Hartshorne (pp. 167-74) and his appreciation of Hartshorne's insights constitute an outstanding brief introduction to that seminal figure for our shared readers. And his cogent critique of Nash and Demarest ("Some Conservative Misunderstandings of Process Thought," pp. 177-79), if seriously attended to, would short-circuit much misconstrued rhetoric that typically threatens the sort of dialogue we aspire to in this symposium. Nevertheless, there is a different agenda at work here – one more reflective of evangelical thought's penchant for precise distinctions and mutually exclusive *choices.* From his title – "Process Theism and the Open View of God: *The Crucial Difference*" (my italics) – through his statement of purpose on pp. 163-64 of his essay ("our objective here is to locate the place where two visions of God – process theism and open theism – diverge") and continuing on through the length of the essay, Rice makes numerous finely drawn distinctions and vigorously defends his choices.

In a sense, this critique of Rice is a "no-brainer"; as I remember our colleague Clark Pinnock describing his original vision for this book, theologians and philosophers were to offer their assessments of the value inherent in and the learnings possible from an evangelical-process dialogue, and we understood ourselves from the beginning to be arranged along a continuum of commitments from strongly evangelical to strongly process. Any such dialogue would of course involve drawing distinctions and making judgments about more and less adequate doctrinal positions. I myself, where I find biblical testimony and widespread religious intuitions supporting an understanding of God's metaphysical ultimacy and God's *chosen* reciprocity with the world, come down on the side of the open theists on the question of the nature of the divine limitation that both they and process theists affirm.

Rice calls this limitation "divine restraint" and connects it with the historically well-attested "kenotic" tradition, which he finds most recently exemplified by Nancey Murphy and George Ellis. "Murphy and Ellis view God's nonintervention as a matter of divine policy rather than metaphysical necessity. God does not intervene, because he chooses not to, not because it lies beyond his capacity to do so."

But I do not programmatically approach the intersection of process thought and more specifically Christian theisms – whether they be "classical" or "open" – with a set purpose of validating one or the other. Rather, I envision the divine reality as a vast and wonderful mystery that we humans are graced to know along the edges, as it were, of its intersection with the self-aware reality that is most immediately ourselves. The conceptual systems and the ritual words and actions through which we structure and express that knowing are at the same time radically perspectival and potential bearers of truth. As numerous philosophers and theologians have taught us in this generation, theological language – if not all descriptive language – is analogical; we describe partially, and combine and connect our metaphors to construct models of reality with different degrees of fit, coherence, and illuminating power relative to the divine reality.[2] Our descriptions gather about the divine reality like the four and twenty elders surrounding God's throne in John's Apocalypse (Revelation 4:4), and their truth function, in the nature of the case, may partake more of "complementarity" than the law of the excluded middle.[3]

I am not advocating theological relativism here. I do believe in a God of truth and in the existence of more and less appropriate descriptions of God's reality. Furthermore, I believe that our descriptions of God shape our expectations and behaviors, so their degree of truthfulness matters. For instance, process theists and open theists agree that a genuinely responsive God exists in relationship with humans and other creatures who have substantial freedom vis-à-vis God, and therefore we agree that prayer to God and lives of freely cho-

2. For a good description and analysis of the contemporary discussion, see Garrett Green, *Imagining God: Theology and the Religious Imagination* (Grand Rapids: Eerdmans, 1998).

3. The reference is to the complementary function in scientific theories of multiple models that may seem incompatible when taken literally; the classic case is the description of light as both wave function and particulate field.

sen discipleship genuinely affect the course of our life together. But given our radical finitude, and our dramatic differences in temperament, personal experience, and cultural context, I prefer to imagine a plurality of conceptualities in continual dialogue and mutual transformation, rather than some eventual resolution in terms of one or the other of them.

I myself have my standpoint, along the evangelical/process relational boundary – if truth be told, just over on the evangelical side of the boundary. Therefore I typically privilege Holy Scripture as a normative theological source among a plurality of sources, as illustrated above in my remarks about the divine self-limitation. Indeed, I follow Rice on many of the distinctions he draws. "Process thought and Christian theology belong to different realms of discourse." Of course: one attempts to give a comprehensive explanation of generic human experience; the other interprets and applies a specific, concrete religious experience. "My belief is that process thought helps on the level of the universal and the categorical – in other words, on the level of God's relation to the cosmos – but becomes less helpful as it moves into attempts to describe the more particular, historical aspects of Christian faith." Once again, of course: categories are exemplified by specific, contingent realities; they can never generate the realities, nor can the realities be reduced to the categories. But it is precisely because philosophical categories and concrete faith assertions play different roles in our discourse about reality that I am uncomfortable speaking as forthrightly as Rice does about where "process theism and the open view of God diverge."

"Of course they diverge," one might say, "but not necessarily because one is right and the other is wrong. Rather, it is because they are about radically different ways of processing experience." Case in point: in process philosophy, "the ultimate metaphysical fact is God-and-world. . . . For the open view of God, the situation is radically different. The ultimate metaphysical faith is not God-and-world, but God, period." This appears to be an irreconcilable difference and to pose a paradigmatic case of the law of the excluded middle. But the process God emerges as an implicate of a metaphysical analysis of the world, as Rice himself explains, so of course God is always found with the world and vice versa. Biblical theism purports to introduce to us, as a deliverance of faith, the original limiting condition – God alone – of the same

God-and-world reality within which and only within which the biblical theist experiences God. (Thus most traditional theists today agree with Hume et al. that reason and experience alone cannot carry us beyond our experience to its unaccompanied origin and limiting condition; i.e., the traditional philosophical proofs for the existence of God fail.)

So why must we oppose process theism and an explicitly biblical theism at this point? Metaphysical analysis gives a conceptuality of God-and-world, which – one might argue – is as far as we get outside revelation; the faith vision of biblical theism gives us God both with and beyond the world. One might argue that to fault process metaphysics in light of the concrete faith of the Bible for not having an ultimately transcendent Divine Ultimate manifests the same kind of category mistake religious creationists make when they fault secular scientists for not acknowledging a transcendent Creator, and then attempt to make their biblically attested God do the work of worldly causes. Why not let each conceptuality do its work, and let them complement each other, rather than forcing decisions on issues that may lie on opposite sides of categoreal boundaries?

If I had the space, I would respond in a similar vein to Rice's disjunctive treatment of the process and the open views of divine love and divine power. As I argued in my own essay, religious convictions entertained in supposed neutrality as to worldview frame their conceptual content, often uncritically, in terms of some worldview absorbed from the dominant culture. Better to choose intentionally a worldview for its power and integrity on its own terms, and bring our religious experience, pure and unadulterated, into dialogue with it, also on its own terms. Where the religious content lends vivid concreteness to the worldview, and the worldview a universalizing context to the religious content, so much the better for both of them. But that does not mean that they must be exhaustively harmonized from the point of view of either.

Rice says: "I still think that philosophical reflection has an important role to play in Christian thought. Christianity has always been a missionary religion. From the beginning its adherents faced the task of communicating their convictions to the world around them. To be faithful to our heritage we must look for ways to give our beliefs serious intellectual expression." I heartily agree. I think all of us in this dialogue have tried to do just this. I also must say in all candor that if thinkers such as Rice and Griffin all insisted on the sort of both/and strategy I am advocating in this response to Rice, there would be no open theism and process theism positions as such to compare and contrast. I honor the technical skill and the firm commitments exemplified in these positions that are more determined than my own. But I submit that in my meandering along boundaries, I am in my own way exemplifying both the openness and evolving character of the process worldview and the "walking by faith" (cf. Hebrews 11:8) characteristic of evangelical faith. "For now we see through a glass, darkly . . ." (1 Corinthians 13:12, KJV).

5 An Adequate God

WILLIAM HASKER

The theme of this essay is "an adequate God." But does that make sense? Is God merely "adequate"? Do we really want to say that the "creator of heaven and earth, of all things visible and invisible," is "adequate"? Clearly, it is *our conceptions* of God that must be evaluated as adequate or inadequate, not God himself.[1] But "adequate" in what sense? The medievals defined truth as *aedequatio intellectus ad rei*, the "adequation of the intellect to the thing." But "adequacy" in this sense is difficult to assess in the case of God, who is not in a straightforward way available for us to compare with our conceptions of him. Let us ask, then, a question that may be slightly easier to answer: What conception of God is adequate for the faith and life of the Christian church? That faith and life, at least, are in some way available for our assessment, though what conclusions we should draw about them may not be immediately obvious.

To be sure, the reference to the "faith and life of the church" cannot be taken as a comprehensive statement on theological methodology; indeed, no such statement can be attempted here. Like many others, I am impressed with the wisdom implicit in the "Wesleyan quadrilateral" of Scripture, tradition, reason, and experience. But to say

1. I follow biblical, and traditional Christian, usage in using masculine pronouns to refer to God, while recognizing that neither sex nor gender properly applies to the divine being.

this leaves us with the large and challenging task of specifying the relationships among the four elements in the quadrilateral, and of showing in detail how they interact in reaching specific theological conclusions. That task lies far beyond the scope of this essay. I may note, however, that the use of the faith and life of the church as a touchstone is at the very least highly consistent with the Wesleyan quadrilateral. The church has always sought to be faithful to Scripture and to its own traditions; it has sought to present its teachings in such a way as to be congruent with right reason; and the "experience" mentioned in the quadrilateral is an integral part of the church's life. Perhaps some process theologians will object that the proposed criterion gives in effect too much weight to tradition, as opposed to reason and experience. That is a fair comment; on the other hand, if a particular school of theology finds itself compelled to reject conclusions that have been seen as essential by a strong consensus of Christian thinkers throughout the history of the church, that fact deserves serious notice. Christian tradition is by no means an absolute authority, even when a particular tradition is supported by a broad consensus. But neither should such a tradition be abandoned without compelling reasons.

My present concern is to compare the understanding of God in process theism[2] with the view associated with the phrase, "the openness of God."[3] But before I pursue the undeniable differences, I want to speak of some important areas of agreement between the two views. One such agreement is the following: God is really related to his creatures, where "really related" means that it makes a difference to God how things are with the creatures. For example, God's state in knowing that the Berlin Wall came down in 1989 is a different state than God would have been in had he known, instead, that the wall was still standing in 1998. On a personal note, let me state that I first became clearly convinced of this through reading Charles Hartshorne's *Divine Relativ-*

2. My discussion of process theism is based largely on John B. Cobb Jr. and David Ray Griffin, *Process Theology: An Introductory Exposition* (Philadelphia: Westminster, 1976); and John B. Cobb Jr., *A Christian Natural Theology: Based on the Thought of Alfred North Whitehead* (Philadelphia: Westminster, 1974), as well as some of Charles Hartshorne's writings.

3. See Clark Pinnock, Richard Rice, John Sanders, William Hasker, and David Basinger, *The Openness of God: A Biblical Challenge to the Traditional Understanding of God* (Downers Grove, Ill.: InterVarsity Press, 1994).

ity.[4] Prior to reading Hartshorne, I had puzzled over the medieval doctrine that, while the creatures are really related to God, God has only a "relation of reason" to the creatures.[5] That God is really related to the creatures is a genuine and important point of agreement between process theism and the open view of God.

A second point of agreement, which builds on the first, is that God is affected by the state of his creatures, and suffers when things go badly for them. Here again, I am indebted to process thinkers for nudging me out of my state of perplexed indecision about the medieval doctrine of divine impassibility. The decisive impetus in this case came from John Cobb and David Griffin's trenchant critique of the views of Anselm and Thomas Aquinas concerning the divine compassion.[6] Both of these worthies held, in essence, that God acts as we would expect a compassionate being to act, but that any feeling of sympathy or compassion is altogether alien to God. Once I saw clearly what the doctrine of impassibility amounted to, it seemed entirely evident to me that such a doctrine cannot possibly be true. "As a father pities his children, so the Lord pities those who fear him" – that is the faith and, still more, that is the experience of the people of God through the ages.[7]

Yet a further area of agreement between process theism and the open view concerns the nature and implications of human freedom. Both of our views reject the compatibilist notion of freedom, which holds that free will is compatible with causal determination. In rejecting this, we also reject the notion of God as all-controlling, as the sole determiner of everything that takes place in the universe. Instead, we affirm the incompatibilist, or libertarian, view according to which one

4. Charles Hartshorne, *The Divine Relativity: A Social Conception of God* (1948; reprint, New Haven and London: Yale University Press, 1964).

5. Let me add a word here by way of explanation. Like many Christian philosophers of my generation, I first encountered a philosophically serious theism in the classical theism of Augustine, Anselm, and Thomas Aquinas. We rightly understood them to have devoted careful and profound thought to the proper understanding of God, and as a result their views tended to be privileged in a certain way for us, even though a number of those views were eventually rejected.

6. See Cobb and Griffin, *Process Theology,* 44-46.

7. For a powerful critique of divine impassibility from a standpoint that is close to the one adopted here, see Nicholas Wolterstorff, "Suffering Love," in *Philosophy and the Christian Faith,* ed. Thomas V. Morris (Notre Dame, Ind.: University of Notre Dame Press, 1988), 196-237.

is free only if one would be able, under exactly the same circumstances, to refrain from the act that one has in fact chosen, and to do something else instead. This view, to be sure, is held in common with many of our fellow Christians in various traditions. But the further conclusion drawn from this is more controversial: Since the future is genuinely open, since it is possible for a free agent to act in any of several different ways, it follows that it is not possible for God to have complete and exact knowledge of the entire future.[8] This does not, we go on to say, compromise divine omniscience. Just as, by common consent, omnipotence is defined as God's ability to do whatever it is logically possible for a perfect being to do, so also omniscience should be defined as God's knowing whatever it is logically possible for a perfect being to know – and logically the free, contingent future can be known not with certainty but only with a degree of probability.

Let me emphasize that I mention these points of agreement here not merely out of the irenic desire to establish some common ground before entering areas of controversy. The agreements in question – that it makes a difference to God how things are in the world, that he cares what befalls us and rejoices and suffers along with us, and that he allows us genuine freedom to affect the open future – these are real, and extremely substantive, areas of mutual agreement, and they stake out clearly our common opposition to some important trends in traditional theology. But there are also major differences between our two views, and these I must now address. I consider them under three main topics: God creates; God acts; and God communicates.

God Creates

The traditional Christian doctrine of creation may be stated concisely, since it is generally well known. God is the sole eternal, self-existent being. The divine eternity has often been understood as timelessness, but the open view holds rather that God is everlasting – without beginning or end, but nevertheless undergoing a sequence of experiences, even apart from God's relation to the creation. The created universe, com-

8. For my own development of this and related arguments, see *God, Time, and Knowledge* (Ithaca: Cornell University Press, 1989).

prising all of concrete reality with the exception of God himself, came into existence ex nihilo, out of nothing, by the sheer will and command of God. Furthermore, all created things depend on God for their existence from moment to moment; this is the divine "conservation" of created reality. As to the particular character of the creation, its original nature was wholly determined by God, and its subsequent changes occur (apart from instances of direct divine intervention) according to the inherent powers with which God has endowed the various creatures, exercised in ways that God may or may not actively endorse, but which he has chosen to permit to occur. Highly characteristic of the entire situation is the one-sided ontological dependence of the universe on God – a dependence, however, that does not exclude that creatures have in many respects exercised their God-given and God-sustained powers in ways contrary to God's intentions for them. Combining this point with the earlier emphasis on the real relation of God to the creatures, one may say that God is ontologically independent of the creatures and yet also, by his own gracious decision, relationally dependent on them. God has freely chosen to create beings that act in ways he does not directly control, and by which he is affected in significant ways.

The standard process conception of the world-God relationship stands in marked contrast with all of this. There are, for instance, Whitehead's well-known formulas in *Process and Reality*, in which God and the world are juxtaposed:

> It is as true to say that God is permanent and the World fluent, as that the World is permanent and God is fluent.
>
> It is as true to say that the World is immanent in God, as that God is immanent in the World.
>
> It is as true to say that God transcends the World, as that the World transcends God.
>
> It is as true to say that God creates the World, as that the World creates God.[9]

Significantly, Whitehead goes on to say, "God and the World are the contrasted opposites in terms of which Creativity achieves its supreme

9. Alfred North Whitehead, *Process and Reality* (New York: Macmillan, 1929), 528.

task of transforming disjoined multiplicity, with its diversities in opposition, into concrescent unity, with its diversities in contrast."[10]

These formulas conflict strongly with the church's faith in creation, and were no doubt so intended by Whitehead, who, as Cobb remarks, often "opposes the various connotations of the term 'creator' as applied to God."[11] When Whitehead's philosophy was appropriated for Christian theology, it became impossible simply to dismiss the notion of creation, given its deep entrenchment in Christian tradition. But it is also well-nigh impossible for process thinkers to affirm creation in anything approaching the traditional sense. Creation, for process thought, is not ex nihilo; it is rather a sort of divine "shaping" of realities already in existence, a shaping that depends for its effect on the response of those already existent realities. Hartshorne compares God's creating with the way in which any social being – humans being the prime example – "creates," in part, the life of the society to which she or he belongs: "The more important members of a society contribute more largely and vitally to the actuality of other members. The supreme member of a society would contribute most vitally and largely to the actuality of all."[12] He also observes that what distinguishes God's creation from ours is that "the preceding phase was itself created by God, so that he, unlike us, is never confronted by a world whose coming to be antedates his own entire existence."[13] This is true enough, but the Whiteheadian symmetry still holds: it is also the case that each previous stage of God's life was in part "created" (i.e., conditioned) by the world, so that the world "is never confronted by a Deity whose being antedates its own entire existence." From the standpoint of the church's faith in creation this conception of God as, in effect, primus inter pares is deeply unsatisfying.

But does this really matter? Is this traditional conception of creation a genuine part of the vital faith of the community? Or is it, as Hartshorne implies, merely the result of some early, and not overly successful, attempts to "harmonize Greek philosophical and Judaic reli-

10. Ibid.

11. *Christian Natural Theology,* 203-4.

12. *Divine Relativity,* 29. For a more extensive discussion, see "Creation Through Evolution," chap. 3 of Hartshorne's *Omnipotence and Other Theological Mistakes* (Albany: SUNY Press, 1984).

13. *Divine Relativity,* 30.

gious views"[14] – a harmony, to be sure, that is hampered by "a dubious interpretation of an obscure parable, the book of Genesis"?[15]

I think it matters a great deal. Consider, for example, Yahweh's challenge to Job in the concluding chapters of that book:

> Where were you when I laid the earth's foundation?
> Tell me, if you understand.
> Who marked off its dimensions? Surely you know!
> Who stretched a measuring line across it?
> On what were its footings set,
> or who laid its cornerstone –
> while the morning stars sang together,
> and all the angels shouted for joy?
>
> (Job 38:4-7, NIV)

After a good deal more in this vein, Job replies,

> I know that you can do all things;
> no plan of yours can be thwarted. . . .
> Surely I spoke of things I did not understand,
> things too wonderful for me to know. . . .
> My ears had heard of you
> but now my eyes have seen you.
> Therefore I despise myself
> and repent in dust and ashes.
>
> (Job 42:1, 2, 5-6, NIV)

Isn't the majesty of God as creator seen here as an integral aspect of the very Godhood of God? Could we reduce the creative role of God to that prescribed by Whitehead without undermining the entire conception of God that is being presented? To be sure, the language in the book of Job, as in many other parts of Scripture, is dramatic and poetically evocative rather than conceptually exact. One must exercise great care and circumspection in moving from such poetic and evocative language to articulated conceptual schemes such as

14. "Creation Through Evolution," 73.
15. *Divine Relativity,* 30.

those of the traditional doctrine of creation or of process theism. But not just any conceptual scheme is adequate to just any set of poetic metaphors, and I submit that the match between the Whiteheadian metaphysics and the powerful imagery of Job is awkward in the extreme.

In Isaiah, it is precisely the greatness of the Creator that provides the guarantee of an efficacious redemption:

> For this is what the LORD says –
> he who created the heavens,
> he is God;
> he who fashioned and made the earth,
> he founded it;
> he did not create it to be empty,
> but formed it to be inhabited . . .
> "Turn to me and be saved,
> all you ends of the earth;
> for I am God, and there is no other."
>
> (Isaiah 45:18, 22, NIV)

Passages such as these in Job and Isaiah, I submit, are not exactly redolent of armchair speculation. In framing his own conception of the divine, Whitehead was deliberately repudiating a view of God such as is presented in these passages; there is no point in our pretending, at this late date, that the two disparate conceptions can be reconciled.

Excursus on John B. Cobb Jr.

Or is there another way the process thinker can take here? I said above that it is well-nigh impossible for process thinkers to affirm creation in anything approaching the traditional sense. The reason for the qualification "well-nigh" is that at least one process thinker has proposed modifications in the Whiteheadian scheme that have the potential to bring it a great deal closer to the traditional doctrine of creation than the ideas surveyed thus far. I am referring to John B. Cobb Jr., who undertakes, in chapter 5 of *A Christian Natural Theology,* "to develop a doctrine of God more coherent with Whitehead's general cosmology and metaphysics than are some aspects of his own doctrine."[16] Let us see what Cobb has to offer.

One important shift recommended by Cobb is that we should think of God not as a single "actual entity" (as Whitehead did), but rather as a "living person" and thus as a "society or sequence" of occasions of experience (p. 188).[17] An even more important shift, however, concerns the role played by the "initial aim" in the coming-to-be of an actual occasion. As Cobb says, "God's role in creation centers in the provision to each actual occasion of its initial aim" (p. 203). The initial aim represents God's "ideal purpose" for the occasion in question; this purpose will be realized to a greater or lesser extent, depending on the "subjective aim" adopted by the occasion itself in its process of concrescence. So much is common among Cobb, Whitehead, and other Whiteheadians. Cobb's distinctive move, however, is to amplify the importance of the initial aim in comparison with other elements of the situation. He admits that "in some of [Whitehead's] statements he seems to imply a general equality of functioning between the initial aim and other elements in the initial phase." But, he claims, "in his detailed analyses no such equality obtains" (p. 204). Cobb's remarks in support of this need to be cited at some length:

> In the first place, the initial aim determines the standpoint that the occasion will occupy, its locus and extent in the extensive continuum. This, in turn, determines what occasions will be in its past, in its present, and its future. That means that the initial aim determines which occasions will constitute the past and therefore, the initial data of the new occasion. . . .
>
> For these reasons we may properly think of the initial aim as the originating element in each new occasion. Since Whitehead regards God as the sole ground of the initial aim, he systematically attributes to God the all-decisive role in the creation of each new occasion, although he draws back from so strong a formulation. (pp. 204-5)

16. *Christian Natural Theology,* 176. Page references in the text are to this work.

17. Due to limitations of both space and competence, I do not attempt here an exposition of the basic conceptions of process philosophy. Readers in need of such an exposition will find one in the first chapter of Cobb and Griffin's *Process Theology.*

Attention must also be given to the relation between God and "creativity." In some passages, Whitehead seems to subordinate God to creativity: "Neither God, nor the World, reaches static completion. Both are in the grip of the ultimate metaphysical ground, the creative advance into novelty."[18] Consider also Whitehead's previously quoted assertion that "God and the World are the contrasted opposites in terms of which Creativity achieves its supreme task of transforming disjoined multiplicity . . . into concrescent unity." Both of these passages suggest strongly that Creativity itself is the ontological ultimate, with God and the World being somehow instrumentalities through which Creativity achieves its "task." Cobb maintains, however, that one cannot grant creativity, as properly understood, the primordial causative and explanatory role such statements suggest. Creativity is not an actual entity of any kind; it is, in the final analysis, "another word for the change itself" (p. 210) that characterizes all actual entities. Cobb goes on to ask,

> Does the notion of change, or becoming, or process include in it some sense that this changing must have gone on forever and must continue to do so? On the contrary, it seems just as possible that it will simply stop, that there will be then just nothing. There is a radical and evident contingency about the existence of new units of creativity (actual entities). (pp. 210-11)

This in turn means that

> If the question as to why things are at all is raised in the Whiteheadian context, the answer must be in terms of the decisions of actual entities. We have already seen that the decisive element in the initiation of each actual occasion is the granting to that occasion of an initial aim. Since Whitehead attributes this function to God, it seems that, to a greater degree than Whitehead intended, God must be conceived as being the reason that entities occur at all as well as determining the limits within which they can achieve their own forms. God's role in creation is more radical and fundamental than Whitehead's own language usually suggests. (pp. 211-12)

18. *Process and Reality*, 529.

Putting all this together, I submit that Cobb has come very close indeed to the traditional doctrine of the divine conservation of all creaturely entities – to what has sometimes been called "continuous creation." For consider: Any continuing entity consists of a series of "actual occasions."[19] These occasions do not give rise to themselves, nor are they produced by the occasions of the past. There is, furthermore, no a priori guarantee that the sequence of occasions will continue; that they do so is determined by the appearance of the "initial aim" for each new occasion in the sequence, and this initial aim is contributed by God. In other words, the persistence of any entity in existence depends wholly on the divine activity – which is just what is affirmed by the doctrine of divine conservation. The existence of all created entities depends radically on the sustaining activity of God. On the other hand, God must (I think) be seen as contributing his own initial aim for each new occasion of experience of which his life consists. This gives a clear meaning to the traditional doctrine that God alone is self-existing and self-sufficient, in contrast with other things whose existence depends on him.

Indeed, Cobb suggests the possibility of going even farther than this. "I am not sure that the *possibility* 'that creativity originally had only a single instantiation' is strictly ruled out by Whitehead's metaphysics, but I am not interested in arguing this question here" (p. 205 n. 65). For creativity originally to have only a single instantiation would mean, of course, that in the beginning God was the only actual being in existence; other beings, then, would come to exist when God conferred on them their appropriate initial aims. Is this not a fair equivalent, within process thought, of creation ex nihilo? And since, in the case of the first entities created, there would be no previous entities other than God by which their initial aims might be conditioned, it will be the case after all that the creation's "original nature was wholly determined by God, and its subsequent changes occur . . . according to the inherent powers with which God has endowed the various creatures." At this point it seems extremely plausible that the remaining differences between the doctrine of creation

19. I shall not raise here the question whether this is indeed the best way to think about the existence of continuing entities. That question goes to the heart of Whitehead's general metaphysic, whereas my concern here is to explore the possibilities for a doctrine of creation within that metaphysic, as it has been developed and revised by Cobb.

suggested by Cobb and the traditional one are matters of philosophical detail rather than fundamental theological principle.

To be sure, Cobb presents this idea as a speculative possibility, and does so in a way that suggests that other Whiteheadians might not agree that it is possible. This suggestion is surely correct, with David Griffin serving as a prime example.[20] I am unable to adjudicate the disagreement about what is implied by Whitehead's metaphysics. But I think it is clear that the possibility in question is implied by Whitehead's metaphysics as modified and interpreted by Cobb. Consider the passage previously quoted from Cobb:

> Does the notion of change, or becoming, or process include in it some sense that this changing must have gone on forever and must continue to do so? On the contrary, it seems just as possible that it will simply stop, that there will be then just nothing. There is a radical and evident contingency about the existence of new units of creativity (actual entities). (pp. 210-11)

If the continuing occurrence of new units of creativity is "radically and evidently contingent," then surely the same must be true of the occurrence of nondivine units of creativity in the first place. If it is metaphysically possible for creation to have an end, it is also possible for it to have a beginning. On Cobb's principles, creation ex nihilo[21] becomes a genuine possibility.

In response to this, process thinkers may question whether creation ex nihilo, in the sense of an absolute temporal beginning, is after all an essential element in the traditional doctrine of creation. This question requires a somewhat complex response. Creation ex nihilo is at least strongly suggested by several biblical passages,[22] and has been a

20. When this chapter was presented orally, Griffin asserted, "I wish my teacher [i.e., Cobb] had not said it was possible that there be only a single instantiation of creativity."

21. Some thinkers apply the term *creatio ex nihilo* to the assertion that all created reality is radically dependent on God, regardless of whether there was a first moment of creation. For purposes of clarity, I always use the term in such a way that a first moment is implied.

22. For example, John 1:1-3; Romans 4:17; Colossians 1:15-16; and Hebrews 11:3. It seems probable, on the other hand, that Genesis 1:1-2 presupposes the existence of a primeval chaos.

consistent element in Christian teaching about creation since the early centuries of the church. It should be noted, furthermore, that the doctrine has not been and cannot be refuted scientifically: what would a scientific proof of the eternal existence of the cosmos look like?[23] At the worst, we might find ourselves in a position similar to that of Thomas Aquinas, who held that the question of the temporal beginning of the world was undecidable by reason but that a first moment of creation must be affirmed on the basis of revelation.[24]

Having said this, I must add the following: If God should have chosen to create a universe everlastingly, with no temporal beginning, there is no reason why this would imperil any other significant theological assertion. If it is within God's power to create a universe with a beginning, it is also in his power to create a universe without a beginning. What is essential, however, is that it is possible for the universe to have a temporal beginning, and the reason this is essential is that without this possibility the world would be metaphysically necessary for God, a view that Christian theology has always rejected.[25] One of the chief problems with the doctrine of an "eternal creation" is that it strongly suggests, even though it does not logically imply, the necessity of the world for God. Thus my response to the question above is as follows: While a temporal beginning of the created universe can and should be affirmed, what is theologically essential is not so much an actual temporal beginning as the metaphysical possibility of such a beginning. As we have seen, this possibility is guaranteed by Cobb's interpretation of Whiteheadian metaphysics, though it is rejected by many other process theists.

A final question: If God could exist apart from any universe, does

23. At present, to be sure, the implications of Big Bang cosmology seem to favor a temporal beginning for the creation, though this certainly should not be cited as an absolute proof.

24. Thomas was unusual, among medieval Christian thinkers, in holding that the temporal beginning of the cosmos was not rationally demonstrable. I judge that he was correct in rejecting the arguments that were put forward to prove this conclusion.

25. The necessity of the world for God was accepted by some medievals strongly influenced by Neoplatonism, such as the Muslim Avicenna and the Christian John Scotus Erigena. Such views were rejected alike by mainstream Muslims, Jews, and Christians. See David B. Burrell, *Freedom and Creation in Three Traditions* (Notre Dame, Ind.: University of Notre Dame Press, 1993).

this mean that the love and the relationality of God, so important to both the open and the process views, are merely contingent attributes of God? Not at all. What it does mean is that the love and relationality of God *toward the creation* are merely contingent — though even here, given that there is a creation, it is necessarily the case that God is related to it and loves it. But wholly apart from creation, love and relationship abound within God, in the eternal loving mutuality of the persons of the Trinity, the Father, the Son, and the Holy Spirit. A disquisition on the Trinity is clearly beyond the reasonable boundaries of the present essay. But at this point the Trinity needs to be mentioned all the same, because of the inner connection between the doctrine of the Trinity and that of creation.

Before leaving this topic I wish to say a word about my intentions in this section. It is not my claim that Cobb's version of the Whiteheadian metaphysics, as presented here, is the "right" or the "best" version of that metaphysics. My objective, rather, has been to explore the possibilities offered by Cobb's presentation for something that closely approximates the traditional Christian doctrine of the creation of all things by God. Whether this understanding of process thought is acceptable to its proponents is for them to say; I for one will be most interested in their response.

God Acts

Arguably, the Christian God is known first and foremost as an *agent,* one who is active in the world and in human life. Indeed, if God were not an agent it is difficult to see how we could know anything about him. Creation ex nihilo is an act of God, and so is the divine conservation in existence of the entities already created. At present, however, we are concerned with particular actions of God — things God does in one time and place, and not in other times or places. Both Scripture and Christian tradition are filled with accounts of such actions. Broadly speaking, the divine actions can be placed in two general categories: acts of personal influence, and acts involving the control of nature. Examples of the former category would include the work of the Holy Spirit in conversion and in enabling believers to develop spiritually, as well as in communicating to specific persons various insights and understandings. Examples of the latter category include the extensive range of biblical miracles – "signs and wonders." These, of course, exhibit a great deal of variety among themselves; they include miracles of healing, the sudden quieting of a dangerous storm, a bush burning without being consumed and a voice issuing from it – the list goes on and on. From the standpoint of traditional theism, there is nothing particularly problematic about God's ability to perform such miracles, since God is credited with omnipotence, defined as the power to do anything that is neither logically contradictory nor in conflict with God's moral perfection.

Process theism views these two classes of divine actions in somewhat different ways. The acts of personal influence are fairly readily accommodated by God's provision of the initial aim for each of the occasions of experience that serially make up a person's life. The initial aim does not, of course, control the person's response; there is no "irresistible grace" in this system. But with this reservation (which is generally agreeable to proponents of the open view) divine actions in this category need not create insurmountable difficulties.[26]

Divine acts involving the control of nature pose a more serious problem. To be sure, a divine "influence" that "shapes and guides" nature in certain directions is readily accommodated by process theism. (The process account of evolution, as directed by the divine "stimulus" inherent in God's provision of the initial aim for each occasion, is quite attractive.)[27] But the "persuasive" nature of divine action is taken to preclude the unilateral control over nature that is involved in the traditional view of miracles. Whatever "wonders" may occur must be ultimately explicable in terms of the inherent powers of the natural entities involved, as guided by the divine "initial aim" for each actual occasion. Some miracles of healing may pass muster, since it seems that human minds, when endued with sufficient faith, do possess remarkable capacities to bring about physical healing. But there will be no water from

26. In the final section of this chapter, I discuss some limitations of process theism's treatment of the acts of personal influence. Even so, it remains true that process theism more readily accommodates these divine actions than acts involving the control of nature.

27. For a discussion of evolution in this light, see chap. 4, "A Theology of Nature," in Cobb and Griffin's *Process Theology*.

wine, no miraculous multiplication of bread and fishes – and no bodily resurrection of Jesus from the dead.

Process thinkers are aware that this rejection of miracles seems to constitute a significant restriction of divine power, and thus arguably a diminution of the divine excellence and perfection. In response, they appeal in part to the "widespread belief that the nexus of natural cause and effect excludes divine 'intervention.'"[28] They also appeal to the problem of evil as a reason for rejecting the possibility of miraculous divine intervention, and they argue for the moral superiority of persuasion over control as the mode of divine activity in the world.[29]

From the standpoint of traditional Christianity, this stance is highly problematic. It may be true that disbelief in miracles is widespread among contemporary elite. But the notion that there are compelling scientific and philosophical arguments against the possibility of such divine actions is an Enlightenment myth we need to rid ourselves of. Science gives an account of the way natural entities function and interrelate with other natural entities; it cannot speak to the issue of what happens when a supernatural power (such as God) intervenes in the natural order.[30] Further, there are no compelling metaphysical arguments against miracles that do not already presuppose the truth of some competing worldview. There are, to be sure, certain epistemological difficulties, developed by Hume and his modern followers, about our ability to identify miraculous divine actions as such. But these difficulties, while genuine, are by no means conclusive.[31] A little reflection will show that it is unlikely that such epistemological objections could constitute a decisive barrier to reasonable belief in miracles. If God is able to perform miraculous actions, and desires to do so, isn't it reasonable to suppose that he would be able to do it in ways that per-

28. See *Process Theology,* 51.

29. Ibid., 50-54.

30. "To say that water has miraculously turned into wine, for example, is not to say that water has turned into wine under the exact set of natural conditions under which the relevant laws tell us this will not occur. It is to maintain that an additional nonnatural causal factor, namely direct divine activity, was also present in this case" (Michael Peterson et al., *Reason and Religious Belief: An Introduction to the Philosophy of Religion,* 2nd ed. [New York: Oxford University Press, 1998], 193).

31. For a balanced overview of the current discussion, see chap. 8, "Miracles: Does God Intervene in Earthly Affairs?" in ibid.

mit right-thinking persons to recognize the actions as coming from God?

Unfortunately for process theists, the appeals to the moral superiority of persuasion and to the problem of evil tend to cancel each other out. If persuasion is always and unconditionally morally superior to direct control, then there is no need to establish metaphysical limits on divine power, since a perfectly good God could be relied on not to use his power inappropriately. But the problem of evil implies strongly that persuasion is not in all cases morally superior to the use of power to control. The core complaint in the problem of evil is, Why didn't God prevent this? But this implies that a being with the sort of power God is said to have morally ought to use that power to prevent grave evils. In other words: in certain circumstances, it is morally preferable that power be used coercively, if this is necessary in order to prevent serious harms from occurring. To be sure, almost all of us will agree that, other things being equal, it is better for God to work persuasively, since only in that way can the desired relationship of friendship and mutual love between God and human beings be established. But that it is always wrong for power to be used in the form of direct control is something very few of us strongly believe.[32]

David Griffin agrees with this; he holds that the limitation on divine power is not ethical but metaphysical.[33] This avoids the problems cited in the previous paragraph, but it brings with it a new difficulty: If coercion is ethically justifiable in some circumstances, then it would seem that the most adequate conception of God would be of a being possessing both persuasive and coercive power, and using each as befits the occasion at hand. It may be true that metaphysical limits on divine power are implied by the Whiteheadian metaphysic. But that can scarcely be used to settle the present question; after all, it is precisely the ability of that metaphysic to support an adequate conception of God that is at issue.

In response to this Griffin has developed an extensive argument

32. The argument of this paragraph is indebted to chap. 3 of David Basinger, *Divine Power in Process Theism: A Philosophical Critique* (Albany: SUNY Press, 1988).

33. See Griffin's *Evil Revisited: Responses and Reconsiderations* (Albany: SUNY Press, 1991), 152-57. Griffin states that he has never used the ethical superiority of persuasion over coercion to justify the limitation on divine power. He acknowledges, however, that other process theologians have not always been so careful (ibid., 154).

purporting to show that the traditional conception of omnipotence is incoherent.[34] He claims that one cannot consistently hold both that God has created an actual world (i.e., a world containing actual beings other than God), and that God has unilateral power to prevent evil in that world. As a brief summary of his argument, consider the following:

> If the world is an actual creation, and not simply a complex idea in the divine mind, or simply aspects or "modes" of God, then all-powerful *cannot* mean having *all* the power. And if there are many centers of power, then no state of affairs in which these entities are involved can be completely determined by any one of them. . . . Although an actual world without genuine evil is possible, it is impossible for an omnipotent being to guarantee such a world.[35]

Spelled out a bit more fully, Griffin's argument can be represented as follows:

1. Necessarily, any actual being must possess some power of self-determination, and must be able to cause things it is not caused to cause.
2. Necessarily, any being with the power of self-determination is able to do evil.
3. Necessarily, if a being has the power to do a certain thing, then no other being has the power to prevent it from doing that thing.

Therefore,

4. Necessarily, if there is a universe containing actual beings other than God, these beings have power to do evil and God cannot prevent them from doing evil.[36]

34. Griffin's argument develops ideas suggested by Hartshorne, but the argument as given by Griffin is much more fully developed and so is better suited for the present discussion.

35. *God, Freedom, and Evil: A Process Theodicy* (Philadelphia: Westminster, 1976), 269-70.

36. Since the second and third premises are not clearly stated as such by Griffin, it may be helpful to provide a brief justification for their inclusion. If creatures could be

The argument is valid; if the premises are true, then so is the conclusion. But if even one premise is false, then the conclusion is not established. In this case I believe that all three premises are false, though this may be more obvious for some of the premises than for others. The first premise denies the possibility of any real being whose behavior is completely causally determined by previous events. This means, of course, that the physical objects posited by classical (pre-quantum) physics logically could not exist. To say the least, it is a pity someone did not point this out to Isaac Newton, who could have spared himself and his successors hundreds of years of incoherence! More recently, Einstein could have avoided spending several decades in futile resistance to quantum mechanics, if he had been enlightened as to the conceptual absurdity of his deterministic stance.

The second premise rules out the possibility of a being capable of self-determination yet incapable of doing evil. For traditional theology, however (and, one would hope, for process theology as well), God is the preeminent example of a self-determining Being whose absolute moral perfection renders him incapable of doing evil.

The third premise, however, is the one that is most obviously unacceptable. I have the power to drive my car to the store and purchase a loaf of bread. But if a freight train plows into my car as I cross the tracks, I will be unable to exercise my power to buy the loaf of bread. To be sure, what this says is that I do not have *absolute* power with respect to purchasing the bread, but only *qualified* power — power that is contingent on noninterference by the freight train and other such "superior powers." That is true enough — but qualified power is the only sort of power we finite beings have or need to have. Thus, in spite of Griffin's argument, there is no contradiction in saying that you and I and other finite realities have powers that we are able to exercise in most situations, but that God has the power to overrule our finite powers when he sees fit to do so. The traditional conception of omnipotence has not been shown to be incoherent.

---

self-determining but lack the power to do evil, then there could be a world of self-determining creatures in which evil was impossible. And if creatures can be self-determining and yet that power of self-determination can be overridden by a superior power, the claim that God cannot have the power to prevent evil collapses immediately. Furthermore, all of the premises must be necessarily true; this is essential if one is to maintain the charge of incoherence against the traditional doctrine.

Having said all this, I must now say that the problem of evil does require our attention. But it is important to be clear about what the argument from evil is being used to prove. The question is not, Which conception of God presents God as the greatest, most exalted being that could possibly exist? That question has already been addressed by the previous discussion. With respect to divine power, the answer seems to be that the greatest possible divine being would be one that uses love and persuasion to the greatest extent possible, yet retains the ability to use controlling power when the situation demands it. The question posed by the problem of evil is rather this: Is it tenable to believe in a God of such wondrous power, given the many, varied, and often excruciatingly horrible evils that infect our world?

In an essay devoted to other matters, I cannot readily address this question in passing. But I need to say at least a little about it, lest the reader conclude that traditional theism is without resources at this point.[37] Process theists already concede one important part of the answer: In dealing with free and responsible creatures such as human beings, it is far better that in the vast majority of instances God should act through love and persuasion, rather than unilaterally intervening. But while process theists generally acknowledge the force of this "free will defense" insofar as it involves evils that are caused by human beings, they observe rightly that it fails to account for "natural evils" that are not traceable to responsible creaturely actions. Hartshorne claims that the "only solution of the problem of evil 'worth writing home about' . . . uses the idea of freedom, but generalizes it."[38] It does seem plausible that some notion of freedom that is analogous to the free agency attributed to human beings is applicable to at least the higher animals. Whether it makes sense to attribute freedom – as opposed to mere randomness – to the causally undetermined trajectories of quarks and electrons seems more dubious. But there does seem to be sense to the idea that nature in its general constitution has an inner order and integrity that is intrinsically good and ought not to be violated without good reason, even by God. There is also the additional point, made forcefully by John Hick:

37. For a good general discussion of the problem of evil, from a perspective that harmonizes well with the open view of God, see Michael L. Peterson, *God and Evil: An Introduction to the Issues* (Boulder: Westview, 1998).

38. *Omnipotence and Other Theological Mistakes,* 13.

> Suppose that, contrary to fact, this world were a paradise from which all possibility of pain and suffering were excluded. . . . No one could ever injure anyone else: the murderer's knife would turn to paper or the bullets to thin air; . . . the mountain climber, steeplejack, or playing child falling from a height would float unharmed to the ground; the reckless driver would never meet with disaster. . . .
>
> One can at least begin to imagine such a world – and it is evident that in it our present ethical concepts would have no meaning. If, for example, the notion of harming someone is an essential element in the concept of a wrong action, in a hedonistic paradise there could be no wrong actions – nor therefore any right actions in distinction from wrong. Courage and fortitude would have no point in an environment in which there is, by definition, no danger or difficulty. Generosity, kindness, the *agape* aspect of love, prudence, unselfishness, and other ethical notions that presuppose an objective environment could not even be formed. Consequently such a world, however well it might promote pleasure, would be very ill adapted for the development of the moral qualities of human personality.[39]

All this leaves standing what may, in the end, be the most troubling aspect of the problem of evil, which lies in the question, Why didn't God intervene to prevent *this?* – where "this" refers to some especially horrible and pointless instance of evil. Let us admit, right away, that often we do not know why God does not intervene; we may indeed wish devoutly that he had done so, and may have no very good idea about why the evil in question was permitted. Yet even here, faith is not without resources to give an account of itself.

To begin with, the mere fact that you or I do not understand why God has acted in a certain way provides very little evidence that God has not in fact acted in that way or that he lacks good reason for doing so. In order for the argument from evil to make any headway, the argument must identify some general principle stating that, under certain sorts of circumstances, God would be morally obliged to intervene or would be morally deficient in some way if he failed to do so. Should

39. John Hick, *Philosophy of Religion*, 3rd ed. (Englewood Cliffs, N.J.: Prentice-Hall, 1983), 47-48. For my own adaptation of Hick's "soul-making theodicy," see "Suffering, Soul-Making, and Salvation," *International Philosophical Quarterly* 28 (March 1988): 3-19.

God, then, routinely prevent all serious evils, whether they result from free creaturely actions or from the operation of natural forces? As we have already seen, God's doing this would eliminate almost all the motivation we ordinarily have to deal constructively with such evils ourselves, either by preventing them or by mitigating their effects once they have occurred. As Hick says, "an environment intended to make possible the growth in free beings of the finest characteristics of personal life must have a good deal in common with our present world.... If it did not contain the particular trials and perils that . . . our world contains, it would have to contain others instead."[40]

A more subtle position allows for this by holding that God morally ought to intervene to prevent evils whenever his intervention would do more good than harm. According to this view, some evils are justifiably permitted in that God's preventing them would either lead to other, even greater evils or would prevent the occurrence of good states of affairs that are sufficient to outweigh the evils in question. But evils of which this is not true – "gratuitous" evils, as they are often called – God must indeed prevent, assuming that God is both morally good and has the power to prevent the evils in question.

Many theists have risen to the bait thus offered, and have maintained that God does prevent all genuinely gratuitous evils, so that the evils he permits, and that actually occur, are all such that God's preventing them would either lead to even greater evils or would prevent greater goods from coming to pass.[41] This position is difficult to refute conclusively, but it places the believer in an extremely uncomfortable position. There are many instances of evil concerning which we are not only unable to specify the "greater good" that comes about as a result of the evil's being permitted, but the very idea of "justifying" such evils is apt to seem repugnant. To take refuge in agnosticism when confronted with the inevitable parade of horrific examples is but a weak response.

A better reply is available, however. Instead of claiming, seemingly in defiance of the evidence, that each and every evil serves the purpose of some greater good, it is better simply to reject the assertion that God,

40. *Philosophy of Religion,* 48.

41. For a number of articles discussing the problem of evil from this perspective, see Daniel Howard-Snyder, ed., *The Evidential Argument from Evil* (Bloomington: Indiana University Press, 1996).

in order to be morally good, must prevent the occurrence of all genuinely gratuitous evils. This rejection can be buttressed by a variation of the argument already cited from Hick. We have seen that, if God were to prevent all evils whatsoever, almost all our own incentive and motivation to deal constructively with such evils would disappear. But what would be the consequence if, instead, God were to prevent all gratuitous evils — all those evils whose occurrence would not lead to any greater good? If we knew that this was God's policy, would not our own motivation to prevent or alleviate such evils be greatly reduced? For whatever the evil in question, we could be certain that, if the evil occurs, it has been allowed to occur by God only because its occurrence will lead to some greater good, or to the prevention of some other equal or greater evil. By preventing some evil that would otherwise have occurred, we are most certainly not increasing the total goodness of the world, and may very well be causing the world overall to be worse than it otherwise would be! Thus the claim that God does and must prevent all genuinely gratuitous evils runs counter to God's intention to make of us responsible moral individuals; such a claim should not, then, be endorsed by any Christian believer.[42]

To sum up: While the phenomena of evil and suffering are deeply perplexing and troubling to all of us, I have maintained that there is no compelling moral principle stating that a good God must intervene to prevent such evils from occurring. God loves us, and is calling us to salvation and to fellowship with himself, but in most circumstances he does not directly intervene to spare us from the suffering occasioned either by human actions or by the forces of nature. We may be unable, in a great many cases, to understand why God permits particular evils to occur. But our profound ignorance in these matters is a poor argument that a powerful and loving God does not exist or does not care for us. In

42. I am happy to be able to say that, in many cases, Christians who endorse such views nevertheless continue, inconsistently, to battle valiantly against evil as they encounter it in everyday life. Sometimes, however, the acknowledgment "It is God's will," in the face of evil and suffering, comes too soon, when there is still much that human beings can and should do to avert the evil in question. For a more extensive discussion of this argument, see my "Necessity of Gratuitous Evil," *Faith and Philosophy* 9/1 (1992): 23-44; David O'Connor, "Hasker on Gratuitous Natural Evil," *Faith and Philosophy* 12/3 (1995): 380-92; and my "O'Connor on Gratuitous Natural Evil," *Faith and Philosophy* 14/3 (1997): 388-94.

this age of the world, God does indeed persuade but he seldom compels. His ultimate triumph lies in the future – and when he shall choose, he has abundant power to bring about that triumph.[43]

The most serious objection to process theism's view of divine power concerns that view's rejection of so much that seems central to the biblical drama of salvation. To be sure, not all the wonders of the Bible are of equal importance for that drama. Some Christians could with little sense of loss allow the floating ax head, or the tale of Jonah and the large fish, to be consigned to the realm of pious legend. But the Gospel miracles and, most central of all, the resurrection of Jesus Christ from the dead are nonnegotiable for the historical church and for the vast majority of Christians today. If adequacy for the faith and life of the church is a criterion for good theology, it could turn out that this process conception of divine action is adequate only for a rather small subset of the actual Christian community.[44]

Cobb to the Rescue Again?

Can Cobb's views, as surveyed in the previous section, contribute anything further to a process conception of divine action? I believe they can, but in order to show this I need to develop his ideas in ways that go beyond what he himself has said, and that he might not fully endorse. Let us begin with the idea that God provides the initial aim for each ac-

43. Cf. 2 Peter 3:9 (NIV): "The Lord is not slow in keeping his promise. . . . He is patient with you, not wanting anyone to perish, but everyone to come to repentance."

44. For a more extensive critique of the process view of divine power, see Basinger, *Divine Power in Process Theism*. Yet another criticism of this view, which cannot be pursued in detail here, lies in the suspicion that the God of process theism does after all possess a considerable measure of coercive power. Basinger, among others, argues this (see his chap. 1, "Divine Persuasion: Could the God of Process Theism Do More?"). Barry L. Whitney holds that God's power is purely persuasive, but he also thinks process theists have a good deal of work to do in articulating their views to make it clear that this is in fact the case. As he says, "if God *could* coercively establish natural laws, or if God *appears* coercively at times to lure creaturely acts and decisions within the limits imposed by the laws, then it is reasonable to ask why God does not coerce at other times to eliminate evils and suffering" ("Hartshorne and Theodicy," in *Hartshorne, Process Philosophy, and Theology*, ed. Robert Kane and Stephen H. Phillips [Albany: SUNY Press, 1989], 53-69; the quotation is from 62).

tual occasion. Apart from God, there would *be* no actual occasion, and the so-called continuing object would cease to exist. Furthermore, God "determines the standpoint that the occasion will occupy, its locus and extent in the extensive continuum." In this regard, Cobb observes that "the continuum tells no tales as to how it shall be atomized. The actual standpoints to be realized may be large or small and may have a variety of shapes. Any given region may be divided in an infinite number of ways."[45] Furthermore, "the initial aim determines which occasions will constitute the past and therefore, the initial data of the new occasion." Thus, "by determining the standpoint of each occasion, God determines also just what other occasions it will prehend."[46] Moreover, "how [the becoming occasion] objectifies [the initial data] is determined by the initial aim."[47] Finally, "the initial aim also determines at what kind of satisfaction the occasion will initially aim and thereby influences, without determining, the satisfaction actually attained."[48]

Now, in order to recognize the significance of all this, we need to recall one further fact: In Whiteheadian thought, the appropriation of the data from past occasions by the becoming occasion is the concrete embodiment of what we term the "laws of nature." So if God really has the extensive control over this appropriation suggested by the quotations above, it seems extremely unlikely that the possible range of divine actions is limited to what is allowed by the laws of nature as we commonly think of them.[49] God, it would seem, enjoys a considerable amount of freedom to bring about results that go beyond what is permitted by the ordinary natural laws – in a word, to perform miracles. To be sure, process theists may not wish to describe such events as "supernatural" or as "violations of the laws of nature." They may be inclined, rather, to hold that what we call the "laws of nature" are simply descriptions of the way nature ordinarily behaves, but that these "laws"

45. *Christian Natural Theology,* 153.

46. Ibid.

47. Ibid., 205.

48. Ibid., 153-54.

49. It might be possible in theory to maintain that the variations in God's control, as outlined in the text, are adequately accounted for by the range of possibilities opened up by quantum-level indeterminacy. But this, I think, would trivialize the "options open to God" that are set forth in Cobb's statements. Quantum indeterminacy, after all, can be completely ignored in most real-life situations.

do not possess the ultimate ontological status often ascribed to them. Process thinkers are also likely to reject the sharp distinction of natural versus supernatural as artificial and misleading. After all, on the suggested view, in performing "signs and wonders" God is doing just what he always does, namely providing the initial aim for new actual occasions. It is just that the results of the initial aims in these particular cases are unusual, spectacular, and contrary to normal expectations.

These differences, however, are theologically of secondary importance. Numerous thinkers have found useful such concepts as "natural law" and "natural-supernatural," but these concepts are not theologically indispensable: they are not found in the Bible, nor are they part of the "deposit of faith." What is theologically important is not these concepts, but whether God can perform, and has in fact performed, the mighty works ascribed to him in the Bible. Cobb's view, as construed here, suggests that God may indeed be able to perform these works.

How much freedom does our revised process theism accord to God? I find it impossible to answer this question; even an approximate answer would need to be worked out by someone far more thoroughly versed in process thought than I am. It may be, however, that a general answer is not needed at this point. Rather than deciding in advance what God can and cannot do, a promising strategy may be to proceed as follows: First, examine the evidence to see whether good candidates for "miraculous" divine actions actually exist. Then, when such candidates are found, process theists can apply themselves to the task of working out, on the basis of process thought, possible ways in which the surprising results could have been brought about by God.[50] If this approach is acceptable, it may open up additional possibilities for a fruitful dialogue between process theology and evangelical theology. Many evangelicals would welcome a debate on the evidential basis for belief in miracles, especially if that debate is not encumbered with a prior assumption that miracles are impossible.[51]

Finally, I should like to ask Cobb, and other process theists, to con-

50. I have learned from a student of David Griffin that Griffin has worked out a way in which the miraculous multiplication of loaves (see Mark 6:30-44 and parallels) could be explained using a process perspective. Griffin would insist, for the reasons given in the text, that his explanation is not "supernaturalistic."

51. See, e.g., Stephen T. Davis, *Risen Indeed: A Christian Philosophy of Resurrection* (Grand Rapids: Eerdmans, 1993).

sider yet a further modification of Whitehead's thought. Cobb attributes to Whitehead, and apparently accepts himself, the view that for God there is an eternally unchanging, primordial ordering of the "eternal objects" (roughly, universals). Furthermore, this "ordering is such as to specify the initial aim for each occasion."[52] Cobb explains this by saying that "every possible state of the actual world is already envisioned as possible and every possible development from that actual state is already envisioned and appraised. Thus, the one primordial ordering of eternal objects is relevant to every actuality with perfect specificity."[53] This proposal is metaphysically neat and, in a certain way, attractive. But Cobb, let us recall, has put forward the supposition that God is a living person. Now surely process thinkers will agree that it is characteristic of living persons to enjoy greater freedom and a more spontaneous creativity than is implied by routinely applying to each new possible situation an ordering of valuations that has been predetermined in advance. It would seem that a theology that is so solicitous for the freedom of finite persons ought also to attribute meaningful freedom to God himself! So here is my proposal: I would ask Cobb, and other process thinkers, to contemplate the possibility that God's primordial ordering of the eternal objects does indeed constrain, but need not uniquely determine, the preferred divine response to the various situations that arise. There is, after all, no compelling reason why value theory needs to hold that there is a unique "best" response in each and every situation – indeed, I should think that the greater plausibility lies on the other side of that question. A God who is, like ourselves, a free person, seems a far more suitable recipient of our praise and adoration than one whose sole function is to execute an a priori set of value orderings.[54]

52. *Christian Natural Theology,* 155.

53. Ibid., 155-56.

54. David Griffin has suggested in discussion another way in which God's freedom might be secured. In Griffin's view, the ordering of the eternal objects is itself a matter of divine volition, and may be different for different cosmic epochs. This does indeed provide for God a degree of freedom not allowed by Cobb's presentation. It also seems to contradict the views attributed by Cobb to Whitehead, namely that "God's ordering of the eternal objects is primordial, and that in a sense which clearly means eternally unchanging," and that "this timeless envisagement of possibilities constitutes God's primordial nature" (*Christian Natural Theology,* 155; Cobb refers to *Process and Reality,* §§46 and 74). An ordering that "constitutes God's primordial nature" would hardly seem to be a matter of divine volition.

God Communicates

God creates, God acts, but God also communicates. If God were speechless, how should we know his thoughts toward us? The Bible chronicles a large variety of ways in which God communicates with human beings. There are laws written on stone tablets, and laws written on the heart. There is the voice speaking from the burning bush, and the voice from heaven on the road to Damascus. There are the thunderings of the prophets, and the musings of the authors of the wisdom literature. A study of the modalities of divine revelation would be an enormous undertaking, one that lies far beyond our scope on an occasion such as this. But one feature that stands out, in the biblical view of God's self-disclosure, is the *specific and definite* character of some of these revelations.[55] They are specific, in being delivered to a particular person (or group of persons) at a particular time and place. They are definite, in communicating unambiguously a particular content that constitutes the will of God for that person at that time and place. As a case study, let us consider the conversion of Saul, the persecutor of the early Christians, by which he became Paul, the apostle to the Gentiles. This conversion took place in the famous encounter on the road to Damascus and events immediately thereafter.[56] As a result of his experiences, Paul became convinced of the following:

1. Jesus of Nazareth, the central cult figure in the sect Saul had been persecuting, is "the Lord" – roughly, the supreme religious authority.
2. Jesus had personally appeared to Saul, confronting him with the wrongness of his policy of persecuting the Christians and, indirectly, Jesus himself.

55. In an earlier version of this material, I emphasized the *clarity* of divine communication. As a result of discussions with James Keller, I now realize that this was a mistake. "Clarity," in the sense prized by logicians and analytic philosophers, was seldom if ever a primary concern of the biblical writers. They freely used poetic images, evocative metaphors, and culturally charged concepts in a way that is religiously powerful but seldom logically transparent. (That is one reason there is so much work to be done by exegetes and theologians!) It is hoped that the present emphasis on "specific and definite" communication achieves a better fit with the actual character of the biblical text.

56. See Acts 9:1-18; 22:3-21; 26:12-18.

3. Jesus had selected Saul, now called Paul, to carry his message throughout the world, primarily to the Gentiles.
4. Paul had become aware of 1-3 because God had revealed these matters to him, both in the original encounter with Jesus and through subsequent experiences.

On the basis of these beliefs, Paul entered upon a course of action that entailed massive changes in his life plan, his prospects, and his very identity. As an apostle of Christianity to the Gentiles, he endured continuous and sometimes life-threatening conflict with the leaders of his own Jewish people. His treasured identity as a Jew was frequently called into question, though never finally abrogated. He frequently risked his life, and repeatedly endured beatings and imprisonment. In the end, he suffered martyrdom for the sake of his faith in Christ. I submit that this change of direction on Paul's part is unintelligible, and would probably have been wholly impossible, apart from his belief in 1-3 as stated above. His confident belief in 1-3 would itself be unintelligible apart from his belief in 4, that God had specifically revealed these matters to him. These beliefs, I assert, were constitutive of Paul's identity as the apostle to the Gentiles. But if this is true, it suggests a further observation, one that is relevant to us today: It is difficult, indeed it may be impossible, for us coherently to endorse Paul's mission and his message while rejecting the beliefs that were for him constitutive of that mission. To put it bluntly, if we do not believe that God revealed to Paul what his mission was to be, we call in question everything about that mission, Paul's subsequent life, and his message.

With this example under our belt, let us examine process theism's view of divine communication. It is just at the point of specific and definite divine communication to human beings that process theism encounters serious difficulties.[57] To be sure, God as conceived by process theism is not uncommunicative. On the contrary, he is constantly communicating to all beings his "ideal will" for them, in the form of the "initial aim" for each occasion of experience. But two factors make this less than satisfactory. First, the initial aim is originally perceived primarily on an unconscious level; it emerges into consciousness, if at all,

57. The thoughts in this section are strongly indebted to chap. 6 of Basinger's *Divine Power in Process Theism.*

only after extensive processing has occurred at deeper levels of the personality. For this reason, process thinkers sometimes urge us to consider our prereflective, intuitive responses as more reliable than conclusions arrived at by reflective thought.[58] But this advice, however appropriate in some circumstances, brings with it difficulties of its own. First, it is abundantly clear that the unconscious mind contains, and is subject to, many influences different from, and even inimical to, the impulses we may receive from God. Second, in many situations — for instance, complicated ethical questions involving social or environmental policy — we simply cannot derive answers directly from intuition; in such cases, reflective analysis is unavoidable.

A further difficulty arises from the universality and uniformity of the divine action postulated. Quite simply, God is always and in all places communicating his ideal will, in the form of the initial aim for each occasion, to the greatest extent possible. It might seem, initially, that this is a strength of the process view rather than a weakness. It means, however, that there is nothing further God can do to ensure that his message is rightly received. He cannot get someone's attention with a burning bush, or speak to some particular individual in a special way, in order to be sure of getting his message across. God has already done all he can do; the rest is entirely up to us. This means that differences in the reception of the divine message are due entirely to differences in the preparation and spiritual receptivity of the human recipient. To put it bluntly, the only reason we should especially listen to Isaiah, Paul, or Moses is that we judge them to have been unusually wise and good individuals, and thus (we think) more receptive to the divine will than the rest of us. The note of "Thus says the Lord" has disappeared entirely. But of course, Paul and Moses and Isaiah did not think the validity of their message came from their own superior discernment; rather, it was for them the Lord's own word. But don't we then have to ask: If they were wrong about that, were they really such discerning individuals after all? To revert to our previous example: If Paul was wrong in thinking God had spoken to him, why should we suppose he was right about much of anything else — at least about anything that we moderns are unable to verify directly for ourselves?

Once again, I beg leave to introduce a modest proposal. If our

58. For details see ibid., 100-109.

conception of God, and of God's working, is modified in the ways suggested in the last section, the prospects for God's communication with human beings improve greatly. If God enjoys the freedom of action appropriate to a living person, then God can indeed select certain situations, and certain individuals, in order to communicate his message more directly, to the end that they in turn may pass it along to the rest of us. If God has the power to bring about occurrences that go beyond the ordinary laws of nature, then such "signs and wonders" can be used to call attention to, and indeed to authenticate, the messengers he has chosen to use. It would be a considerable task to work out the details of this proposal and develop its detailed implications. It seems evident, however, that the more we ascribe to God in the way of both freedom and power over nature, the better the prospects become for definite, unambiguous communication from God to human beings.

In this essay I have surveyed both some similarities and some major differences between process theism and the open view of God. I have also looked at a modification of process theism that, remaining within the general Whiteheadian metaphysical framework, would allow the process theist to move closer to mainstream, historical Christianity on a number of issues. Whether this is a promising avenue for process theology to follow, others must decide. In any case, the exploration has been for me – and, I hope, for at least some readers – a source of both instruction and enjoyment.[59]

59. An earlier version of this material was presented at the international Whitehead conference held at Claremont in August 1998. My thanks to John Cobb, David Griffin, Nancy Howell, James Keller, and other participants in the discussion at that time; their comments have resulted in major improvements in the chapter. My thanks also to David Basinger for providing thought-provoking written comments.

In Response to William Hasker

DAVID RAY GRIFFIN

The point of the title of William Hasker's essay, "An Adequate God," is that the divine reality portrayed by process theists is not adequate, whereas that portrayed by classical free will theists is. In this response, I first reply to his critique of process theism. In the second section, I summarize the ways in which I regard the Deity portrayed by Hasker as less adequate.

As a preliminary matter, it is first necessary to reflect on the key notion in this exchange, adequacy, which begs the question: Adequacy to what? In philosophy, it usually means adequacy to the world as we know it. In his opening paragraph, however, Hasker says that his concern is to have a conception of God that is adequate "for the faith and life of the Christian church." His rationale for thus limiting his scope is that this faith and life are available to us, whereas God is not, but that is an irrelevant antithesis. The relevant point is that the nature of the world is accessible to us in roughly the same way as is the nature of Christian faith. Granted that we cannot directly compare our concepts with the divine reality itself, the question is: In terms of which criteria should we assess the relative adequacy of various concepts of God? It is certainly the case that a concept, to be considered a *Christian* concept of God, must be adequate to Christian faith. But if we are to claim that our concept of God not only is Christian but should also be accepted as *true* (in the modest sense of at least not less true than other concepts about the ultimate nature of reality), then surely it must also be adequate to the nature of the world as known through experience and reasoning thereon. However, although one of my central criticisms of Hasker is his far too narrow construal of the criteria of adequacy, I do not reject his concern for adequacy to Christian faith. Accordingly, I meet his challenge at this level, arguing in the first section that process theism is more adequate to Christian faith than Hasker alleges, then in the second section that his concept of God is less adequate to Christian faith than he claims. Before concluding that second section, however, I summarize several respects in which his concept is also inadequate to the world as we know it.

The Alleged Inadequacies of Process Theism

I devoted the final section of my essay (chapter 1 above) to the task of showing that process theology can be more adequate to Christian faith than has widely been thought. Perhaps that discussion, which was not available to Hasker when he wrote his essay, has now led him to change his assessment somewhat. My assignment, nevertheless, is to respond to the critique of process theism given in his essay. Although doing so requires that I must deal with some of the same issues that I discussed earlier, this response differs by virtue of responding specifically to the four dimensions of Hasker's claim that process theism is not adequate to the Christian faith – namely, its faith in creation, miracles (especially the resurrection), revelation, and divine perfection.

Creation out of Nothing

At the core of Hasker's charge of inadequacy to the Christian faith in creation is the fact that process theism rejects creation ex nihilo – at least if the *nihil* is understood to mean absolute nothingness, in the sense of the complete nonexistence of finite actualities. This rejection is said to be problematic because theology needs "to be faithful to Scripture and to its own traditions" (p. 228). The more important of these in Hasker's mind is clearly Scripture, as shown by his willingness to jettison various traditional ideas, such as divine impassibility, nontemporality, and predestination, because they are contrary to Scripture. His criticism of process theism, therefore, hinges on the claim that the traditional doctrine of creation ex nihilo is biblical.

That claim, however, is extremely problematic. Hasker himself admits that the passage long assumed to be the locus classicus of this doctrine, Genesis 1:1-2, probably supports "the existence of a primeval chaos" (n. 22). He even seems implicitly to admit that there is no biblical passage that clearly affirms the traditional doctrine of creation out of nothing, as he merely points to several biblical passages in which this doctrine is said to be "at least strongly suggested." Furthermore, even if these passages did clearly support creation out of absolute nothingness (over against creation out of relative nothingness, discussed below), which they do not, Hasker's claim would still be in tension with the scriptural method endorsed in *The Openness of God,* which is not to base doctrines on proof texts but on the "broad sweep of biblical testimony."[1] Judged from this perspective, the doctrine of the creation out of absolute nothingness is, according to a growing consensus of scholars, not biblical. On this score, I had pointed to Jon Levenson's *Creation and the Persistence of Evil,* which shows that the notion of creation out of chaos was central to the Hebrew liturgy. Equally germane is Gerhard May's *Creatio Ex Nihilo: The Doctrine of "Creation out of Nothing" in Early Christian Thought,*[2] which discusses the motives of early Christian theologians for adopting this doctrine in spite of its lack of clear scriptural support.

Some of Hasker's criticisms of process theism could be understood as echoing the conviction of these early Christian theologians, namely, that creation out of absolute nothingness is necessary for Christian faith even if it is not biblical. But his claims, thus interpreted, are not well supported. One of these claims is that process theism is antithetical to the "majesty of God as creator" expressed in various biblical books. But the magnificence of the creation, and thereby of its creator, is one of the central convictions of process theists. Another claim

1. Richard Rice, "Biblical Support for a New Perspective," in Clark Pinnock et al., *The Openness of God: A Biblical Challenge to the Traditional Understanding of God* (Downers Grove, Ill.: InterVarsity Press, 1994), 15.

2. Jon D. Levenson, *Creation and the Persistence of Evil: The Jewish Drama of Divine Omnipotence* (San Francisco: Harper & Row, 1988); Gerhard May, *Creatio Ex Nihilo: The Doctrine of "Creation out of Nothing" in Early Christian Thought,* trans. A. S. Worrall (Edinburgh: T. & T. Clark, 1994).

by Hasker, made in relation to some comments by Hartshorne, is that process theists regard "God as, in effect, primus inter pares." One of the central themes of Hartshorne's writings, however, has been the many ways in which God is different in kind from all other individuals, being, for example, the only individual who exists necessarily, everlastingly, and omnipresently, the only one with an absolutely unchanging essence, and the only one who knows and loves all finite beings. The charge that Hartshorne regards God as merely the "first among equals" goes beyond caricature to complete distortion. Still another claim made by Hasker is that process theism, by virtue of affirming a version of creation out of chaos, understands creation as "a sort of divine 'shaping' of realities already in existence." This charge, which implies that God would have confronted a realm of actualities that had itself not been evoked into existence by God's creative activity, I already answered in my essay.

These distortions of process theism aside, the central question is why Hasker thinks the insistence on creation out of absolute nothingness is so important. Part of the answer seems to be the "reverence by association" to which I referred in my essay, through which secondary and tertiary doctrines, by virtue of being seen at one time as necessary to support some primary doctrine, come to be regarded as important in their own right. That this phenomenon plays a role in Hasker's thinking is suggested in a discussion in which, after conceding that no "significant theological assertion" would be imperiled by the doctrine that God chose to create a universe everlastingly, he adds: "What is essential, however, is that it is possible for the universe to have a temporal beginning, and the reason this is essential is that without this possibility the world would be metaphysically necessary for God, a view that Christian theology has always rejected." In a footnote (n. 25), he points out that some medieval thinkers, such as John Scotus Erigena, did accept the necessity of the world for God, which means that his claim is really that such necessity has always been rejected by "mainstream" theologians. In any case, part of the reason why it is important to reject the idea that the world is metaphysically necessary for God seems to be that mainstream Christian theologians have always done so.

Hasker does, however, also evidently think that these mainstream theologians have been right to reject this idea because its acceptance would imperil some "significant theological assertion." The general issue here is the conflict between Christian monotheism and various types of "dualism," which I briefly discussed in my essay, showing that the version of "semi-dualism" affirmed by process theism does not have any of the negative consequences for primary Christian doctrines that were entailed by the types of dualism that the church, in insisting on creation ex nihilo, had been concerned to oppose. I will now show that process theism can even affirm the secondary doctrines that Hasker regards as essential, at least to the extent that they can be affirmed without imperiling the primary doctrine of God's unbounded love.

One problem with Hasker's discussion is that, in spite of process theology's distinction between *a* world, in the sense of some realm or other of finite actualities, and *our* world, in the sense of this particular cosmic epoch, he continues to phrase the issue, as in the quotation above, simply in terms of whether *the* world is metaphysically necessary for God, thus ignoring a crucial distinction. Process theologians agree with the mainstream of Christian thought that "the world," in the sense of our universe, with its electrons and protons, its prokaryotic and eukaryotic cells, and its dolphins and humans, is not metaphysically necessary but is a free creation of God. We even agree that our universe was in one sense created out of nothing: As I suggested in my essay, the state of chaos out of which our universe was created contained, by hypothesis, no enduring individuals, not even ones as elementary as quarks. Although this state of chaos contained finite actualities, these were extremely trivial momentary events, lasting perhaps on the order of a billionth of a second, none of which was organized into what Whitehead calls "enduring objects" (or "serially ordered societies"). There were, therefore, no "things" in the sense in which we ordinarily understand this term, namely, enduring entities retaining their identity through time. Therefore, the creation of the first elementary particles, such as quarks, involved a creation out of no-thing. This creation out of chaos can, accordingly, also be called creation out of relative nothingness. Any claim that such a doctrine was meant to be ruled out by any of the biblical passages to which Hasker refers – such as Hebrews 11:3, which says that "the world was created by the word of God, so that what is seen was made out of things which do not appear" (RSV) – would be implausible.

In explaining the important implications of the doctrine of creation out of absolute nothingness, Hasker says: "As to the particular character of creation, its original nature was wholly determined by God." In my speculative account, I suggested that, "in the first instant of the creation of a particular universe," the divine persuasion would be able to instill a complex set of finely tuned contingent principles, thereby producing "quasi-coercive effects."[3] In other words, the "original nature" of the "particular [contingent] character" of our particular universe would have been "wholly determined by God." This does not mean, of course, that every feature of our universe was determined by a divine volition, because our cosmic epoch, besides embodying the contingent principles that resulted from the divine decision at its outset, also embodies a set of necessary, metaphysical principles, which would (by hypothesis) be embodied in every particular universe. Even these metaphysical principles, however, are not to be thought of as imposed on God from some alien realm. Rather, as I suggested in my essay, these principles are inherent in the very nature of things because they are "inherent in the nature of God and thereby the God-world relation." Thus all the features of the original nature of our universe can be regarded as "wholly determined by God," even though only those features that are contingent, being unique to our particular universe, can be thought of as rooted in the divine *will* (as distinct from the divine *nature*).

In going further by insisting that there are no truly metaphysical principles — on the grounds that all the principles embodied in our universe are contingent, being the result of a divine decision that could have been otherwise — Hasker exemplifies the doctrine that I call "extreme voluntarism," which insists that not only the particular character of our universe, but even whether there is to be a realm of finite existents at all, must be up to God. I have argued that one reason why Christians should resist this extreme voluntarism is that, by implying that God can interrupt the world's cause-effect relations at will, it creates an insoluble problem of evil, thereby imperiling the primary doc-

3. This point provides an answer to Barry Whitney's question to Hartshorne, cited by Hasker (n. 44), as to why, "if God *could* coercively establish natural laws . . . , God does not coerce at other times to eliminate evils and suffering." The answer is that the divine establishment of the laws of physics is only a *quasi*-coercive effect.

trine of God's unqualified love for the world. Hasker, of course, believes that by denying God's power to intervene at will, we imperil other vital doctrines. Before coming to these, I must deal briefly with Hasker's suggestion that process theism could be revised to allow for creation out of absolute nothingness.

Hasker bases this suggestion on a footnote in John Cobb's 1965 book, in which Cobb said he was not sure that Whitehead's metaphysical position rules out the possibility that God might have originally been the only instantiation of creativity. Having already been quoted by Hasker (n. 20) as saying that I wished that Cobb had not made this suggestion, I here give three reasons for discounting it. First, when the book in which this comment appeared was written, Cobb was in a phase that he later termed "Whiteheadian scholasticism," by which he meant the attempt to show how far Whiteheadian philosophy could be used to support traditional Christian doctrines. Second, Cobb's remark was extremely tentative, saying only that he was "not sure" that this possibility was ruled out. Third, Whitehead himself had clearly ruled out this doctrine, saying, for example, that he rejected the "theology of a wholly transcendent God creating out of nothing an accidental universe,"[4] endorsing instead the idea that, just as "God's nature is a primordial datum for the World," "the World's nature is [also] a primordial datum for God"[5] (note that it is only the world's "nature" that is a primordial datum for God, not our world in its concrete details), and saying that "the relationships of God to the World . . . lie beyond the accidents of will," being instead "founded upon the necessities of the nature of God and the nature of the World."[6] One might, to be sure, dismiss those statements as showing only that Whitehead himself rejected the idea that there could be only a single instantiation of creativity, not that his metaphysical position as such rules it out. But the latter is entailed by the fact that, according to his position, the three terms *God, creativity,* and *temporal creatures* are each meaningless apart from the other two.[7] It is also entailed by the very description of creativity as a process in which "the many become one," so that there is an advance

4. Alfred North Whitehead, *Process and Reality* (1929), corrected ed., ed. David Ray Griffin and Donald W. Sherburne (New York: Free Press, 1978), 95.

5. Ibid., 348.

6. Whitehead, *Adventures of Ideas* (New York: Free Press, 1967), 168.

7. *Process and Reality,* 225.

"from disjunction to conjunction."[8] It would be a severe distortion of Whitehead's meaning to suggest that the "many" might have at one time been a purely temporal many, comprised exhaustively of a series of divine occasions of experience.

Miracles, Especially the Resurrection

Although the second dimension of Christian faith discussed by Hasker is divine action in general, he sees the main inadequacy of process theism under this heading to be the fact that it "preclude[s] the unilateral control over nature that is involved in the traditional view of miracles." To discuss this matter, it is important to get clear on exactly what the issue is. In saying that for process theologians "there will be no water from wine, no miraculous multiplication of bread and fishes," Hasker suggests that we necessarily reject the occurrence of those types of events that have traditionally been regarded as miracles. But that is not so, as I have shown in my writings on parapsychology.[9] The real issue is that process theists deny that such events, if they happen, should be regarded as miracles in the traditional sense, meaning events in which the world's ordinary cause-effect relations have been supernaturally interrupted. The resulting question is whether this denial implies the inadequacy of process theism, as Hasker alleges.

This is an issue in which it is especially clear that the adequacy of a position needs to be gauged not simply in terms of traditional Christian beliefs but also in terms of what we now know about the world. One thing that has been learned is that the kinds of events traditionally called (physical) miracles, such as levitation (which would be involved in "walking on water"), the multiplication of food, and extraordinary healing, have been reported in virtually all traditions in virtually all pe-

8. Ibid., 21.

9. In my essay above (chapter 1), I had mentioned my book on the topic, *Parapsychology, Philosophy, and Spirituality: A Postmodern Exploration* (Albany: SUNY Press, 1997). But the ways in which Whiteheadian philosophy allows for the possibility of various types of paranormal phenomena are explained much more fully in an earlier essay, "Parapsychology and Philosophy: A Whiteheadian Postmodern Perspective," *Journal of the American Society for Psychical Research* 87/3 (1993): 217-88.

riods of human history.[10] How would Hasker respond to this fact? One solution would be to say that all the other reported events were based on superstition, deception, bad observations, and the like, so that only the extraordinary feats reported in the Bible really happened. But this would be a desperate solution, especially given the fact that many of the other reports have much better evidential support. Another solution, adopted by some theologians in the medieval and early modern periods, is to accept that the reported events in non-Christian contexts did occur but to contend that they were merely "preternatural" occurrences, brought about by Satan to deceive people, not genuinely supernatural events, which God alone can produce. But this move would be equally desperate. By contrast, process theism is compatible with the interpretation provided by most scientists involved in the study of paranormal events, which is that they are brought about by extraordinary but fully natural powers. Just as Hasker considers his rejection of the traditional doctrines of impassibility and predestination as a step forward, not a sign of inadequacy, the same is true, I suggest, for the rejection of the traditional view of miracles.

The most important reported event of this type, as Hasker indicates, is the resurrection of Jesus. My endorsement of the importance of this event is shown by the fact that my essay's list of primary Christian doctrines includes "a salvation for us in a life beyond bodily death" and the conviction that God "acted decisively to realize the divine purposes in the life, death, and resurrection of Jesus of Nazareth." Process theism would indeed be inadequate to Christian faith if it would preclude these affirmations. Hasker has assumed that it would. To sort out the truth of the matter, we must ask separately about three distinguishable features of the resurrection as understood by Hasker: (1) the genuineness of the resurrection appearances, in the sense of their having been produced by the continued existence of the personality of Jesus, a view

10. For a classic account, see James Frazer, *The Golden Bough: A Study in Magic and Religion* (London: Macmillan, 1923). Although Frazer reported similar beliefs about paranormal phenomena from various cultures, he regarded them all as superstitious. For more recent studies, which take the similarities to mean that we are dealing with "natural kinds," rather than culturally induced phenomena, see James McClenon, *Wondrous Events: Foundations of Religious Belief* (Philadelphia: University of Pennsylvania Press, 1994); and Michael Murphy, *The Future of the Body: Explorations in the Further Evolution of Human Nature* (Los Angeles: Jeremy Tarcher, 1992).

that implies the reality of life after death; (2) the resurrection as a supernatural miracle; and (3) the *bodily* resurrection. As indicated in my essay, I accept the first but deny the second, holding instead that the same divine modus operandi through which God first evoked life and then human life can also evoke life after death for human personalities. Also, the appearances of Jesus as reported in the Gospel accounts are similar in most respects to reports of appearances of the recently deceased in other times and places,[11] a fact that provides an empirical basis for not regarding the resurrection of Jesus as a supernatural event. With regard to the third issue, it is hard for me to see it as crucial, partly due to the evidence provided by Gregory Riley, which I mentioned in my essay, that the earliest Christians evidently thought in terms of the "resurrection of the soul," with the notion of the resurrection of the body arising only later, in a polemical context. This doctrine has every appearance of being one of those secondary doctrines that, having provided support for a primary doctrine in an earlier context, has taken on undue reverence by association.

Revelation

Hasker's position on divine revelation is clearly the weakest part of his case, being challenged even by other evangelical theologians. Having in an earlier version of his essay made claims for the "clarity" of the biblical revelation, as he indicates (n. 55), he now speaks instead of some of these revelations as "definite," meaning thereby that they "communicat[e] unambiguously a particular content." It was precisely this feature of his earlier claim about clarity, however, that was problematic, because this claim is undermined by the fact that there have been theological conflicts, rooted at least partly in contrary scriptural passages, about virtually every aspect of Christian doctrine. As we have seen, for

11. See Michael C. Perry, *The Easter Enigma: An Essay on the Resurrection with Special Reference to the Data of Psychical Research* (London: Faber & Faber, 1959); and John J. Heaney, *The Sacred and the Psychic: Parapsychology and Christian Theology* (New York: Paulist, 1984), chap. 9, "Apparitions and the Resurrection of Jesus." On apparitions as evidence for life after death, see George Tyrrell, *Apparitions,* published in one volume with Tyrrell's *Science and Psychical Research* (New Hyde Park, N.Y.: University Books, 1961); or chap. 7 of my *Parapsychology, Philosophy, and Spirituality.*

example, although Hasker believes that the Bible teaches creation out of absolute nothingness, this position is, to say the least, not unambiguously taught. The position taken on the Bible by other "openness" theologians, as I mentioned in my essay (chapter 1 above), is that the Bible contains "diverse statements if not diverse perspectives" on most topics, so that what one sees depends on one's "angle of vision."[12] That process theism does not support unambiguous revelation, therefore, provides no basis for calling it inadequate.

Divine Perfection

Although Hasker does not make the notion of divine perfection a separate category, in effect he regards it as a fourth respect in which process theism falls short. But his argument is no more successful here than elsewhere. He claims that process theists "are aware that [their] rejection of miracles seems to constitute a restriction of divine power, and thus arguably a diminution of the divine excellence and perfection." This claim about our "awareness," however, is contradicted by Hasker's recognition that I, following Hartshorne, have argued that "the traditional conception of omnipotence is incoherent." The point is that if that traditional conception is incoherent, it provides no standard in terms of which to become "aware" that the power of the God of process theism is imperfect, in the sense of less than the power of some (genuinely) conceivable being.[13] I do not, therefore, agree that our view involves a restriction or limitation on divine power, because, as Hartshorne says in a statement I have endorsed,[14] "to speak of limiting a conception seems to imply that the conception, without the limitation, makes sense."

Even given this clarification, however, Hasker would still consider the process deity imperfect, because he rejects my argument that the traditional doctrine of omnipotence is incoherent. One of his rebuttals is based on the premise that, in Hasker's formulation, "any actual being

12. Rice, in *Openness of God,* 16, 57.

13. *God, Power, and Evil: A Process Theodicy* (Philadelphia: Westminster, 1976; reprinted with a new preface, Lanham, Md.: University Press of America, 1991), 272-73.

14. Ibid., 273.

must possess some power of self-determination." Seeking to rebut this premise with ridicule, Hasker points out that it implies that "the physical objects of classical (pre-quantum) physics . . . could not exist," adding that it is a pity that someone did not point this fact out to Newton and Einstein so that much incoherence and conceptual absurdity could have been avoided. My reply is that, yes, it is a pity. The difference between us here appears to be twofold. First, whereas Hasker wrote "logically" at the point marked by the ellipsis in the above quotation, I would write "metaphysically." Hasker's choice of terms suggests that he, in line with much analytic philosophy, assumes that it makes sense to talk about logical possibility in isolation from metaphysical possibility, even when discussing possible worlds, whereas I consider this position confused, because any discussion of what is possible with regard to actualities involves metaphysical premises.[15] Second, Hasker seems to assume that, if a concept is incoherent, then it would in all cases be easy for reasonably clear thinkers, such as Newton and Einstein, to discern this fact, whereas I, in harmony with Hartshorne,[16] hold that the discernment of what is possible and impossible is often, as in the present case, extremely difficult.

The remainder of Hasker's rebuttal depends on the use of two premises that, besides being, as Hasker points out, "not clearly stated as such by Griffin," also *would* not be stated by me. One of these premises, "any being with the power of self-determination is able to do evil," is easily shown by Hasker to be absurd, because it would imply that God could do evil. But the premise that my argument actually uses says only that any finite being with the power of self-determination cannot be guaranteed by God not to do evil (with which Hasker agrees). The other premise falsely assigned to my position is that "if a being has the power to do a certain thing, then no other being has the power to prevent it from doing that thing." By rebutting this premise on the basis of a commonplace example involving a car, a freight train, and a human body, Hasker, like David Basinger before him, "refutes" my argument by distorting it, primarily by ignoring the crucial distinction between

15. See David Ray Griffin, *Evil Revisited: Responses and Reconsiderations* (Albany: SUNY Press, 1991), 137-40.

16. Charles Hartshorne, "A Reply to My Critics," in *The Philosophy of Charles Hartshorne*, The Library of Living Philosophers, vol. 20, ed. Lewis Edwin Hahn (La Salle, Ill.: Open Court, 1991), 569-731, at 653.

genuine individuals, such as human souls, which cannot be unilaterally determined by another, and aggregational societies, such as cars, freight trains, and human bodies, which can be so determined.[17]

Thinking that he has, with these arguments, rebutted the claim that his conception of God is incoherent, Hasker concludes by claiming to have shown that this conception "presents God as the greatest, most exalted being that could possibly exist." It presents a being greater in power than the deity of process theism, he argues, because the process deity has only persuasive power whereas his deity also "retains the ability to use controlling power." Besides having all the problems to which I have already pointed, however, Hasker's conclusion also ignores my argument, articulated in response to Basinger's critique, that we human beings have controlling power (coercive power in the metaphysical sense) only by virtue of having bodies, so that, assuming that God does not have a body (at least aside from the world as a whole), we have no analogical basis for intelligibly attributing this kind of power to God.[18] In sum, Hasker seems to have ignored his own warning, which I had cited in my essay, that "difficulties have arisen because people have been too ready to assume that they can determine, easily and with little effort, what perfection *is* in the case of God."[19]

The Inadequacies of Hasker's Concept of God

Having used most of my allotted space in the first section, my discussion of the adequacy of Hasker's own concept of God must be relatively brief. This is not, however, problematic: Given the points I have already made about classical free will theism in my essay and in this response, I can here for the most part simply summarize those points.

17. For my exposure of Basinger's distortion of my position, even to the point of repeated misquotation, see *Evil Revisited,* 57-60, 109-13, 116-17. Hasker, unfortunately, cites Basinger's "extensive critique of the process view of divine power" (n. 44) without referring to this exposure.

18. See my *Evil Revisited,* 112-13.

19. Hasker, "A Philosophical Perspective," in *Openness of God,* 132.

Inadequacy to Christian Faith

The problem of evil, as Hasker acknowledges, provides the primary challenge to the adequacy of his position to do justice to the Christian faith, with its witness to the love of God. But Hasker's treatment of this problem makes no advance on the unsatisfactory solutions proffered by other classical free will theists. For example, although I have repeatedly provided extensive critiques of John Hick's soul-making theodicy,[20] Hasker's position, as he points out (n. 39), is simply a variant on it, and yet he offers no response to the critiques that I and others have given of it. Hasker is to be commended for not trying to deny the occurrence of gratuitous evil, for his acknowledgment that the classical free will position leads to the constant raising of the question as to why God did not intervene to prevent "some especially horrible and pointless instance of evil," and for his forthrightness in admitting that he often has no answer to this question.

But these personal virtues on his part do nothing to lessen the fact that the conception of God whose adequacy he extols fails to allow for an adequate solution to the problem of evil. His admission that his omnipotent God does not prevent all gratuitous evils means rejecting the widespread intuition, which usually serves as one of the premises of the formal statement of the problem of evil, that a perfectly good being would want to prevent all gratuitous evil, which leaves us wondering what definition Hasker would offer of a morally perfect being. What we can call his "motivation defense" for God's policy of nonintervention implies that we are supposed to be morally better, in the sense of more concerned to prevent and eliminate gratuitous evil, than is God. Finally, this defense leaves the problem of animal suffering, especially the hundreds of millions of years of suffering that occurred prior to the rise of human beings, with no answer at all (assuming that God is not worried about destroying the motivation of birds, rabbits, and horses to "deal constructively" with evil themselves). Hasker's insistence on retaining traditional theism's conception of divine power, along with the doctrine of creation ex

20. See *God, Power, and Evil,* chap. 13; *Evil Revisited,* 14-22; and my critique of Hick's position in *Encountering Evil: Live Options in Theodicy,* ed. Stephen T. Davis (Atlanta: John Knox, 1981), 53-55.

nihilo used to support that conception, provides a classic example of the way in which undue reverence for secondary and even tertiary doctrines can endanger the primary doctrines of the faith they were meant to safeguard.

Besides undermining the creative side of what Charles Wesley called God's "pure unbounded love," the classical free will position also threatens its responsive side, making divine power and will more fundamental than divine compassion (as I argued in my essay). Hasker's response to this criticism is to say that, although "the love and relationality of God *toward the creation* are merely contingent . . . , given that there is a creation, it is necessarily the case that God is related to it and loves it." But this remains a bare assertion, with no explanation as to why this extremely voluntaristic creator must "necessarily" love its creatures. This question is especially pressing given the insistence of classical free will theism, to which I referred in my essay, that the fact that God's relation to the world is one of love is based on a voluntary decision. This insistence seems to leave the door open for the possibility, implied by many traditional theists, that God is indifferent to, or even filled with hate for, most of the creatures.

Inadequacy to the World

Because being adequate to the world as we know it is not even mentioned by Hasker as a criterion for assessing differing conceptions of God, it is not surprising that his conception fails in this regard. Unlike many versions of classical theism, his position is, as I mentioned above, adequate to the fact that the world is filled with gratuitous evils. But it fails in several other respects, most obviously with regard to the Bible, extraordinary events, and evolution.

With regard to the Bible, Hasker's Christian theism leads to the expectation that it should contain a kind of revelation that it does not. Hasker himself says, in a statement meant to commend his position, that "the more we ascribe to God in the way of both freedom and power over nature, the better the prospects become for definite, unambiguous communication from God to human beings." One of the main implications of biblical scholarship over the past three centuries, however, is that the Bible does not contain or even reflect such communication.

We seem to have here a clear example of the empirical disconfirmation of a theological hypothesis.

Closely related is Hasker's treatment of those extraordinary types of events that have come, in parapsychological circles, to be known as "paranormal" events. As is now knowable, thanks to historical and anthropological studies, investigations of spontaneous paranormal occurrences, and laboratory experiments, the capacity to produce strong psychokinetic effects seems to be a natural if rare ability that occurs in all populations,[21] something like the extraordinary capacities for mathematical feats and musical composition. In the light of this available knowledge, Hasker's retention of the traditional Christian view, that a tiny percentage of these extraordinary events – namely, those reported in the Bible – should be interpreted not as psychokinetic events but as supernatural miracles, is anachronistic. To the extent that his conception of God leads to the prediction that miraculous interruptions of the world's causal processes will occasionally occur, another empirical disconfirmation of this theological hypothesis has arguably been provided by the modern study of paranormal events.

With regard to the mismatch between Hasker's conception of God and the evolutionary nature of our world, the only point that I would add here, beyond what I said in my essay, is that the anachronistic nature of Hasker's conception of the God-world relation occurs here too. Hasker's anthropocentric theology could have been articulated in the early eighteenth century, long before the discovery that modern human beings have existed on the order of only one-thousandth of one percent of the history of the universe. Surely that discovery should have some effect on our conception of the divine purpose behind the creation of the world and the divine modus operandi! I repeat the point that although classical free will theism can be adjusted so as not to be in outright contradiction with the evolutionary nature of our universe, this theological hypothesis provides no illumination as to why our world should have come about in this way.

One final problem with Hasker's theism, which I have discussed

21. See my *Parapsychology, Philosophy, and Spirituality,* chap. 2, "White Crows Abounding: Evidence for the Paranormal."

elsewhere,[22] is its inadequacy for reconciling the worldview of the theistic religious communities with that of the scientific community. For the latter, the most fundamental ontological conviction is arguably what I call "minimal naturalism," meaning simply the conviction that there can be no supernatural interruptions of the world's normal pattern of cause-effect relations. Hasker attempts to regard scientific naturalism as a purely methodological stance, with no ontological implications, so that, although scientists qua scientists cannot refer to supernatural acts of God, they and others can continue to affirm their existence in other contexts. But it is most unlikely, I have argued, that this move will ever be acceptable to the ideological leadership of the scientific community.

Hasker might reply that what I call naturalism in the minimal sense is simply an unproved hypothesis, so that to point out that his theology is not "adequate" to it is to beg the question. But the belief in occasional supernatural interruptions has been increasingly undermined by scientific progress, such as by the sciences of parapsychology, anthropology, and historiography, including biblical criticism. I have, in any case, made the present point about the inadequacy of Hasker's theism in terms not of minimal naturalism as such but of the need for a theological position that could finally overcome the late modern conflict between the worldviews of the scientific and religious communities.

Hasker began his critique of process theism by saying that traditional views, especially if they have been regarded as essential by a strong consensus of thinkers throughout Christian history, should not be abandoned "without compelling reasons." I have offered several reasons, which seem compelling to me, for abandoning the traditional view of omnipotence, along with its supporting doctrine of creation ex nihilo.

22. David Ray Griffin, *Religion and Scientific Naturalism: Overcoming the Conflicts* (Albany: SUNY Press, 2000), chap. 3.

Index